THE **Spiritual Meaning** OF **Scripture**

THE **Spiritual**
Meaning OF
Scripture

Your Greatest Opportunity.
Your Mental Wellbeing.
Your Religion and Science.

Howard B. Becker

If you care to just stop for just a moment, cast off the noise of the world and look honestly, sincerely, and humbly within yourself to ask the question "what's it's all about," you'll find "a still small Voice" softly answering out from within your soul.

I dedicate this book in gratitude to being brought to where my knees bent and my neck bowed, and I listened, rather than rejecting the Lord's Testimony about how we may eternally share in the Joy of His Heavenly Love for us.

I would also like to dedicate this book to all who have, are now, and will soon be experiencing this very same Miracle unfolding within them.

It is without a doubt, the Opportunity of our lifetimes!

> "And Jacob awakened out of his sleep, and he said,
> Surely the Lord is in this Place; and I knew it not."
>
> Genesis 28:16

Contents

Author's Note

*I*n the secular world, it is common for people to discuss the differences between the letter of the law and the spirit of the law. Answers are sought about the intent and purpose of the law. Justice is pursued, requiring good judgment.

Making good judgments is called wisdom.

I have written *The Spiritual Meaning of Scripture* to focus on the spiritual meaning and Intent of Scripture so that it will not become ignored, glossed over or obscured by overemphasis on the letter of the Word.

This book explores the Spirit of the Word, seeking answers about the Lord's Purpose for the Creation of your soul. And as Scripture is God's Testimony to you—to all of us, there is no better way to gain understanding about the Way He Intends to fulfill that Purpose within your life.

And because you are finite and God is Infinite, you have been Gifted with the ability to become transformed into a very special person, unique, and invaluable to Him and to others, no two individuals ever being the same. Understanding how to get there from here offers you the Greatest Opportunity of your lifetime.

~

I am Howard Becker. Like many, I've had questions about my own spiritual journey. I have wrestled with many of the same questions that permeate today's noisy, chaotic world of conflicting beliefs and competing religious doctrines. Through exploring the spiritual meaning of the stories, examples and lessons of the Bible, I have found good, sensible and sustainable answers to those questions, even the most difficult ones. I have found that other than being willing to approach, or re-approach Scripture with an open mind and heart, there are no prerequisites required to comprehend the meaning of these precious answers.

With all love, humility, and respect I invite you to join me in exploring these answers, for they are the most important things of all.

Together we will seek them and find them. With all my heart, I believe this journey will help deliver you to a place where you will find ever-deepening understanding about the spiritual Meaning and Purpose of the Bible for the rest of your life, as it has mine.

This book makes no demand to belong to a particular religious denomination. It contains no ulterior motive for organizational or institutional recruitment. It is simply based on spiritual Principles that are True, timeless, common, and invaluable to all of us. It informs us about what matters most in life.

Throughout, I've included verses of Scripture that relate to the subject matter of the chapter cited—all are taken from the *Authorized King James Bible*. Many Words have been capitalized to help edify their spiritual meanings. I greatly recommend that you read each chapter in chronological order, as each builds upon the preceding one.

Most likely, you will have favorite Scriptural entries. I encourage you to treat them as devotionals for everyday living. With all hope and confidence, I believe that this book will help you tremendously in your relationship with your Maker, and with all around you.

You've picked up the right book!

Setting the Stage for The Spiritual Meaning of Scripture

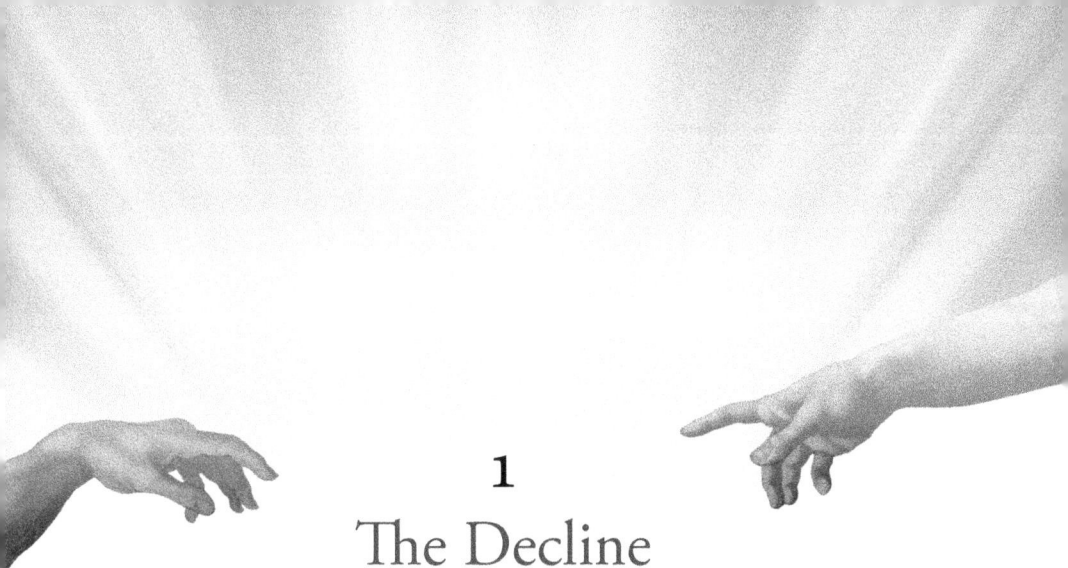

1
The Decline

God needs to Communicate to you ....

*F*ormal religious membership has been significantly declining, predominantly in the United States and Europe, and filtering to many other countries throughout the world. Legacy religious institutions are being left with legacy members, aging and dying out. Attendance within established religious communities is challenged and gasping for air and new life.

Why?

- Younger members are questioning formal religious dogmas, and not always finding answers that resonate with their common sense.

- Evangelical movements are turning to various political ideals, which are very often *religious* in name only.

- Far too many religious institutions have been riddled by sexual abuse scandals, committed and suppressed by their own leaders.

- Too many leaders in power use religion to make themselves appear righteous when they are anything but.

- Literal Biblical teachings are conflicting with the discoveries of modern science.

• Many have become disillusioned—especially younger generations—about the conflicts, inconsistencies, and hypocrisies they are finding in formal religious institutions.

All of these factors are contributing greatly to the growing drift of individuals who are losing interest and disconnecting in droves. They no longer identify themselves as members of organizations that were once deemed the core of families in America and defined the American way of life.

Can you blame them?

In March 2021, Gallup reported this growing loss in its news article: *U.S. Church Membership Falls Below Majority for First Time.*

Americans' membership in houses of worship continued to decline last year, dropping below 50% for the first time in Gallup's eight-decade trend. In 2020, 47% of Americans said they belonged to a church, synagogue or mosque, down from 50% in 2018 and 70% in 1999.

The U.S. remains a religious nation, with more than seven in ten affiliating with some type of organized religion. And far fewer, less than half, have a formal membership with a specific house of worship. While it is possible that part of the decline seen in 2020 was temporary and related to the coronavirus pandemic, continued decline in future decades seems inevitable, given the much lower levels of religiosity and church membership among younger versus older generations of adults.

In March 2023, *The Wall Street Journal*-NORC poll reported in its article: *America Pulled Back from Values That Once Defined It,*

Among other shrinking American core values, only 39% of respondents said religion was very important to them. That was down sharply from when the *Journal* first asked the question 25 years ago in 1998, when 62% deemed religion to be very

important. Today, 31% of young respondents said religion was very important, compared to 55% of those 65 and up.

According to an article published in the *Atlantic* magazine on July 29, 2023 by Jake Meador:

> Forty million Americans have stopped attending church in the past 25 years. That's something like 12 percent of the population, and it represents the largest concentrated change in church attendance in American history.

As I read these results, and many more like them, I wasn't surprised. Although the declining trend in formal religious membership is clear, the sense that there is something much Greater than ourselves will never depart from the human race. The need to connect with that inner awareness continually beckons us to seek answers about why and how we may. Those answers have not been hidden from us, neither are they far off. They are actually much closer to our minds, hearts, and souls than we realize.

The letter of the Word embodies the Spirit of the Word.

And so, the decline of formal religion is not to be compared with a decline in our need to connect with a Higher Calling. Rather, our need to make that Connection has never been greater.

⁓

As you and I explore the spiritual meaning of Scripture, it is important to realize that the letter of the Word embodies the Spirit of the Word, just as your physical body encompasses the spirit within your soul. And just as you are physically dead without your spirit living within you, so the letter of the Word is dead without the Spirit Living within it.

It is therefore vital to recognize that it is the Spirit of the Word that gives the letter of the Word its True meaning and Life ... *not the other way around.* Thinking otherwise leads to countless misunderstandings about what God is attempting to Communicate to you about His Plan and Purpose for the Creation of your life.

~

Within, I've included a chapter dedicated to many of the spiritual terms found throughout the Bible. Another addresses the Biblical Story of our Creation. Later chapters discuss the Principles that Govern our mental, emotional, and spiritual wellbeing. When taken together, you will discover they provide answers that dissipate any conflict between the letter of the Word and the Spirit of the Word.

The verses of Scripture cited have all been taken from the Authorized King James Bible. I have capitalized many words to edify their spiritual meaning. All discussion is Scripture-based.

2
Introducing
Timeless Principles

The Keys that unlock your innermost happiness
and genuine fulfillment in life.

*T*hroughout *The Spiritual Meaning of Scripture* you and I will explore the answers surrounding the spiritual meaning of the stories, examples, and lessons of and from the Bible.

Even the most difficult ones.

There is no demand to belong to a particular religious denomination. You will find no ulterior motive for organizational or institutional recruitment.

It is simply based on spiritual Principles that are timeless, common, and invaluable to you … to all of us. It identifies and educates as to what matters most in life.

~

The human race loves to investigate the laws of physical science. The principles of physics, chemistry, biology, mathematics, time-space, and many other physical "laws" are studied, tested, and continually validated and revalidated worldwide. Their confirmations enhance our understanding about the order of the physical universe, and when used with good judgment, they work together to greatly benefit our lives and the lives of those around us.

Likewise, many studies in psychology and psychiatry are conducted to enhance our understanding about what benefits our mental and emotional wellbeing. Yet, considering the importance of what supports all of these benefits, it should not be a stretch to seek understanding about the spiritual Principles that are fundamental to establishing the Goodness within them.

He Promises to bring all things Good into fruition within your life.

Rather, gaining understanding about these Principles should be your highest priority in life, for as you apply them in the Way the Lord has Shown that you must, He Promises to bring all things Good into fruition within your life. Throughout the Bible, He invites you to learn about these Sacred Principles, and then confirm their validity for yourself.

> *"Have ye not known? have ye not heard? hath it not been told you from the beginning? have ye not understood from the foundations of the earth?"*
>
> Isaiah 40:21

~

He continually Calls upon you to learn about them, teaching you that you can easily understand them and prove them for yourself if you honestly, sincerely, and humbly open your mind and heart, and try.

> *"I have not spoken in secret, in a dark place of the earth: I said not unto the seed of Jacob, Seek ye Me in vain: I the Lord speak Righteousness, I declare things that are Right."*
>
> Isaiah 45:19

Gaining spiritual understanding about the Lord's Testimony to you is life-altering. It Enlightens your sense of Reason while Inspiring you to develop into the person that you are capable of becoming.

In the Old Testament, the Truth of that understanding is described as an eternal Light placed over the altar of our lives, Exodus 27:20-21 and Isaiah 60:19-20. In the New Testament, John 1:4 and Revelation 22:5 designate that Truth as the *Light of men.*

Receiving the Truth of that understanding will Give meaning and Purpose to everything you think, feel, and do in life. And so, for your Good and for the Good of all, the Lord asks you to learn from Him and then trust Him, relying on what He has been teaching all of us since the beginning of human existence. In Psalms 118.23, He Promises that what He will develop within you as you abide by that understanding will be nothing less than Marvelous in your eyes.

> "*Give ye ear, and hear My Voice; hearken, and hear My Speech.*"
>
> Isaiah 28:23

Throughout the Bible, the Lord uses physical things to teach you about spiritual things. By doing so, He employs the things you have become familiar with since your earliest childhood to teach you about the things that affect your mental, emotional, and spiritual wellbeing. In this manner He uses the letter of the Word to Communicate with you about the Spirit of His Word.

This is His Speech. It is the Way He Gives you understanding about why and how you must live your life, and it is the language spoken throughout the Heavens.

> "*If I have told you about earthly things, and ye believe not, how shall you believe if I tell you about Heavenly things?*"
>
> John 3:12

The very first Words in the Bible are "In the Beginning." These Words describe a spiritual awakening within your mind and heart about the Truth of Love. They describe the time when spiritual Reality begins to dawn within you about what leads to innermost happiness and genuine fulfillment in life. From this Glorious Beginning, the Lord begins to divide the darkness from the Light within your soul.

> The Word "Water" describes genuine spiritual knowledge about Divine Truth.

Within the first book and chapter of Genesis, the stage is set.

> "*In the Beginning God Created the Heaven and the earth.*
>
> "*And the earth was without form, and void; and darkness was upon the face of the deep. And the Spirit of God moved upon the face of the Waters.*
>
> "*And God said, Let there be Light: and there was Light.*"
>
> Genesis 1:1–3

The Word: *Water* describes genuine spiritual knowledge about Divine Truth.

The Words: *And the Spirit of God moved upon the face of the Waters* illustrate the Lord internally Inspiring you with spiritual knowledge about Divine Truth. When willfully applied to the Way you live your life, that knowledge acts as an internal cleansing, dissipating falsities and evils of all sorts from preventing you from recognizing what matters most in life. When acknowledged and accepted, that spiritual understanding moves everything within you for the Better.

And so, throughout the Bible the Lord describes spiritual knowledge about Divine Truth as Life-Giving. He Offers it to you freely in Order to prepare you to spiritually grow and prosper in all that you think, feel, and do.

Spiritually, nothing Good will continue to grow and prosper within you without willfully applying that knowledge to the Way you live your life.

The Words: *And God said, Let there be Light: and there was Light* reveal that Holy understanding dawning within your life.

> "O send out Thy Light and Thy Truth: let them lead me; let them bring me unto Thy Holy Hill, and to Thy Tabernacles.
>
> "Then will I go unto the Altar of God, unto God my exceeding Joy: yea, upon the harp will I praise Thee, O God my God."
>
> Psalms 43:3–4

Throughout the Bible, the Lord describes you as a "temple" and as a "church." He describes you in this manner because you have the spiritual potential to eternally host the Joy and Goodness of His Love within your mind and heart. Everywhere He teaches about the Way you, all of us, must live our lives in Order to receive, retain, and forever share in those incomparable Blessings. Using that understanding to make good judgments about why and how you must is spiritual Wisdom.

> "Doth not Wisdom cry? And understanding put forth Her Voice?
>
> "She standeth in the top of High Places, by the Way in the Places of the Paths.
>
> "She crieth at the Gates, at the entry of the City, at the coming in at the Doors."
>
> Proverbs 8:1-3

Everywhere the Lord teaches about your need to heed His Call. He
Beckons you, and me, to turn away from the pride of self-intelligence
and to turn toward Him for knowledge about the Way we must live our
lives. Through that understanding He Guides you to take steps, to enter
through Gates and to open the Doors which will allow the Truth and
Goodness of His Love for you to come to Rest in Peace and Goodwill
within your soul.

With each story, lesson, and example recorded in the Bible, He Reasons
with you about why and how you must. All the while He asks you to
abide by the Principles that He is asking you to keep foremost during
your entire spiritual journey in this world. Those are the Principles of
His Righteousness, and they are embedded within the Commandments
He has Given to all of us. To you. And so, He asks you to "Post" those
Sacred Principles upon the "gates" of your mind and heart, teaching you
that these are the Standards that He has established to protect you from
mental, emotional, and spiritual harm as He develops your full potential
into becoming a "Place" for His Abode.

> "And thou shalt write them upon the door Posts of thine house,
> and upon thine gates.
>
> "That your Days may be multiplied, and the Days of your
> children, in the Land which the Lord sware unto your fathers
> to Give them, as the Days of Heaven upon the earth."
>
> Deuteronomy 11:20–21

The spiritual potential of your mind and heart is described throughout
the Bible as a "land." It is that potential that the Lord Wills to prepare into
becoming a fertile ground. Through that preparation He seeds your mind

and heart with spiritual understanding so that the Goodness of His Love for you may take root, grow, and prosper within your soul. As you work with Him to tend that growth, He Promises to deliver you into "the Land which the Lord sware unto your fathers to Give them, as the Days of Heaven upon the earth."

> "*Now He that planteth and He that watereth are One: and every man shall receive his own reward according to his own labor.*
>
> "*For we are labourers together with God: ye are God's husbandry, ye are God's building.*"
>
> 1 Corinthians 3:8-9

In themselves, spiritual curiosity, religious affiliations, and mere confessions of the mouth are ineffectual in unlocking the full spiritual potential of your soul. The Lord teaches you that your full spiritual potential can only be unlocked as you wholeheartedly apply what He is Showing you to be True and Right to each and every aspect of your life. And so everywhere in Scripture He beseeches you to remove any stumbling blocks that would have you think otherwise. He Promises that as you do so, He will Gift you with Thoughts and Affections that are much Higher and much more Perfect than anything you could have ever conceived on your own.

> "*Go through, go through the Gates; prepare ye the Way of the people; cast up, cast up the Highway, gather out the stones; lift up a Standard for the people.*"
>
> Isaiah 62:10

Each stage of your spiritual progression in life is described as a "Day" in the Bible. Each successful progression is depicted as a "night" turning into "morning." As you continue to abide by what the Lord is teaching you to be True and Right, those progressions will multiply and propagate within you with newly conceived thoughts and affections received from the Lord's Thoughts and Affections.

The Words in Deuteronomy 11:21, *That your Days may be multiplied, and the Days of your children* illuminate that propagation. In this manner your mind and heart become spiritually born again, formed, and made into an image to His Truth and as a likeness to the Goodness of His Love for you.

> *"Jesus answered and said unto him, Verily, verily, I say unto thee, Except a man be born again, he cannot see the Kingdom of Heaven."*
>
> John 3:3

"If ye keep My Commandments, ye shall abide in My Love; even as I have kept My Father's Commandments and abide in His Love."

John 15:10

"He that hath an ear, let him hear what the Spirit saith unto the churches."

Revelation 2:29

In my *Author's Note,* I shared that I was born to a Jewish father and a Catholic mother. And although my mother converted to Judaism when I was three, she instilled a great affection and respect for the Christian faith within our family.

Being brought up in a Reformed Jewish house of worship, I studied the Hebrew language as it applied to the Old Testament and was Bar Mitzvahed at age thirteen. Sabbath services and weekend religious study classes were attended regularly at our local Jewish Temple until I was fifteen, when I graduated with confirmation in that religious education. And although I had come to feel a deep bond with God during that time, I drifted away from religious thought and practice shortly thereafter.

During my late teens and early twenties, I was fully occupied with my educational goals, earning a Bachelor of Arts in psychology and a Master's degree in business administration, after which I began full-time employment. I gave no further reverence or consideration to religious thought or practice, period.

What took their place could best be described as an immersion in self-centered thoughts, selfish desires, and their corresponding egotistical behaviors. Everything was about me, worldly success, and the *pleasures of life.* I was a true master of them all.

In my mid-twenties I experienced circumstances that stopped me in my tracks. Those circumstances brought me to a startling and very humbling recognition that there was something much deeper to life than anything I had previously been willing to acknowledge. That realization led me to seek sensible answers about what that "something" was, and about what it implied for the way I was living my life.

My quest began for those answers. I started by examining and reexamining various philosophies and religions, both ancient and current. I visited many religious houses of worship, attending their various services and speaking with their leaders and teachers, asking them countless questions about their core beliefs and religious doctrines. In many ways their answers were beneficial, but perplexing in many other ways.

According to a February 2021 report from the Center for the Study of Global Christianity, there are currently more than 200 differing Christian denominations in the US alone, and a staggering 45,000 globally. Each has both subtle and not-so-subtle differences in belief and doctrine.

Wikipedia reveals that there are several Jewish religious movements also known as denominations. Each has significant differences in belief and doctrine. Most perplexing of all is that each of these many Christian and Jewish denominations claim to be exclusively correct.

I was confused with what seemed like a tug-of-war within and between the many Christian and Jewish denominations I encountered. I was left wanting. And I recognized that same "wanting" was being experienced by countless others.

As I reflected upon these many competing religious factions, certain Principles became apparent that united all the best of them into One. I came to recognize these as the age-old Principles of Righteousness expounded in the Bible, from beginning to end. I realized that they formed the foundation for all the Truth and Goodness existing and perpetuating within the human race.

I began to comprehend that these Sacred Principles override any differences between us, you and I included, and are indispensable for our individual and collective mental, emotional and spiritual wellbeing. I began to understand that these Principles are the Keys to unlocking our innermost happiness and genuine fulfillment in life.

As I continued in my everyday working career, I began teaching business classes. During those classes, I attempted to incorporate the Principles I had come to recognize as the most important of all into what I was teaching. They became the core of each class. I taught graduate courses in entrepreneurship, management, and business ethics in the MBA program for 20 years at California Lutheran University. Although I was surrounded by the Lutheran environment, I never became a formal member of the Lutheran church.

He will Gift you with Thoughts and Affections which are much Higher than your own.

Rather than joining any specific religious denomination, I have tried to keep my focus centered upon the Principles that unite us all together in understanding the most important things of all.

It is now time for me to share the spiritual meaning and implications of those invaluable Principles with you.

3
Our Creation Story

Your realization that the Principles of Righteousness
lead to all things Good within your life is the beginning
of all genuine spiritual understanding.

> *The entrance of Thy Words Giveth Light: it Giveth understanding to the simple.*
>
> Psalms 111:30

Spiritually, the Word "simple" does not describe the unintelligent or uneducated; rather, it describes not being confused about what brings innermost happiness and genuine fulfillment into your life.

> *And God saw the Light, that it was Good: and God divided the Light from the darkness.*
>
> *And God called the Light Day, and the darkness He called night. And the evening and the morning were the first Day.*
>
> Genesis 1:4-5

Each stage of your spiritual progression is described by a *Day* in the Bible. Each successful progression is depicted as a *night* being turned into a new *morning*. That foundational awareness is presented by the Words: *And God saw the Light, that it was Good: and God divided the Light from the darkness.*

As you continue to receive understanding from the Lord, new thoughts and affections from His Thoughts and Affections will continue to spring forth and multiply within your life. In this manner you become as one of His children in mind, heart, and soul.

> "*And Jesus called a little child unto Him, and set him in the midst of them,*
>
> "*And said, Verily I say unto you, Except ye be converted, and become as little children, ye shall not enter into the Kingdom of Heaven.*
>
> "*Whoever therefore shall humble themselves as this little child, the same is the greatest in the Kingdom of Heaven.*"
>
> Matthew 18:2-4

Your honest, sincere, and humble realization that the Principles of Righteousness lead to all things Good within your life is the beginning of all genuine spiritual understanding. As you live your life accordingly, the Lord puts all things in their proper Order within your thoughts and affections. From that new Order, He brings a new sense of Reason into all that you think, feel, and do.

> "*And God said, Let there be a firmament in the midst of the Waters, and let it divide the Waters from the waters.*"
>
> Genesis 1:6

The Words: *Let there be a firmament in the midst of the Waters* describe the Lord forming this new spiritual rationality within you. As this new sense of Reason grows and matures, it brings clarity into your ability to discern the differences between Truth from falsity and Right from wrong, spiritually described by the Words: *and let it divide the Waters from the waters.*

"And God made the firmament, and divided the waters that
were under the firmament from the Waters that were above the
firmament and it was so."

Genesis 1:7

As you continue to apply yourself to living your life in the Way the Lord is teaching you that you must, He Gifts you with all the spiritual sensibility you need to make Good Judgments during your spiritual journey ahead.

The Words: *And God made the firmament and divided the waters that were under the firmament from the Waters that were above the firmament* illustrate His increasing your ability to separate falsity from Truth and wrong from Right in all you think, feel, and do in life.

The Words: *and it was so* confirms your reception of that incomparable Gift.

"And God called the firmament Heaven. And the evening and
the morning were the second Day."

Genesis 1:8

Becoming spiritually rational enables you to choose wisely about the things that affect your mental, emotional and spiritual wellbeing, described by the Words *And God called the firmament Heaven.*

The Words: *And the evening and the morning were the second Day* describe coming into that new state of spiritual Enlightenment.

"And God said, Let the Waters under the Heaven be gathered
together unto One Place, and let the dry land appear and it
was so."

Genesis 1:9

The Words: *Let the Waters under the Heaven be gathered together unto One Place* illustrate your new perspective coming into Single focus about the most important things of all.

The Words: *let the dry land appear* verify that new perspective establishing an internal state of surety and confidence within you about that spiritual Reality.

In Reality, your spiritual journey has really just begun.

As you willingly work with the Lord to develop that *dry land* into what is fertile and productive, you become a willing laborer, tenant, and husbandman of the things that bring His Goodness into fruition within your life. Isaiah 28:23-26, Matthew 13:1-9, and 21:23 all reveal the Truth of that spiritual Reality.

The Words: *and it was so* confirm that continuing spiritual development unfolding within your soul.

> "*And God called the dry land earth; and the gathering of the*
> *Waters called He Seas: and God saw that it was Good.*"
> Genesis 1:10

The Words: *And God called the dry land earth* describe your mind and heart developing into something Amazing to behold.

The Words: *and the gathering of the Waters called He Seas* describe spiritual knowledge converging into deep and expansive spiritual comprehension within you. That knowledge is filled with Life-Giving Principles about the the most important things of all.

> "*And God said, Let the earth bring forth grass, the*
> *herb yielding seed, and the fruit tree yielding fruit after his*
> *kind, whose seed is in itself, upon the earth: and it was so.*

> *"And the earth brought forth grass, and herb yielding seed after His kind, and the Tree yielding fruit, whose seed was in itself, after His kind: and God saw that it was Good.*
>
> *"And the evening and the morning were the third Day."*
>
> Genesis 1:11-13

The Words: *And God said, Let the earth bring forth grass, the herb yielding seed, and the fruit tree yielding fruit after his kind* reveal the increase of all things True and Good within your life.

The Words: *whose seed is in itself, upon the earth* represent like begetting like —as the more you tend to those *things,* the more of the same they will bring forth within your mind, heart, and soul.

And although this *third Day* in your evolving spiritual development is indeed Marvelous to behold, there is still much more work left to be done. In Reality, your spiritual journey has really just begun.

~

> *"And God said, let there be Lights in the firmament of Heaven to divide the day from the night; and let them be for Signs, and for Seasons, and for Days, and Years.*
>
> *"And let them be for Lights in the firmament of the Heaven to Give Light upon the earth: and it was so."*
>
> Genesis 1:14-15

As you continue to live your life in the Way the Lord is Showing you that you must, He continues to Enlighten you about all things True and Right.

The Words: *And God said, let there be Lights in the firmament of the Heaven to divide the day from the night* describe His continuing to Illuminate the differences between Truth and falsity and Right from wrong in all that you think, feel, and do.

The Words: *and let them be for Signs* depict the Principles of His Righteousness continuously being Raised Up as Standards to Guide you during your spiritual journey ahead.

The Words: *and for Seasons, and for Days, and Years* spiritually describe the internal changes you will necessarily undergo as you allow the Lord to reform you and transform you into the person that He has Purposed for you to become.

The Words: *and it was so* confirm a further advance in your mental, emotional, and spiritual evolution.

> "*And God made two great Lights; the greater to rule over the Day, and the lesser to rule the night. He made the Stars also.*"
>
> Genesis 1:16

The Words: *And God made two great Lights* describe what the Lord has established to Guide you in times of gladness and in times of trial.

The Words: *The greater to rule over the Day* describe His Guidance during times of gladness.

The Words: *The lesser to rule the night* describe His Guidance during your trials and tribulations.

The Words: *He made the Stars also* describe the individual lessons He Provides to help you find Direction and navigate, even during the most trying times of your life.

> "*And God set them in the firmament of the Heaven to Give Light upon the earth.*"

*"And to rule over the Day and over the night, and to divide the
Light from the darkness: and God saw that it was Good.*

"And the evening and the morning were the fourth Day."

Genesis 1:17-19

The Words: *And God set them in the firmament of Heaven to Give Light
upon the earth* describe the Lord further Elevating your ability to discern
things True and Right within your life. They are described as being *set in the
firmament of Heaven* because they Give you the ability to discern Thoughts
that are much Higher and much more Perfect than anything you could
ever conceive on your own.

The Words: *And the evening and the morning were the fourth Day* describe
your having come into a more fully developed and much clearer spiritual
comprehension about the Truth of Love.

~

*"And God said, Let the Waters bring forth abundantly the moving
creature that hath Life, and the fowl that may fly above the
earth in the open firmament of Heaven."*

Genesis 1:20

Willfully applying genuine spiritual knowledge to the Way you live your
life allows the Lord to develop your full potential to host the incomparable
Blessings that He has Prepared for you to receive since your inception.
And although *creatures* are used to describe both positive and negative
spiritual characteristics in the Bible, those described as having *Life* contain
positive attributes such as innocence, commitment, and perseverance, all
of indispensable service to you as you continue to walk in the Light of
His Righteousness. Uplifted and Inspired by the realization of all the
Good the Lord is bringing into your life, your new thoughts about these
Wonderful things are spiritually described as *the fowl that may fly above
the earth in the open firmament of Heaven.*

> "*And God Created Great whales, and every Living creature that moveth, that the Waters brought forth abundantly, after their kind, and every winged fowl after His kind: and God saw that it was Good.*"
>
> Genesis 1:21

Great whales portray the most encompassing Principles existing within spiritual knowledge about the Truth of Love. Throughout the Bible the particulars of those Principles are described as "fish."

The Words: *and every Living creature that moveth, that the Waters brought forth abundantly, after their kind* reveal the endless arrays of positive characteristics that come forth from abiding by those spiritual Principles. Inspired and Uplifting, succeeding thoughts are portrayed as *every winged fowl after His kind.*

The Joy of that internal experience continually validates all He has Given you.

As these positive spiritual characteristics and Elevated thoughts all *move* and *soar* within you *after their kind,* they transform the Way you think, feel, and act in life. The Words *and God saw that it was Good* describe those Wonders being *brought forth abundantly* within you by the Lord as you continue to live your life in the Way He is Showing you that you must.

> "*And God Blessed them, Saying, be fruitful, and multiply, and fill the Waters in the seas, and let the fowl multiply in the earth.*"
>
> "*And the evening and the morning were the fifth Day.*"
>
> Genesis 1:22-23

As the Lord brings forth the Goodness of His Love within your mind and heart you are spiritually described as becoming *fruitful.* As His Goodness propagates within your soul it *multiplies* in Goodwill toward all others. These incomparable Blessings are active, always bringing forth like kind in Ways that will far exceed your greatest expectations.

The Words: *and fill the Waters in the seas, and let the fowl multiply in the earth* illuminate the Joy of that internal experience, continually validating all that He has freely Given you to know about things that are True and Right.

The Words: *And the evening and the morning were the fifth Day* describe that new Marvelous spiritual state continuing to unfold within you.

~

"*And God said let the earth bring forth the Living creature after His kind: cattle, and creeping thing, and beast of the earth, after His kind; and it was so.*

"*And God made the beast of the earth after His kind, and the cattle after their kind, and everything that creepeth upon the earth after His kind and God saw that it was Good.*"

Genesis 1:24-25

All things True and Good within your life originate from the Lord's Unselfish Love for you. Your developing ability to grow in hosting those *Living* spiritual characteristics is spiritually described as *And God said let the earth bring forth the Living creature after His kind.*

Bringing forth *cattle* describes gaining the capacity to receive all the mental, emotional, and spiritual nourishment you will need to sustain you during your spiritual journey ahead.

Bringing forth *creeping thing* describes the Lord providing the sensual things that serve His Purpose for the Creation of your soul.

Bringing forth *the beast of the earth after His kind* describes His propagating spiritual attributes that willingly serve His Divine Truth within your life.

The Words: *and it was so* confirm that spiritual understanding.

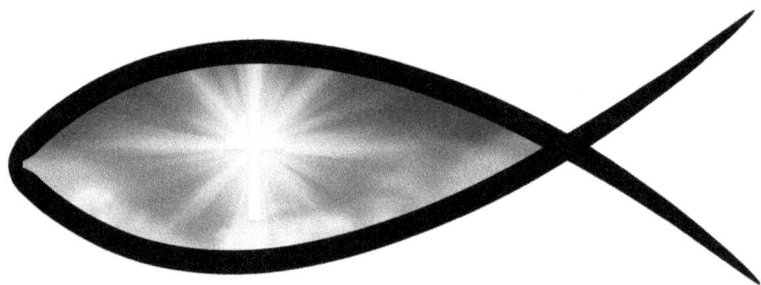

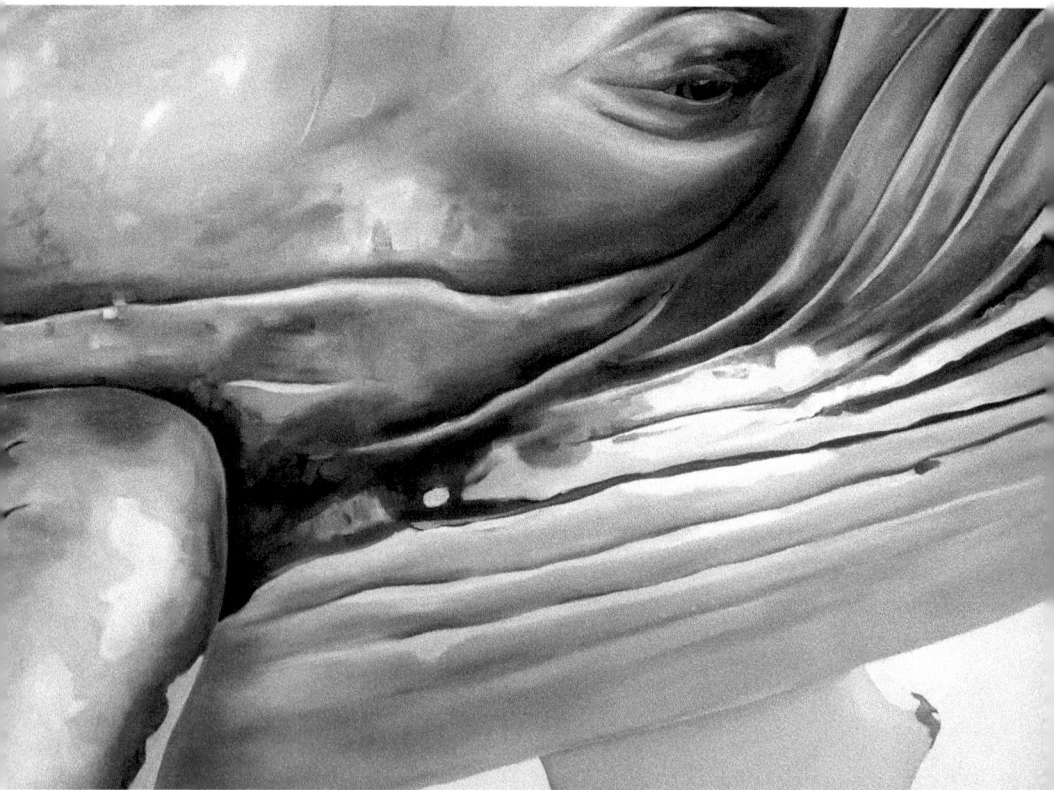

The Most Encompassing Principles of All. Oil painting by Marie McKenzie, 2023

The Words: *and God saw that it was Good* once again describe the continuing internal evolution of your mind, heart, and soul.

~

"*And God said, Let us make man in our Image, after our Likeness and let them have dominion over the fish of the sea, and over the fowl of the air, and over the cattle, and over all the earth, and over every creeping thing that creepeth upon the earth.*"

Genesis 1:26

That there is One Loving God is proclaimed throughout the entire Bible, from Beginning to End. And because His Love for you is Infinite, and you are finite, you can receive the Qualities and Virtues of His Love for you in combinations that make you special, unique, and irreplaceable to Him and to all others, no two ever being exactly the same.

The Words: *Let us make man in our Image, after our Likeness* describe the Lord bringing the limitless arrays of those incomparable Qualities and Virtues into the minds, hearts and souls of all who willingly live their lives according to the Principles of His Righteousness, nothing withheld.

The Words: *and let them have dominion over the fish of the sea, and over the fowl of the air, and over the cattle, and over all the earth, and over every creeping thing that creepeth upon the earth* describe becoming Blessed with new spiritual understanding about the Way you may take command over the destiny of your own soul.

~

"*So God Created man in His own Image, in the Image of God He Created him; male and female Created He them.*"

Genesis 1:27

The Word *male* is descriptive of your ability to host True Thoughts from the Lord's Thoughts within your mind. The Word *female* is descriptive of your ability to host Unselfish Affections for those Thoughts within your heart. When they become untied together in Righteousness, they have the potential to bring forth unlimited generations of inmost Joy within your soul, then overflowing with Goodwill toward all others around you.

> "*And God Blessed them, and God said unto them, Be fruitful, and multiply, and replenish the earth, and subdue it, and have dominion over the fish of the sea, and over the fowl of the air, and over every Living thing that moveth upon the earth.*"
>
> Genesis 1:28

The Words: *And God Blessed them, and God said unto them, Be fruitful, and multiply* portray His Truth and Affection joined together in Righteousness within you, then propagating like kind within your mind, heart and soul.

As you continue to live your life in the Way the Lord has Shown you to be True and Right, He continually *replenishes* the Joy of those invaluable Blessings within your mind and heart. From that continual replenishment you are Given the ability to *subdue* anything that would try to harm the spiritual integrity of your soul. And through the strength of those Gifts, the Lord Gives you *dominion* over all you think, feel, and do.

⌒

> "*And God said, Behold, I have Given you every herb bearing seed, which is upon the face of all the earth, and every tree, in which is the fruit of a tree yielding seed; to you it shall be for meat.*"

"And to every beast of the earth, and to every fowl of the air, and to every thing the creepth upon the earth, wherein there is Life, I have Given every green herb for meat and it was so."

Genesis 1:29-30

Through your willingness to continue to live your life by seeking Righteousness First in all you think, feel, and do the Lord Provides you with everything needed to develop into the person He has Purposed for you to become. Throughout the Old and New Testaments, He teaches you that you must diligently tend these things. As you do so He Promises that you will grow wiser, stronger, and internally prosperous in mind, heart, and soul. And although the "seeds" that allow these things to grow and prosper within you may seem small and insignificant at first, He teaches you that they contain the most important things of all.

"Now the parable is this: The seed is the Word of God."

Luke 8:11

The Words: *and it was so* describe that spiritual understanding, unfolding within all who are wise enough, brave enough, and humble enough to live their lives accordingly.

"And God saw every thing that He had made, and, behold, it was very Good. And the evening and the morning were the sixth Day."

Genesis 1:31

The final stage of your spiritual evolution as you continue to walk in the Light of the Lord's Righteousness is described by the *Sixth Day* in the Bible. It depicts your having become ready to fully inherit the incomparable Blessings that He has Prepared for you to receive since your inception.

"Thus the Heavens and the earth were finished, and all the host of them.

"And on the Seventh Day God ended His Work which He had Made; and He Rested on the Seventh Day from all his Work which He had Made.

"And God Blessed the Seventh Day and sanctified it: because that in it He had Rested from all His Work which God Created and made."

Genesis 2:1-3

The *Seventh Day* describes a perpetual state of Joy, Peace, and Goodness coming to fruition within your soul. It describes a state of being wherein the Lord will have liberated you from all that had previously prevented you from coming into, and remaining within that invaluable Heavenly state of being. That liberation allows Him to Rest from all the Work that He has done to shape you and form you into the person He has Purposed for you to become. In that *Day,* He will have fulfilled the Promise of His Covenant within your life. You do honor the work of His Love and Wisdom by remembering why and how you must keep that Sabbath Day Holy in all that you think, feel, and do. Keeping that Day Holy within your life is your work of Love for Him, and for the Good of all around you.

"And these are the generations of the Heavens and of the earth when they were Created, in the Day that the Lord God made the earth and the Heavens."

Genesis 2:4

From the Beginning of your existence the Lord has Willed to separate
the Light from the darkness within your life. As you willingly seek His
Righteousness First in all you think, feel, and do,
He leaves it up to you.
He Promises to save you from mental, emotional,
and spiritual harm as He delivers you into an eternal state of Heavenly
Joy. Doing so with all your mind, heart, and strength constitutes the work
required to Love Him above all else, and to love others in the Way He has
Loved you.

The Words: *And these are the generations of the Heaven and the earth*
when they were Created, in the Day that the Lord God made the earth and
the Heavens describe those Sacred Promises being fulfilled within your life.

> "*For the Lord God is a Sun and Shield: the Lord will Give*
> *Grace and Glory: no Good thing will He withhold from them*
> *that walk Uprightly.* "
>
> Psalms 84:11

The potential for Truth and Goodness to seed, grow, and prosper within
humanity is limitless. Allowing the Lord to fully develop that latent
potential within each of us will put our world into a creative, innovative, and
prosperous trajectory like none other. Yet He leaves it up to every one of
us, from our own free will, to work with Him to bring that incomparable
Offering into fruition within our lives.

> "*Speak unto the children of Israel, that they bring Me an*
> *offering of every man that bringeth willingly with his heart*
> *ye shall take My Offering.* "
>
> Exodus 25:2

~

"*And every plant of the field before it was in the earth, and every herb of the field before it grew: for the Lord God had not caused it to rain upon the earth, and there was not a man to till the ground.*"

Genesis 2:5

The Words: *And every plant of the field before it was in the earth, and every herb of the field before it grew* reflect our latent spiritual potential to receive, retain, and forever share in the Goodness of the Lord's Love for us.

The Words: *for the Lord God had not caused it to rain upon the earth* describe our mental, emotional, and spiritual state of being prior to acknowledging, accepting, and applying genuine spiritual knowledge to the Way we live our lives.

The Words: *and there was not a man to till the ground* reveal a lack of understanding about the overriding importance of working to internalize these invaluable spiritual things.

> "But there went up a mist from the earth, and Watered the whole face of the ground."
>
> Genesis 2:6

Internalizing the spiritual knowledge the Lord freely Offers you is Life-Giving. The Words: *But there went up a mist from the earth, and Watered the whole face of the ground* describe welcoming that understanding into your life. Your willingness to do so prepares everything within your mind, heart, and soul to change, grow, and continually evolve for the Better.

> "And the Lord God formed man of the dust of the ground, and Breathed into his nostrils the Breath of Life; and man became a Living soul."
>
> Genesis 2:7

Prior to acknowledging and accepting your need to live your life in the Way the Lord has Shown you that you must, you are spiritually described by the Word *dust*. Through your willingness to live your life according to His Commandments, you become described as having received *the Breath of Life*. With that understanding received, and tended, you allow Him to spiritually reform you and transform you into becoming *a Living soul*.

~

> *"And the Lord God planted a Garden Eastward in Eden; and there He put the man whom He had formed."*
>
> Genesis 2:8

The Blessings of True Life from the Lord's Life are Marvelous to behold. Yet your need to attend the Righteous Principles that support them is inescapable. Thinking otherwise is spiritual folly.

> *"And the Lord took the man, and put him into the Garden of Eden to dress it and to keep it."*
>
> Genesis 2:15

~

> *"Until the Spirit be poured upon us from on High, and the wilderness be a fruitful field, and the fruitful field be counted for a forest.*
>
> *"Then Judgment shall dwell in the wilderness, and Righteousness remain in the fruitful field."*
>
> Isaiah 32:15-17

You resemble a spiritual wilderness before you allow the Lord to reform you and transform you in the Light of His Righteousness. Without the work required to allow Him to do so, you will remain spiritually inhospitable to the reception of His Truth and Goodness within your mind, heart, and soul.

The Words: *Until the Spirit be poured upon us from on High, and the wilderness be a fruitful field, and the fruitful field be counted for a forest* describe the immeasurable importance of receiving and applying that spiritual understanding to the Way you live your life.

The Words: *Then Judgment shall dwell in the wilderness, and Righteousness remain in the fruitful field* demonstrate the internal effects of living your life accordingly.

How much more clearly can the Lord describe the most important things of all?

> "*With the ancient is Wisdom; and in length of Days understanding.*"
>
> Job 12:12

> "*Jesus answered and said unto him, Are thou a master of Israel, and knowest not these things?*"
>
> John 3:10

Angelo I: Madonna Sistina, oil painting by Raffaello Sanzio

Reflections
Opportunity
Wellbeing
Modern Science and Scripture

Understanding spiritual things spiritually Offers you the Greatest Opportunity of your lifetime. It Guides, Comforts, and Strengthens your mental, emotional, and spiritual wellbeing.

It dissipates any conflict between modern science and the meaning and Intent of Scripture. It eliminates the need to question the validity of our planet's physical evolution over time. It eliminates the need to defend faith in God's Word by needlessly trying to discredit scientific discoveries unfolding through studies of geography, archeology, biology, and physics.

- It eliminates the need to conflict our children about compatibility of these things.
- It eliminates the need to pit common sense and rational thought against letter-of-the-Word misinterpretations about God's Testimony to us.

It prevents us from falling into religious pitfalls of all sorts. It brings Divine Truth back into Singular focus as the Lord leads us in the Way we must live our lives.

It puts all other contentions to Rest within your life.

"Who also hath made us able ministers of the New Testament; not of the letter, but of the Spirit: for the letter killeth, but the Spirit Giveth Life."

2 Corinthians 3:6

THOU SHALT HAVE NO OTHER GODS BEFORE ME.

Exodus 20:3

4

True Thoughts and Unselfish Affections

From His Love for you, the Lord continually returns to you.

$\mathcal{T}$he Lord has Given you this very first Commandment for One Reason and for One Reason only—namely, for your Good and for the Good of all around you.

> *And now, Israel, what does the Lord thy God require of thee, but to fear the Lord thy God, to walk in all His Ways, and to love Him, and to serve the Lord thy God with all thy heart and with all thy soul,*
>
> *To keep the Commandments of the Lord, and His Statutes, that I Command thee this Day for thy Good?*
>
> Deuteronomy 10:12-13

In a positive sense, the Word *fear* means reverence. You reverence the Lord's Promise to save you from mental, emotional, and spiritual harm and deliver you into a state of eternal Heavenly Joy as you live your life in the Way He is Showing you that you must. To do so is *to love Him* above all else. Through your willingness to do so *with all thy heart and with all thy soul,* you befriend His Purpose for the Creation of your soul.

"The Law of the Lord is Perfect, converting the soul: the Testimony of the Lord is sure, making wise the simple.

"The Statutes of the Lord are Right, rejoicing the heart: the Commandment of the Lord is pure, Enlightening the eyes.

"The fear of the Lord is Clean, enduring for ever: the Judgments of the Lord are True and Righteous altogether.

"More to be desired are they than gold, yea, than much fine gold: sweeter also than honey and the honeycomb.

"Moreover by them is thy servant warned: and in keeping of them there is great Reward."

Psalms 19:7-11

As you willingly abide by the Lord's First Commandment, you will quickly come to realize that doing so requires you to love others in the Way that He Loves you. Soon, you will find out that it is impossible to do the One, without also doing the Other.

"Then one of them, which was a lawyer, asked Him a question, tempting Him, and saying,

"Master, which is the great Commandment in the Law?

"Jesus said unto him, Thou shalt love the Lord thy God with all thy heart, and with all thy soul, and with all thy mind.

"This is the First, and Great Commandment.

"And the Second is like unto it, Thou shalt love thy neighbor as thyself.

> "On these Two Commandments hang all the Law and
> the prophets."
>
> Matthew 22:35-40

As you come to recognize that the Lord is Righteousness Himself, the meaning of loving Him "with all thy heart, and with all thy soul, and with all thy mind" will become quite apparent. That realization will manifest the Truth about the Way you must think, feel, and act toward all others.

> "And the King shall answer and say unto them, Verily I say unto
> you, Inasmuch as ye have done it to one of the least of these My
> brethren, ye have done it unto Me."
>
> Matthew 25:40

As many times as the Lord has Offered humanity understanding about the meaning of having *no other gods before Him*, it is amazing how many times we have devised our own definitions, and then anointed them as *articles of faith*. Those redefinitions cause us to lose focus about our spiritual task at hand.

From the Beginning to the Ending in the Bible, the Lord warns you about dire effects of losing focus about what must always be, and remain, your First Works. And so, from His Love for you He continually returns to you, addressing your need to recognize and abide what must always be, and remain, your First Love.

In Matthew He reminds you,

> "The light of the body is the eye; if therefore thine eye be Single,
> thy whole body shall be full of Light."
>
> Matthew 6:22

In John He teaches you,

> "If ye love Me, keep My Commandments."
>
> John 14:15

In Revelation He warns you,

*"Remember therefore from whence you art fallen, and repent,
and do the First Works; or else I will come unto thee quickly,
and will remove thy Candlestick out of His Place, except thou
repent."*

Revelation 2:5

*"And the Lord God Commanded the man, Saying, Of every tree
of the Garden thou mayest freely eat:*

*"But of the tree of the knowledge of good and evil, thou shalt
not eat of it for in that day that thou eatest thereof thou shalt
surely die."*

Genesis 2:16-17

Spiritually, *trees* are descriptive of what draws genuine spiritual sustenance
up, into your mind and heart. When rooted within the Principles of Righteousness they bring spiritual Goodness into fruition within your soul.
That fruition contains seeds of the Kind that will multiply and prosper in
Goodwill toward others for endless generations to come.

*"Be not wise in thine own eyes: fear the Lord, and depart
from evil.*

"It shall be health to thy navel, and marrow to thy bones.

*"Honor the Lord with thy substance, and with the first fruits
of all thy increase:*

*"So shall thy barns be filled with Plenty, and thy presses shall
burst out with New Wine."*

Proverbs 3:7-10

The tree of the knowledge of good and evil describes thoughts conceived from pride of your own self-intelligence. What comes forth from that *tree* are errant philosophies and misleading religious doctrines of every sort. And so, throughout the Bible the Lord Instructs you not to allow yourself to become "wise in your own eyes," but rather to trust in what He is teaching you about why and how you must live your life.

> "*Woe unto they that call evil good, and Good evil; that put darkness for light, and Light for darkness; that put bitter for sweet, and Sweet for bitter!*
>
> "*Woe unto them that are wise in their own eyes, and prudent in their own sight!*"
>
> Isaiah 5:20-21

> "*Thus saith the Lord, of hosts, Hearken not unto the words of the prophets that prophesy unto you; they make you vain; they speak a vision of their own heart, and not out of the mouth of the Lord.*
>
> "*They say unto them that despise Me, The Lord hath said, Ye shall have peace; and they say unto everyone that walketh after the imagination of his own heart, No evil shall come upon you.*"
>
> Jeremiah 23:16-17

> "*Then if any man shall say unto you, Lo, here is Christ, or there; believe it not.*
>
> "*For there shall arise false Christs, and false prophets, and shall show great signs and wonders; insomuch that, if it were possible, they shall deceive the very elect.*
>
> "*Behold, I have told you before.*"
>
> Matthew 24:23-25

The Word *Christ* means Divine Truth. And although the Lord has always freely Offered us spiritual knowledge about His Divine Truth, time after time, to our own great detriment, we have devised our own "visions" about what constitutes "true and saving faith" in His Testimony to us.

Those who promote those false visions are described as "false Christs, and false prophets." In Numbers 33:55 and Acts 9:5, their zealous attempts to impose their "visions" upon others are described as those who *kick against the pricks.* Nevertheless, from His Love for humanity the Lord continually returns to us, Willing only to restore the spiritual understanding we so greatly need to return into His Love's Embrace.

The union between True Thoughts and Unselfish Affections within your mind and heart is described as a spiritual marriage throughout the Bible.

> "*They that hate Me without a cause are more than the hairs of Mine Head: they that would destroy Me, being Mine enemies wrongfully, are mighty: then I Restored that that I took not away.*"
>
> Psalms 69:4

> "*Blessed are they that do His Commandments, that they may have the Right to the Tree of Life, and may enter in through the Gates into the City.*"
>
> Revelation 22:14

The Lord has Gifted you with the ability to host True thoughts about Divine Truth within your mind. As you place your confidence in those Thoughts, the Lord becomes spiritually described as Resting within you, and you within Him. In that spiritual state of Rest, He brings forth Unselfish Affections within your heart. Innocent in all their Ways, those Thoughts and Affections are wholesome and pure because they have come forth from the Mind and Heart of the Lord, Who is Righteousness Himself.

"And the Lord God caused a deep sleep to fall upon Adam, and he slept: and He took one of his ribs, and closed up the flesh instead thereof;

"And the rib, which the Lord had taken from man, made He a woman, and brought her unto the man.

"And Adam said, This is now bone of my bones, and flesh of my flesh: she shall be called Woman, because she was taken out of Man."

Genesis 2:21-23

The union between True Thoughts and Unselfish Affections within your mind and heart is described as a spiritual marriage throughout the Bible. Through their union, the Lord brings forth innumerable Blessings of Joy and Goodness within your life. You honor the fidelity of that marriage as you abide by the Principles of His Righteousness in all that you think, feel, and do. As you do, He brings forth like kind *to a thousand generations* within you, without ever having anything shameful to hide.

"Therefore shall a man leave his father and mother, and shall cleave unto his wife and they shall be one flesh.

"And they were both naked, the man and his wife, and were not ashamed."

Genesis 2:24-25

Willfully leaving behind your prior concepts about what brings innermost happiness and genuine fulfillment into your life in reverence to what He is Showing you to be True and Right allows your mind and heart to become joined together as One with the Lord.

The Words: *Therefore shall a man leave his father and mother* reflect your need to do so.

The Words: *and shall cleave unto his wife* are telling of your need to then cherish the fidelity of that new union within your life with the dedication and commitment deserved.

> "*Mercy and Truth are met together; Righteousness and Peace have kissed each other.*"
>
> Psalms 85:10

> "*The Kingdom of Heaven is like unto a certain King, that made a marriage for His Son.*"
>
> Matthew 22:2

~

As you willfully choose to live your life according to the Lord's Commandments, you will never become ashamed when your thoughts and affections are exposed in the Light of His Righteousness. And yet, you have been Given the free will ability to make those decisions on your own. The Lord entrusts you with that ability because it allows you to prove the differences between Truth and falsity and Right from wrong for yourself. That proving allows you to learn what Heaven is, and what Heaven is not. It allows you to validate the Truth of His Testimony to you in Ways that would be otherwise impossible.

That *proving* teaches you about the most important things of all. Yet, your free will Gift is also a two-edged sword, for if you have been Given to know these things and then choose to live your life hypocritically, your last state of being will be much worse than your first.

~

> "Bring ye all the tithes into the storehouse, that there may be meat
> in Mine house, and prove Me now herewith saith the Lord of
> hosts, if I will not open you the windows of Heaven, and pour
> you out a Blessing, that there shall not be room enough to
> receive it."
>
> Malachi 3:10

Throughout the Bible, the number "ten" pertains to the Lord's Commandments. These contain all the Principles of His Righteousness. "Tithes," or a "tenth" describe your willing efforts to abide by each and every aspect of those Holy Principles. To do so is to "offer" the Lord the most valuable things of all, for from those offerings, you allow Him to unlock your ability to host the incomparable Blessings that He has had in store for you since the beginning of time.

> "And Jesus said, For Judgment I am come into this world, that
> they which see not might see; and that they which see might be
> made blind.
>
> "And some of the Pharisees which were with Him heard these
> Words, and said unto Him, are we blind also?"
>
> John 9:39-40

The Lord came into our world to restore Good Judgment about the Way we must think, feel, and behave in life. Keeping that spiritual understanding Holy within your life is your responsibility.

~

The Fall of Man, Julius Schnorr von Carolsfeld

> "Now the serpent was more subtle than any beast of the field
> which the Lord God had made. And he said unto the woman,
> Yea, hath God said, Ye shall not eat of every tree of the Garden?
>
> "And the woman said unto the serpent, We may eat of the fruit
> of the trees of the Garden.
>
> "But of the fruit of the tree which is in the midst of the Garden,
> God hath said, Ye shall not eat of it, neither shall ye touch it,
> lest ye die."
>
> Genesis 3:1-3

The pride of self-intelligence is the lowest spiritual creature of all. It is completely self-centered, portrayed here as a subtle *serpent*. It continually offers false reasoning about what brings innermost happiness and genuine fulfillment into your life. If allowed, it will seduce you into believing that its own arguments are "true" and "right" and that the spiritual meaning of the Lord's Testimony to you is "false" and "wrong." It will attempt to turn darkness into "light," and "Light" into darkness within your mind, heart, and soul.

> "And the serpent said unto the woman, Ye shall not surely die:
>
> "For God knoweth that in the day ye eat thereof, then your eyes
> shall be opened, and ye shall be as gods, knowing good and evil.
>
> "And when the woman saw that the tree was good for food, and
> that it was pleasant to the eyes, and a tree to be desired to make
> one wise, she took of the fruit thereof, and did eat, and gave also
> unto her husband with her, and he did eat.
>
> "And the eyes of them both were opened, and they knew that
> they were naked; and they sewed fig leaves together, and made
> themselves aprons.

Adam and Eve by Albrecht Dürer

> "And they heard the Voice of the Lord God walking in the
> Garden in the cool of the Day: and Adam and his wife hid
> themselves from the presence of the Lord God amongst the trees
> of the Garden."
>
> Genesis 3:4-8

Throughout your spiritual journey in this world, the pride of your own self-intelligence will have you believe that it is correct and what the Lord has Testified to you is not. It will entice you to think falsely about the most important things of all.

The Words: *And the eyes of them both were opened, and they knew that they were naked* describe the Lord Giving you the presence of mind and heart to recognize the spiritual dangers that lay ahead. It is what you do then that determines your destiny to come.

The Words: *and they sewed fig leaves together and made themselves aprons* describe being made aware of those dangers—yet choosing to justify your own poor choices instead.

Using those justifications to form spiritual half-truths is described as hiding yourself *from the presence of the Lord God amongst the trees of the Garden.*

Without reconciling yourself with your need to live your life in the Way the Lord has Shown you that you must, your thoughts and affections will always look to flee away from being exposed in the Light of Righteousness.

That fleeing away acts to exile you from remaining within the Joy and Goodness that He has Purposed for you to dwell in since your inception. Mentally, emotionally, and spiritually, that casting out is self-inflicted.

> "And the Lord God called unto Adam, and said unto him,
> Where art thou?"
>
> Genesis 3:9

5

The Story of Abraham

Behold, My Covenant is with thee,
and thou shalt be a father of many nations.

The story of Abraham describes what results when you willingly apply yourself to abiding by the Lord's Commandments with all your mind, heart, and strength, nothing withheld. From that willingness Abraham is spiritually described as becoming the *father of many nations.*

> "*And when Abram was ninety years old and nine, the Lord appeared unto Abram, and said unto him, Abram, I am the Almighty God; walk before Me, and be thou perfect.*
>
> "*And I will make My Covenant between Me and thee, and will multiply thee exceedingly.*"
>
> Genesis 17:1-2

Having been prepared by all that had gone before him, Abram was Instructed by the Lord about the next steps required to evolve into a much Higher and much more perfect spiritual state of being.

The Words: *ninety years old and nine* explain the ending of his prior state of being, with a new and much more Glorious one just ready to unfold.

The Words: *the Lord appeared unto Abram,* describe Abram's inner awareness that something much Greater than himself was Calling him to come into that new spiritual state of being.

> The fate of your own internal happiness will be determined by your willingness to keep your Covenant Holy with Him.

The Words: *and said unto him, Abram, I am the Almighty God; walk before Me, and be thou perfect* describe Abram being Inspired by the Lord to walk the extra mile required for his spiritual journey ahead. And just as Abram was being called to do so, so are you.

Any time the number *"ten"* is referenced in the Bible, it pertains to the Principles of Righteousness. Used as a fraction, such as a tenth or a tithe, or in a multiplication, such as one hundred or one thousand, or as thousands of thousands, they all describe the Way those Holy Principles affect the Goodness within your soul. Here Abram, just coming into the age of one hundred, is undergoing a spiritual breakthrough in thought, feeling and behavior.

A *covenant* is a contract, wherein there is consideration offered through the fulfillment of mutual obligations. A willful failure to perform those obligations violates a contract. You enter into a Covenant with the Lord through your promise to seek His Righteousness First in all you think, feel, and do.

He enters a Covenant with you through His Promise to save you from mental, emotional, and spiritual harm and deliver you into an eternal state of Heavenly Joy. And as the Lord has Promised to always fulfill His Covenant to you, the fate of your own internal wellbeing will be determined by your willingness to keep your Covenant Holy with Him.

The Words: *And I will make My Covenant between Me and thee and will multiply thee exceedingly* describe the Lord's Promise to exponentially increase your Joy and happiness as you abide by the Principles of His Righteousness with all your mind, heart, and strength, nothing withheld.

" And Abram fell on his face and God talked with him, saying,

*" As for Me, Behold, My Covenant is with thee, and thou shalt
be a father of many nations. "*

Genesis 17:3-4

The Words: *And Abram fell on his face* depict the heartfelt humility
experienced when recognizing the Opportunity of your lifetime. That
realization is both wonderful to behold, and daunting. Wonderful when
considering the incomparable Rewards you are being Offered, yet daunting
when recognizing the obligations you are assuming as you walk in the
Light of Righteousness with the Lord Himself.

The Words: *and God talked with him, saying* reveals the internal Guidance
and Comfort the Lord affords you as you accept to shoulder that Sacred
responsibility.

The Lord *says* to Abram, *As for Me, behold My Covenant is with thee, and
thou shalt be a father of many nations* describe the Lord placing His trust in
your willingness to do so. The Words: *many nations* depict the innumerable
Blessings of True Thoughts and Unselfish Affections that will perpetually
come forth within you as you wholly apply yourself to uphold that Burden
of Light within your life.

~

*" Neither shall thy name be called Abram, but thy name shall
be Abraham; for a father of many nations have I made thee.*

*" And I will make thee exceedingly fruitful, and I will make
nations of thee, and kings shall come out of thee.*

*" And I will establish My Covenant between Me and thee and
thy seed after thee in their generations for an everlasting
Covenant, to be a God unto thee, and to thy seed after thee. "*

Genesis 17:5-7

Throughout the Bible, receiving a new *name* from the Lord is descriptive of having received a new spiritual character made in the image and as a likeness to His Qualities and Virtues. The Lord changed Abram's name to *Abraham* by implanting the letters *h* and *a*, taken from the Names *Jehovah* and *JAH*.

This implanting describes the Lord then being within you, and you being within Him, as portrayed within John 14:20. With those new spiritual Qualities and Virtues received, what Abraham was then readied to bring forth and perpetuate within his life is described by the Words *for a father of many nations have I made thee*.

The Words: *And I will make thee exceedingly fruitful* express the Goodness you will yield as you continue to live your life according to the Principles of the Lord's Righteousness, nothing withheld.

The Words: *and I will make nations of thee* reveal the breadth and depth of those incomparable Blessings.

The Words: *and kings shall come out of thee* describe the internal effects of allowing Divine Truth to Govern the Way you live your life. For this Reason, the Lord is called the King of Kings in 1 Timothy 6:15 and is exclaimed in Daniel 2:47, Matthew 28:18, Acts 10:36, and Revelation 19:16.

The Words: *And I will establish My Covenant between Me and thee and thy seed after thee in their generations for an everlasting Covenant, to be a God unto thee, and to thy seed after thee* confirm the Lord's Promise to fulfill His Purpose for your Creation … for the Creation of each and every one of us.

For this Reason, as written in Jeremiah 23:6 and Malachi 3:1, the Lord is called *THE LORD OUR RIGHTEOUSNESS* and *the Messenger of the Covenant.*

> "Know therefore that the Lord thy God, He is God, the faithful
> God, which keepeth Covenant and Mercy with them that love
> Him and keep His Commandments to a thousand generations."
>
> Deuteronomy 7:9

> "Stand is awe, and sin not: commune with your own heart upon
> your bed, and be still. Selah.

> "Offer the sacrifices of Righteousness, and put your trust in the
> Lord."
>
> Psalms 4:4–5

Claiming to be the legitimate heir to this spiritual knowledge due to physical, historical, or religious lineage, without keeping your Covenant of Righteousness with the Lord as your First Works causes a spiritual blindness and deafness like none other.

> "They answered and said unto Him, Abraham is our father.
> Jesus saith unto them, If ye were Abraham's children, ye would
> do the works of Abraham."
>
> John 8:39

Keeping Our Promises to the Lord

The Story of Abraham is timeless and everlasting. Through it, the Lord teaches you about the everlasting mental, emotional, and spiritual Rewards that await you as you do your utmost to live your life according to the Principles of His Righteousness. Within Psalms 26:2, 66:10-12, and Colossians 3:9-10, He teaches you that just as Abraham was asked to put all his doubts and trepidations about these things aside, so must you. And although no one is perfect in this life, He teaches you to always remember the Reasons about why and how you must apply yourself to do so, nothing withheld.

Engraving, Julius Schnorr von Carolsfeld

> "*And it came to pass after these things, that God did tempt*
> *Abraham, and said unto him, Abraham: and he said, Behold,*
> *here I am.*"
>
> Genesis 22:1

As the Lord is Compassion and Forgiveness Himself, as declared in James 1:13, He tempts no one. Rather, any temptations are a consequence of your need to confront and overcome your own internal faults and weaknesses.

To be confident in the Power of Divine Truth is to have trust in the Lord's Promise to Give you all the strength needed to confront and overcome them. As you live your life trusting in Him, He sets everything in their Rightful Order within your life. As revealed in Psalms 84:11, John 14:21, and Revelation 3:20, from that new Order He changes everything within you for the Better.

The Words: *Behold, here I am* demonstrate Abraham's willingness to trust in the Lord by heeding His Call to turn towards Him in times of temptation, and do His Will. Nothing is withheld.

> "*And He said, Take now thy son, thine only son Isaac, whom*
> *thou lovest, and get thee into the land of Moriah; and offer him*
> *there for a burnt offering upon one of the Mountains which I*
> *will tell thee of.*"
>
> Genesis 22:2

Throughout the Bible, Isaac spiritually depicts your sense of reason. And although your initial conception about what is rational may have been formed through your best intentions, you must always be willing to submit it to the Way the Lord is asking you to live your life. As you willingly do so, He aligns your sense of reason with His, setting everything in their proper Order within your soul.

Through that new Order, He divides the darkness from the Light within

Nothing is withheld. your mind and heart. That new Clarity frees you

from being entangled in any errant philosophy or misleading religious doctrine that keeps you from understanding the Way you may find innermost happiness and genuine fulfillment in life.

The *Words*: *And He said, Take now thy son, thine only son Isaac* tell of your need to take command of your own sense of reason.

The Words: *whom thou lovest* describe even the concepts you cherish most in life.

The Words: *and get thee into the land of Moriah* describe the Lord's Instructing you to bring yourself into a state of being wherein you may receive a new spiritual rationality about most important things of all.

The Words: *and offer him there for a burnt offering* express your need to willingly submit your sense of reason to His.

The Words: *upon one of the Mountains which I will tell thee of* communicate that your submission is to be made based upon Reasons that are much Higher, and much more Perfect than anything you could ever conceive on your own.

～

"*And Abraham rose up early in the morning, and saddled his ass, and took two of his young men with him, and Isaac his son, and clave the wood for the burnt offering, and rose up, and went unto the Place of which God had told him.*"

Genesis 22:3

The Words: *And Abraham rose up early in the morning* spiritually describe a new state of internal awakening.

The Words: *and saddled his ass* describe taking control of his spiritual conscience with conviction to do what the Lord is requesting of him. And although this description may seem farfetched, it is important to realize that spiritually, all beasts of burden mentioned in the Bible describe what serves the Lord's Quest for the salvation and deliverance of your soul. And as an *ass* is sure-footed, it depicts what provides you with internal balance, determination, and the mental and emotional stability needed for your spiritual journey ahead.

That Abraham "saddled" his spiritual conscience is descriptive of your need to take command over your own spiritual conscience in reverence to the Lord's Guidance in your life. That the Lord approaches you from within, "*riding*" Humbly upon your spiritual conscience is described many times in the Bible, as portrayed within Deuteronomy 22:4, Zechariah 9:9, Matthew 21:5, and Luke 14:5.

The Words: *and took two of his young men with him* spiritually communicate taking thoughts filled with newly conceived confidence about Divine Truth to aid you in ascending to what the Lord is teaching you about your need to realize what must always be, and remain, your First Love.

The Words: *and Isaac his son* describe your willingness to bring your spiritual sense of reason into alignment with the Lord's Sense of Reason about these things.

The Words: *and clave the wood for the burnt offering* depict your willingness to hold fast to what He has Given you to know as True and Right. Spiritually, "wood" describes the conduit that brings that understanding Up, into your life.

For this Reason, Exodus 25:10-22 describes the Ark of the Covenant as being hewn in wood, and why in Matthew 13:55 and Mark 6:3, the Lord is portrayed as a Carpenter, and as the Son of a Carpenter. Likewise, as described in Matthew 16:24 and John 19:17-20, the wooden cross of His crucifixion portrays His Sacrifice to bring that understanding about Divine Truth, Up, into your life. Further, as depicted in Genesis 3:24, Proverbs 3:18, Revelation 2:7 and 22:1-2, this Truth is illuminated as *the Tree of Life*.

~

> "*And they came to the Place which God had told him of; and Abraham built an Altar there, and laid the wood in Order, and bound Isaac his son, and laid him on the Altar upon the wood.*"
>
> Genesis 22:9

Many times during your spiritual journey in this world, the Lord will ask you to "have no other gods before" Him. Each time you will come into "the Place that God had told" you about in advance. There He will ask you to have faith and trust in His Guidance about why and how you must live your life. That "Abraham built an Altar there" is descriptive of acknowledging His Testimony to you about these things. That *Altar* will also mark

Through that willing submission, the Lord aligns your thoughts, feelings and behaviors with His.

the "Place" where you may find His Guidance again, and again throughout your entire lifetime in this world. In that "Place," the Lord will ask you to put the things that He has Given you to know as True and Right in their proper Order within your life.

The Words: *and laid the wood in Order* reveal your willingness to do so.

The Words: *and bound Isaac his son, and laid him on the Altar upon the wood* describe taking what you cherish most in life, and submitting it to His Guidance about the Way you must live your life. Nothing withheld.

> "*And Abraham stretched forth his hand, and took the knife to slay his son.*
>
> "*And the Angel of the Lord called unto him out of Heaven, and said, Abraham, Abraham! And he said, Here am I.*"
>
> Genesis 22:10–11

Your willingness to surrender what you cherish most to the Lord's Guidance about the Way you must live your life is spiritually described by Abraham stretching *forth his hand* and taking *the knife to slay his son*. Through that honest, sincere, and humble submission the Lord aligns your thoughts, feelings, and behaviors with His.

The Words: *And the Angel of the Lord called unto him out of Heaven, and said, Abraham, Abraham* demonstrates that new spiritual Order becoming clear within your life.

The Words: *and he said, Here I am* describe your acknowledgment that this is the Voice of Reason, having only your very Best interests at Heart.

> "*And He said, Lay not thine hand upon the lad, neither do thou any thing unto him: for now I know that thou fearest God, seeing thou hast not withheld thy son, thine only son from Me.*"
>
> Genesis 22:12

The Words: *And He said, Lay not thine hand upon the lad, neither do thou any thing unto him* illustrate your having gained a correct orientation for what you value most in life.

Abraham's Sacrifice of Isaac, Julius Schnorr von Carolsfeld

The Words: *for now I know that thou fearest God* confirm your reverent willingness to submit what you cherish most in life to what He has been Showing you to be True and Right, nothing withheld.

The Words: *seeing thou hast not withheld thy son, thine only son from Me* describe your having wholly surrendered yourself to do so, in mind, heart, and soul.

⁓

"*And Abraham lifted up his eyes, and looked, and behold behind him a ram caught in a thicket by his horns: and Abraham went and took the ram, and offered him up for a burnt offering in the stead of his son.*"

Genesis 22:13

Woodcut engraving, Julius Schnorr von Carolsfeld

The Words: *And Abraham lifted up his eyes, and looked* reveal having become Enlightened about what constitutes having True and saving faith in the Lord, and what does not.

The Words: *and behold behind him a ram caught in a thicket by his horns* portray the innocence of his throughs, previously encumbered by errant philosophies and misleading religious doctrines. That encumbrance was perceived as "behind him" because he had progressed beyond it.

Through that progression the Lord liberates your mind and heart from the "thicket" that spiritual half-truths impose upon your ability to think clearly about must always be, and remain, your First Love.

The Words: *and Abraham went and took the ram, and offered him up for a burnt offering in the stead of his son* illustrate the heartfelt gratitude experienced when you realize that your sense of reason has become aligned with the Lord's Sense of Reason. That realization Memorializes your remembrance about what it means to "have no other gods" before Him.

> "*And Abraham called the name of that Place Jehovahjireh as it is said to this Day, In the Mount of the Lord it shall be seen.*"
>
> Genesis 22:14

~

> "*Who shall ascend into the Hill of the Lord? or who shall stand in His Holy Place?*
>
> "*He that hath clean hands, and a pure heart; who hath not lifted up his soul unto vanity, nor sworn deceitfully.*
>
> "*He shall receive the Blessing from the Lord, and righteousness from the God of his salvation.*"
>
> Psalms 24:3–5

Humanity has many differences in histories, cultures, traditions, philosophies, and religions. Nevertheless, if we are willing to surrender ourselves to seeking Righteousness from the Lord First in all we think, feel, and do, we will find all the Reason we will ever need to understand why and how we must live our lives.

In that "Day," we will become mentally, emotionally, and spiritually confirmed about these things, then fully rational about the Way we must live our lives and treat all others around us. The incomparable internal Blessings the Lord Promises to bring into our lives as we willingly abide by that understanding is proclaimed throughout the Bible, from Beginning to End. It is up to each one of us to heed His Call to do so, for our Good and for the Good of all humanity.

> "And the Angel of the Lord called unto Abraham out of Heaven the Second time,
>
> "And said, By Myself have I sworn, saith the Lord, for because thou hast done this thing, and hast not withheld thy son, thine only son:
>
> "In that Blessing I will Bless thee, and in multiplying I will multiply thy seed as the stars of the Heaven, and as the sand which is upon the sea shore; and thy seed shall possess the gate of his enemies;
>
> "And in thy seed shall all the nations of the earth be Blessed; because thou hast obeyed My Voice."
>
> Genesis 22:15–18

> "*Come now, and let us Reason together, saith the Lord: though your sins be as scarlet, they shall be as White as snow; though they be red like crimson, they shall be as wool.*

> "*If ye be willing and obedient, ye shall eat the Good of the Land.*"
>
> Isaiah 1:18–19

> "*But seek ye first the Kingdom of God, and His Righteousness, and all these things will be added unto you.*"
>
> Matthew 6:33

This First Commandment, "Thou shalt have no other gods before Me" constitutes the Lord's Call for you to allow no substitutes, whatsoever, to keep you from remembering about what must always be and remain your First Love. There are no *reasons* great enough to deny your responsibility to keep that remembrance Primary in all you think, feel, and do. Likewise, there are no reasons great enough to allow prior attachments to errant philosophies or misleading religious doctrines to keep you from attending that all-important and Sacred responsibility.

Spiritually, the Promised Land portrays a perpetual state of Heaven Love wherein Good Judgment and understanding about the Way you must live your life reigns Supreme within your life.

How much more clearly can the Lord Communicate with you about why you must align your sense of reason with His, and willingly submit what you cherish most in life to what He is Showing you to be True and Right?

> "*Now the Lord had said unto Abram, Get thee out of thy country, and from thy kindred, and from thy father's house, unto a Land that I will Show thee.*"
>
> Genesis 12:1

"*That thou mayest love the Lord thy God, and that thou mayest obey His Voice, and that thou mayest cleave unto Him, for He is thy Life, and the length of thy Days: that that thou mayest dwell in the Land which the Lord sware unto thy fathers, to Abraham, to Isaac, and to Jacob, to Give them.*"

Deuteronomy 30:20

"*When therefore He was Risen from the dead, His disciples remembered that He had said this unto them; and they believed the Scripture, and the Word which Jesus had said.*"

John 2:22

The Four Evangelists. Workshop of Artus Wolfaerts, byAntwerp 1581–1641

Reflections

Throughout history, many errant philosophies and misleading religious doctrines have come to encumber our sense of reason about the most important things of all. Over time, each variation has laid claim to being exclusively correct. Overtly or implicitly, each denies that anyone can be saved or delivered into a Heavenly state of being unless they strictly comply with their own dogmatic belief structures. Those encumbrances have acted to divide us in mutual understanding about the Truth of Love.

It is High time to reconsider what joins us all together as One with the Lord and with one another and what does not. It is High time to once again put everything in their proper Order within our lives by submitting ourselves to living our lives according to what the Lord has Shown us to be True and Right. Nothing withheld. And it is High time to realign our sense of Reason with His. To do so is to love the Lord above all else, and to love others in the Way that He has, is, and will forever be Showing us that we must.

> *Let not your heart be troubled: ye believe in God, believe also in Me.*
>
> *In My Father's House are many Mansions: if it were not so, I would have told you. I go to prepare a Place for you.*
>
> *And if I go and prepare a Place for you, I will come again, and receive you unto Myself; that where I am, there ye may be also.*
>
> *And whither I go ye know, and the Way ye know.*
>
> John 14:1–4

THOU SHALT NOT MAKE UNTO THEE ANY GRAVEN IMAGE.

PART TWO
Introducing The Second Commandment

CHAPTER SIX
No False Idols **79**

"*Thou shalt not make unto thee any graven image, or any likeness of any thing that is in Heaven above, or that is in the earth beneath, or that is in the water under the earth:*

"*Thou shalt not bow down thyself to them, nor serve them: for I the Lord thy God am a jealous God, visiting the iniquity of the fathers upon the children unto the third and fourth generation of them that hate Me;*

"*And Showing Mercy unto thousands of them that love me, and keep My Commandments.*"

Exodus 20:4–6

6
No False Idols

The Lord's Message to you about the
Way you must live your life is Simple to understand.

This second Commandment is Given to you in three amazing verses. Each opens vast windows into the mental, emotional, and spiritual nature of your mind, heart, and soul.

The First Verse of the Lord's Second Commandment:

> *"Thou shalt not make unto thee any graven image, or any likeness of any thing that is in Heaven above, or that is in the earth beneath, or that is in the water under the earth."*
>
> Exodus 20:4

Spiritually, the Word "image" describes reflections about thoughts.

The Word: *likeness* describes similarities of affections.

True thoughts about Heavenly things are images of Divine Truth, and Unselfish affections are likenesses to the Lord's Love for you. These Heavenly things describe the Thoughts and Affections that come forth from the Mind and Heart of the Lord, Who is Righteousness Himself.

They characterize the Qualities and Virtues of True Life that come forth from His Life. They reveal what it means to receive, retain, and eternally share in in the Joys of Heavenly Love with Him and with one another.

The Words: *Thou shalt not make unto thee any graven image of any thing that is in the Heaven above* warn you to refrain from attempting to make *thoughts formed from the imaginations* of your heart appear *true* and *right*, when they are not.

To make a graven image of *any likeness of any thing that is in the Heaven above* is to attempt to make affections for those thoughts appear *unselfish*, when they are not.

Creating spiritual half-truths from those false thoughts and wayward affections is to make them *in the earth beneath.* Mixing those spiritual half-truths with genuine spiritual knowledge to create errant philosophies or misleading religious doctrines is to make them *in the water under the earth.*

~

"*And if thou wilt make Me an Altar of Stone, thou shalt not build it of hewn stone: for if thy lift up thy tool upon it, thou hast polluted it.*"

Exodus 20:25

Spiritually, making *an Altar of Stone* describes acknowledging that the Principles of Righteousness are Primary for your salvation and deliverance into an eternal Heavenly state of being.

Your thoughts and affections spiritually make you who you are.

The Words: *And if thou wilt make Me an Altar of Stone, thou shalt not build it of hewn stone* describe the Lord's forewarning you against making efforts on your own change the meaning or implications of those Principles to conform to errant philosophies or misleading religious doctrines.

The Words: *if thy lift up thy tool upon it, thou hast polluted it* reveal the effect of attempting to change those Holy Principles to justify "thoughts formed from the imagination" of your own heart.

"And it came to pass, when he heareth the Words of this curse, that he bless himself in his heart, saying, I shall have peace, though I walk in the imagination of mine heart, to add drunkenness to thirst."

Deuteronomy 29:19

The Lord's Message to you about the Way you must live your life is Simple to understand. There is no need for you to change it in any manner whatsoever. Rather, for your Good and for the Good of all around you, the Lord warns you against dangers of doing so. Exodus 32 explains the severity of ignoring those warnings, for doing so will turn your thoughts and affections into false idols of your own making. Doing so is a losing proposition.

"I am the Lord: that is my name: and my Glory will I not Give to another, neither My Praise to graven images."

Isaiah 42:8

"Therefore whoever heareth these Sayings of Mine, and doeth them, I will liken him unto a wise man, which built his house upon a Rock."

Matthew 7:24

"And every one that heareth these sayings of Mine, and doeth them not, shall be likened unto a foolish man, which buildeth his house upon the sand."

Matthew 7:26

The second verse of the Lord's second Commandment seeks to keep us from self-inflicted harm:

> "*Thou shalt not bow down thyself to them, nor serve them: for I the Lord thy God am a jealous God, visiting the iniquity of the fathers upon the children unto the third and fourth generation of them that hate Me.*"
>
> Exodus 20:5

Your thoughts and affections spiritually make you who you are. As you receive and apply the Lord's Thoughts and Affections to the Way you live your life, He becomes the Divine "Father" of all things True and Good that come forth and propagate within your mind, heart, and soul.

When your thoughts and affections are motivated by self-centered love, they are described as being brought forth by "the iniquity of the fathers" of falsities and evils within your life. The resulting self-serving thoughts and selfish affections that then come forth and multiply within your life are described as "the children" of "the third and fourth generation of them that hate Me."

> "*For thou shalt worship no other god: for the Lord, whose Name is Jealous, is a jealous God.*"
>
> Exodus 34:14

The Lord is jealous not to lose a single soul to *the fathers of iniquity.* And so, from His Love for you, He describes Himself as "a jealous God" visiting each of your self-serving thoughts and selfish affections in Order to expose them to you for what they really are.

With each visitation, He Offers you the Opportunity to look within yourself and recognize the dangers they pose to your mental, emotional, and spiritual wellbeing. With each visitation, He Gives you the Opportunity to turn away from them—and leave them behind—before they destroy the remnant of His Goodness remaining within your soul.

The Words: *for I the Lord thy God am a jealous God, visiting the iniquity of the fathers upon the children unto the third and fourth generation of them that hate Me* describe that spiritual Reality. It is your responsibility to confront those dangers with Him, and then embrace the Opportunities He has Given you to overcome them, while you still have the spiritual sensibility to do so.

> "*Now therefore fear the Lord, and serve Him in sincerity and in Truth: and put away the gods that your fathers served on the other side of the flood, and in Egypt; and serve ye the Lord.*"
>
> Joshua 24:14

Your need to reverence what the Lord is teaching you about the Way you must live your life is proclaimed throughout the Bible, from Beginning to the End. The Words "and put away the gods that your fathers served" describe your need to recognize and confront any false thoughts and wayward affections derived from the pride of your own self-intelligence before they overwhelm you.

> "*Their idols are silver and gold, the work of men's hands.*
>
> "*They have mouths but they speak not: eyes have they, but they see not:*
>
> "*They have ears, but they hear not: noses have they, but they smell not:*
>
> "*They have hands, but they handle not: feet have they, but they walk not: neither speak they through their throat.*
>
> "*They that make them are like unto them; so is every one that trusteth in them.*"
>
> Psalms 115:4–8

In a positive sense, the Words "silver and gold" express Thoughts and Affections that are Pure in Truth and Beautiful in Goodness. In a negative sense, they describe what has been fashioned into what only appears to be "pure and beautiful."

They have ears,
but they hear not.

The Words: *Their idols are silver and gold, the work of men's hands* depict counterfeit philosophical and religious doctrines created to take the Place of what the Lord has Shown us to be True and Right.

The Words: *They have mouths but they speak not* portray their proponents knowing the Ways of the Lord, yet not being willing to profess what must always be, and remain above all else, our First Love.

The Words: *eyes have they, but they see not* expands that portrayal. Instead of acknowledging what they have been Given to recognize as Divine Truth, they choose to remain *wise in their own eyes*.

The Words: *They have ears, but they hear not* describe having the ability to comprehend the most important things of all, yet not being willing to obey what the Lord has been teaching us since our inceptions.

The Words: *noses have they, but they smell not*, illustrate having retained some spiritual sensibility, yet not being willing to perceive their own hypocrisies.

The Words: *They have hands, but they handle not* represent possessing the authority to do the things the Lord requires of us, yet not taking that responsibly to heart.

The Words: *feet have they, but they walk not* represent claiming to follow the Lord, but refusing to walk Upright, in the Paths of His Righteousness.

The Words: *neither speak they through their throat* expose surface confessions made about being faithful to the Lord that are devoid of internal willingness to do so.

The Words: *They that make them are like unto them, so is every one that trusteth in them* describe the spiritual effects of becoming an image and as a likeness to self-serving thoughts and selfish affections about the Truth of Love. While their appearance in this life may be hard to detect, their appearance in the life to come is instantly recognizable to all around them.

> "*Many will say to Me in that day, Lord, Lord, have we not prophesied in Thy name? and in Thy name have cast out devils? and in Thy name done many wonderful works?*
>
> "*And then I will profess unto them, I never knew you: depart from Me, ye that work iniquity.*"
>
> Matthew 7:22–23

The Word *day* is descriptive of a mental, emotional, and spiritual state of being. Attempting to justify things that you have falsely declared to be "true" and "right" is self-defeating. Instead of leading you into a state of Enlightened understanding, they misguide you to come into a spiritual state of darkness of your own making.

$\sim$

> "*Why, Seeing times are not hidden from the Almighty, do they that know Him not see His Days?*"
>
> Job 24:1

Job's Words address the perplexity of why, when we proclaim to have received spiritual comprehension from the Lord, we have so often continued to place our own errant philosophies and misleading religious doctrines in front of what He has Shown us to be True and Right. Doing so eclipses our ability to understand the most important things of all.

> "*What profiteth the graven image that the maker thereof hath graven it; the molten image, and a teacher of lies, that the maker of his work trustesth therein, to make dumb idols?*

> "*Woe unto him that saith to the wood, Awake; to the dumb stone, Arise, it shall teach! Behold, it is laid over with gold and silver, and there is no Breath at all in the midst of it.*"

Habakkuk 2:18–19

Your mental, emotional, and spiritual "profitability" is measured by gains of innermost happiness, peace of mind and heart, and genuine fulfillment in life. Everywhere the Lord teaches that these invaluable gains are achieved only as you fully invest yourself in living your life in the Way He is Showing that you must.

The Lord's Testimony about why and how you must live your life is simple to understand.

The Words of Isaiah 55:2 and Matthew 25:14-30 set forth these questions:

What lasting meaningful "profit" can you expect to receive if you do not invest yourself in living your life accordingly?

What mental, emotional, and spiritual loss can you expect to suffer if you waste your Opportunity to do so?

The Words: *Woe unto him that saith to the wood, Awake* call out those who promote false concepts about what brings genuine spiritual Truth into fruition within your life.

The Words: *to the dumb stone, Arise, it shall teach!* depict trying to make errant philosophies and misleading religious doctrines seem foundationally sound, when they are not.

The Words: *Behold, it is laid over with gold and silver* portray attempting to make what is wrong and false appear Beautiful and Pure.

The Words: *and there is no Breath at all in the midst of it* reveal the utter lack of spiritual understanding existing within those who insist on proclaiming the correctness of their own misconceptions, even to to their dying breath.

> " *Wherefore the Lord said, Foreasmuch as this people draw near*
> *Me with their mouth, and with their lips do honor Me, but*
> *have removed their heart far from Me, and their fear toward*
> *Me is taught by the precept of men:* "
>
> Isaiah 29:13

Those who persist in being wise in their own eyes "hate" considering that they are wrong. They hate considering that they are misleading themselves and those around them with misplaced zeal for their own false "precepts." They hate being told that they must turn away from their allegiance to those misguided thoughts and wayward affections and leave them behind. Being in a land of "hate" about the Truth of your Salvation is not where you want to be, or remain. There is nothing profitable to be had there.

> " *That this is a rebellious people, lying children, children that*
> *will not hear the Word of the Lord.*
>
> " *Which say to the seers, See not; and to the prophets, Prophesy*
> *not unto us Right things, speak unto us smooth things, prophecy*
> *deceits.* "
>
> Isaiah 30:9–10

The Lord's Testimony to you about why and how you must live your life is not complicated to understand. Throughout history, many have professed to understand it. Many have paid lip service to it, and yet, many have refused to embrace it. Instead they have avoided it, proclaiming much easier "ways" to find "grace" in the eyes of the Lord.

Instead, they have formed their own ideas about the meaning of His Testimony to us, and then adamantly used those misconceptions to dominate the minds and hearts of others.

The Words: *That this is a rebellious people, lying children, children that will not hear the Word of the Lord* describe endless arguments they offer to justify their own misguided concepts about what brings innermost happiness and genuine fulfillment into your life. Instead of accepting what the Lord has so plainly been teaching us about the spiritual causes and effects that Govern the wellbeing of our minds, hearts, and souls they chose to *"say to the seers, See not."*

The Words: *Prophesy not unto us Right things* illustrate how the teachers of errant philosophies and misleading religious doctrines refuse to discuss our overriding responsibility to attend our spiritual task at hand.

> "*But this thing Commanded I them, saying, Obey My Voice, and I will be your God, and ye shall be My people: and walk ye in all the Ways that I have Commanded you, that it may be well unto you.*
>
> "*But they hearkened not, nor inclined their ear, but walked in the counsels and in the imagination of their evil heart, and went backward and not forward.*"
>
> Jeremiah 7:23–24

> "*Who is the wise man, that may understand this? And who is he to whom the mouth of the Lord hath spoken, that he may declare it, for what the land perisheth and is burned up like a wilderness, that none passeth through?*
>
> "*And the Lord saith, because they have forsaken My Law which I set before them, and have not obeyed My Voice, neither walked therein;*

"But have walked after the imagination of their own heart, and after Baalim, which their fathers taught them:

"Therefore thus saith the Lord of hosts, the God of Israel; behold, I will feed them, even this people, with wormwood, and give them water of gall to drink."

Jeremiah 9:12–15

Creating false thoughts and supporting them with misplaced zeal destroys your ability to understand the simplicity and Singularity of the Lord's Message to us all.

The Lord brings harm upon no one.

The Words: *for what the land perisheth and is burned up like a wilderness, that none passeth through?* illuminate the destruction of your ability to process genuine understanding about the most important things of all. Not being able to "pass through" describes the pitfalls and stumbling blocks that cause you to become a mental, emotional, and spiritual wasteland of your own making.

The Words: *for what* ring loudly to all who have maintained the spiritual sensibility to care about what leads to our individual and collective mental, emotional, and spiritual wellbeing.

It is vital for you to understand that the Lord brings harm upon no one, for He is Compassion, Forgiveness, and Mercy Himself. He only Wills to protect you from internal harm as He leads you into an everlasting Heavenly state of being. Rather, it is crucial that you realize that you bring internal harm upon yourself by not living your life in the Way He has Shown you that you must.

The Words: *Because they have forsaken My Law which I set before them, and have not obeyed My Voice, neither walked therein* defines that spiritual Reality. The proponents of errant philosophies and misleading religious doctrines that teach otherwise are described as those who have walked "after Baalim, which their fathers taught them."

The Words: *behold, I will feed them, even this people, with wormwood* reflect the hollowed-out substitutes that then come to replace genuine spiritual sustenance within one's life.

The Words: *and give them water of gall to drink* call out the noxious results of mixing spiritual half-truths with genuine spiritual knowledge about things that are True and Right. And although these concoctions are described as being brought about by the Lord, that is just the spiritual appearance to those who have compounded the Singularity of Lord's Message with "thoughts formed from the imaginations" of their own hearts. Those who do so will never accept blame, or shame for the harmful effects they bring upon themselves, or others, by their stiff-necked and hardheaded allegiance to the pride of their own self-intelligence.

Those who continue to insist on justifying the pride of their own self-intelligence, and try to convince those around them to think likewise are treading upon Ground that is the most Holy of all to the Lord.

~

"*Every man is brutish is his knowledge: every founder is confounded by the graven image: for his molten image is falsehood, and there is no Breath in them.*

"*They are vanity, and the work of errors: in the time of their Visitation they shall perish.*"

Jeremiah 10:14–15

Whenever the proponents of errant philosophies and misleading religious doctrines are challenged, they attack back viciously.

The Words: *Every man is brutish is his knowledge* portray that reaction. Instead of searching for deeper understanding about the meaning and Purpose of the Lord's Testimony to us, they dive deeper into their own misconceptions, spreading misinformation to mislead even the *elect*, if that were possible.

The Words: *every founder is confounded by the graven image: for his molten image is falsehood* tells of the resulting misdirection formed.

The Words: *and there is no Breath in them* expands on the loss of spiritual understanding that results.

The Words: *They are vanity* describe wasting the Opportunity the Lord affords us to to find our Way back into His Embrace.

The Words: *and the work of errors* describes the futility of trying to circumvent that lost Opportunity by trying to justify our own errant philosophies and misleading religious doctrines instead.

The Words: *in the time of their Visitation they shall perish* describe an utter lack of willingness to reconsider those misconceptions, even when they become exposed in the Light of Righteousness for what they really are.

～

Visitations from the Lord are not supernatural events. Rather, they are very normal occurrences experienced throughout our entire lifetimes in this world.

Anyone who feels their conscience tug when facing temptation to violate a Principle of the Lord's Righteousness is experiencing one.

Anyone who feels the need to reconcile themselves with any offense they have made to the Goodness within others is experiencing one.

Anyone who feels the Inspiration to honestly and sincerely learn about the things that the Lord is Showing them to be True and Right is experiencing one.

Anyone who willingly responds to His Testimony about why and how they must is experiencing one.

Anyone who feels Inspired to walk the extra mile required is experiencing one.

And anyone who feels the Joy and gratefulness of having been Given the understanding they need to do so is experiencing one.

With each Visitation the Lord calls upon you to be wise enough, brave enough, and humble enough to welcome Him into your life. He beseeches you to follow the Guidance He is Offering you, for your Good and for the Good of all around you.

> "*And though the Lord Give you the Bread of adversity, and the Water of affliction, yet shall not thy Teachers be removed into a corner any more, but thine eyes shall see thy Teachers:*
>
> "*And thine ears shall hear a Word behind thee, saying, This is the Way, walk ye in it, when ye turn to the Right hand, and when ye turn to the left.*"
>
> Isaiah 30:20–21

The Third and Final Verse of the Lord's Second Commandment:

> "*And showing Mercy unto thousands of them that love Me, and keep My Commandments.*"
>
> Exodus 20:6

Through the work of your spiritual reformation, the Lord's Compassion and Mercy unfolds within your mind and heart, just as an evening turns into the Light and Warmth of morning, refreshing His Goodness within your soul. That Opportunity is not earned but is Offered freely to you from His Love for you. He has declared this spiritual Truth many, many times throughout the ages of human history. It is now your responsibly to take Him up on this incomparable Offer by offering to live your life in the Way He has Shown you that you must. There is nothing else required.

"*Speak unto the children of Israel, that they bring Me an offering: of every man that giveth it willingly with his heart ye shall take My Offering.*"

Exodus 25:2

"*And there I will meet with thee, and I will Commune with thee from above the Mercy seat, from between the two cherubims which are upon the Ark of the Testimony, of all things which I will Give thee in Commandment unto the children of Israel.*"

Exodus 25:22

"*Know therefore that the Lord thy God, He is God, the faithful God, which keepeth Covenant and Mercy with them that love Him and keep His Commandments to a thousand generations.*"

Deuteronomy 7:9

"*If ye keep My Commandments, ye shall abide in My Love; even as I have kept My Father's Commandments, and abide in His Love.*

"*These things have I spoken unto you, that My Joy might remain in you, and that your Joy might be full.*"

John 15: 10–11

Reflections

There are many errant philosophies and misguided religious doctrines that clamor to stand in Place of what must always be, and remain, your First Love. They are loud and stubborn, always seeking to distract your focus from understanding and acknowledging what must always be, and remain, your First Works. To make *any graven image, or any likeness of any thing that is in Heaven above, or that is in the earth beneath, or that is in the water under the earth,* and then chose to *bow down to them* and *serve them* wastes the Opportunity of your lifetime. It is therefore imperative that you come to understand what profits the Goodness within your soul, and what does not, before it becomes too late.

> "*And that, knowing the time, that now it is high time to awake out of sleep: for now is our salvation nearer than when we believed.*"
>
> Romans 13:11

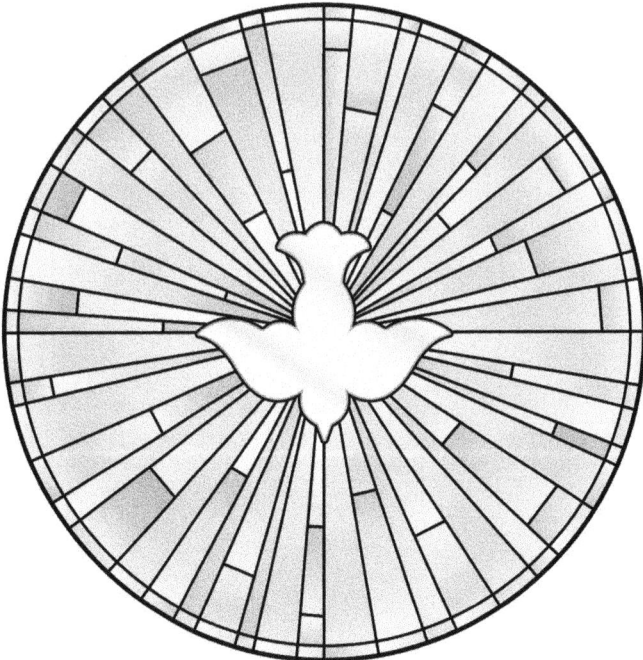

YOU SHALL NOT TAKE THE NAME OF THE LORD IN VAIN

Your life in this world goes by much quicker than you realize.
Thereby never waste your Opportunity to become the person the
Lord has Purposed for you to become. Your everlasting happiness
and Joy depend upon it!

7

The Opportunity
of Your Lifetime

From your willingness to abide by the Lord's Commandments
you help Him fulfill His Purpose for the Creation of your soul.

*I*n Scripture, all "names" portray various spiritual characteristics. The "Name" of the Lord portrays His spiritual Characteristics, displaying His Qualities and Virtues for all to see and understand. Each is filled with expressions of His Love for you, including Truth, Compassion, Forgiveness, Fidelity, Honesty, Sincerity, Humility, and Goodwill toward all. They all radiate through His Grace and Mercy, flowing forth with Purpose to protect you from mental, emotional, and spiritual harm as He leads you into a perpetual state of Heavenly Joy. These Glorious arrays of His Divine Love are Righteous in all their Ways.

> "*Even every one that is called by My Name: for I have Created*
> *him for My Glory, I have formed him, yea, I have made him.*"
>
> Isaiah 43:7

Throughout the Bible the Lord informs you that you have been Created to host the Glorious arrays of His Qualities and Virtues within your mind, heart, and soul. He reveals that as you willingly live your life according to the Way the He has Shown you must, He will spiritually transform you into the person He has Purposed for you to become. To have been Given that Opportunity and then waste it by not living your life accordingly is to "take the Name of the Lord thy God in vain."

> *"Therefore say thou unto them, Thus saith the Lord of hosts;*
> *Turn ye unto Me, saith the Lord of hosts, and I will turn unto*
> *you, saith the Lord of hosts."*
>
> Zechariah 1:3

The Lord comes into your life as Divine Truth, Willing only to fulfill His Love's Quest for your salvation and deliverance into an everlasting state of Heavenly Joy. He teaches you that your reception of those incomparable Blessings will require you to turn away from your self-serving thoughts, selfish desires, and their corresponding behaviors, and leave them behind. All the while He asks you to turn toward Him by living your life according to the Principles of His Righteousness, nothing withheld.

> *"At that Day ye shall know that I am in My Father, and ye in*
> *Me, and I in you."*
>
> John 14:20

> *"He that hath an ear, let him hear what the Spirit saith unto*
> *the churches: To him that overcometh will I Give to eat of the*
> *hidden Manna, and will Give him a White Stone, and in the*
> *Stone a new name written, which no man knoweth saving he*
> *that receiveth it."*
>
> Revelation 2:17

We have all been born into this world capable of overcoming our spiritual faults and weaknesses as we diligently work with the Lord in the Light of His Righteousness. And, as we are finite and He is Infinite, we have all been Given the Opportunity to host the Qualities and Virtues of His Love for us in combinations that make us special and invaluable to Him and to one another, no two ever being the same. The new Qualities and new Virtues you will acquire as you live your life accordingly will constitute your new name, describing your unique ability to host the Goodness of True Life from His Life within your mind, heart, and soul. In that sense, we are all spiritually described as His individual temples and *churches*.

"A Word fitly Spoken is like apples of Gold in pictures of Silver."

Proverbs 25:11

St John the baptist, by Leonardo Da Vinci

The Wrath of Vanity

" *The Words of the Preacher, the Son of David, King in Jerusalem.*

" *Vanity of vanities, saith the Preacher, vanity of vanities; all is vanity.*

" *What profit hath a man of all his labor which he taketh under the sun?* "

Ecclesiastes 1:1–3

Everywhere in the Bible the Lord warns you about the dangers of spiritual vanity. He teaches you that it originates from the pride of your own self-intelligence and covets its own thoughts above His Thoughts. He teaches you that it loves to be worshiped and adorned beyond reproach and hates to be *Commanded,* even if those Commandments have been Given to you for your Good and for the Good of all around you. He teaches you that rather than submitting itself to the Truth of Love, spiritual vanity will passionately promote itself with a blind and misguided zeal, *glorifying* itself with tremendous pomp and ceremony until it turns spiritual Sweetness into spiritual bitterness within your life.

" *For in the multitude of dreams and many words there are also divers vanities: but fear thou God.* "

Ecclesiastes 5:7

The Words: *multitude of dreams* spiritually describe intellectual and religious delusions of grandeur.

The Words: *and many words there are also divers vanities* describe the endless arguments conceived by those who have become "wise in their own eyes." They use those arguments to proclaim that they alone are correct, while implying that all others are wrong. The worst of these overtly declare that all others are in danger of eternal damnation, vainly intimidating the innocent and unsuspecting. Throughout history, there have been many examples of spiritual vanities building themselves up, and each ultimately taking a great fall.

> "*And they said one to another, Go to, let us make brick, and burn them thoroughly. And they had brick for Stone, and slime had they for Mortar.*
>
> "*And they said, Go to, let us build a city and a tower, whose top may reach unto Heaven; and let us make us a name, lest we be scattered abroad upon the face of the whole earth.*"
>
> Genesis 11:3–4

The Word: *brick* spiritually highlights the false concepts that are used to build up errant philosophies and misleading religious doctrines.

The Words: *and burn them thoroughly* describe the misguided passion used to harden those false concepts into appearing irrefutable.

Spiritually, having "brick for Stone" is descriptive of substituting false thoughts for True Thoughts about why and how you must live your life. As these "bricks" become stacked up one upon another, they create entire false belief structures, spiritually described throughout the Bible as the "cities" made from "the thoughts of the imaginations" of your own heart.

The Words: *and slime had they for Mortar to build a tower* spiritually identify the wrongheaded logic used to bond those misleading beliefs together. To *build a tower* in such a *city* is to construct lofty dictates that promote those misguided beliefs. To *make us a name* describes putting sheep's clothing on wolves to make them appear *righteous,* when they are anything but. Such pretense gives the the "right" to exercise false authority over the lives of others. Their fear of losing that authority is expressed by the Words: *lest we be scattered abroad upon the face of the whole earth.*

> *"And the Lord came down to see the city and the tower, which the children of men builded."*
>
> Genesis 11:5

Errant philosophies and misleading religious doctrines exalt themselves by making lofty proclamations about their irrefutable correctness. From those "towers" they promote themselves, overtly or implicitly looking down upon any who may beg to differ. From that perspective they strive to rule over the minds and hearts of their followers, attempting to redefine the Laws of Heaven and earth, as if that were even possible. At the times of their Visitation, the Lord openly exposes them to what they really are. During those exposures, their leaders—more often than not—double down on their own delusions of grandeur.

> *"And the Lord said, Behold, the people is One, and they have all one Language; and this they begin to do: and now nothing will be restrained from them, which they have imagined to do."*
>
> Genesis 11:6

The Lord has Given you a Singular Message about why and how you must live your life. That Message should be easy for anyone to understand who reads the Bible with genuine honesty, sincerity, and humility. Through that understanding He Wills to unite our minds and hearts as One, with His.

The Words: *Behold, the people is One, and they have all One Language* reveal that humanity had, at one time, wholly embraced and enunciated that spiritual understanding.

Should you begin to allow the vanity of the pride of your own self-intelligence to take control over what the Lord is Communicating to you about your need to seek His Righteousness First in all you think, feel, and do, you risk losing your ability to remember what must always be, and remain, your First Love.

The Words: *and this they begin to do* describe the age-old perplexity of why we so often allow vain proclamations of our own making to take control over our lives, even though we have been Given to know better.

The Words: *and now nothing will be restrained from them, which they have imagined to do* describe what results when vanity opens flood gates for falsehoods and evils of all sorts to enter in and overwhelm the remaining spiritual sensibilities within our thoughts and affections.

> *Go to, let us go down, and there confound their language, that they may not understand one another's speech.*
>
> Genesis 11:7

The Lord "confounds" no one about the Way we may receive, retain, and forever share in the Joy and Goodness of His Love for us. No one. Rather, it is we who confound ourselves about these things by developing and promoting errant philosophies and misleading religious doctrines of our own making. The Words: *Go to, let us go down, and there confound their language* spiritually represent the individual and collective misunderstandings that result from our own ill-conceived notions.

The Words: *that they may not understand one another's speech* reveals the divisions and disagreements that then arise among the people of the world.

> *So the Lord scattered them abroad from thence upon the face of all the earth: and they left off to build the city.*
>
> *Therefore is the name of it called Babel; because the Lord did there confound the language of all the earth: and from thence did the Lord scatter them abroad upon the face of all the earth.*
>
> Genesis 11:8–9

As each errant philosophy and misleading religious doctrine continues to promote the correctness of their own "speech," the incoherent arguments they construct all sound like a spiritual "babbel" when exposed in the Light of Righteousness. With their own misguided zeal they scatter their misconceived concepts far and wide. Their rise and fall throughout the history of humanity is well documented.

> "Lo, when the wall is fallen, shall it not be said unto you, Where is the daubing wherewith ye have daubed it?
>
> "Therefore thus saith the Lord God; I will even rend it with a stormy wind in My fury; and there shall be an overflowing shower in Mine anger, and great hailstones in My fury to consume it.
>
> "So will I break down the wall that ye have daubed with untempered mortar, and bring it down to the ground, so that the foundation thereof shall be discovered, and it shall fall, and ye shall be consumed in the midst thereof: and ye shall know that I am the Lord.
>
> "Thus will I accomplish My wrath upon the wall, and upon them that have daubed it with untempered mortar, and will say unto you, The wall is no more, neither they that daubed it."
>
> Ezekiel 13:12–15

The Lord always attempts to bring you into a state of honest, sincere, and humble introspection about the Truth of Love.

A *stormy wind* is descriptive of the result of resisting that spiritual understanding.

The Words: *Lo, when the wall is fallen, shall it not be said unto you, Where is the daubing wherewith ye have daubed it?* reach out to you. They Call upon you to reexamine any

Life of Christ series by James T. Tissot

philosophy or religious doctrine that argues against your need to establish the Principles of His Righteousness as Primary for the Way you must live your life. Any, regardless of their physical, historical, cultural or political lineage, or "pedigree."

The Words: *Therefore thus saith the Lord God; I will even rend it with a stormy wind in My fury; and there shall be an overflowing shower in Mine anger, and great hailstones in My fury to consume it* reveal the self-inflicted effects of striving against what must always be and remain your First Love.

A *stormy wind* is descriptive of the result of resisting that spiritual understanding. An *overflowing shower* vividly describes how falsities overwhelm your ability to think clearly about why and how you must live your life. The inclusion of *Hailstones* depicts misguided zeal, acting to destroy any remaining spiritual sensibility within you, and within others caught in those same tumultuous entrapments.

The Words: *So will I break down the wall that ye have daubed with untempered Mortar* describe the fall of arguments that defend errant philosophies and misleading religious doctrines, as the Lord reveals them for what they really are. That they have been *daubed with untempered mortar* describes the lack of Good Judgment and sound Reason that went into constructing them.

The Words: *so that the foundation thereof shall be discovered* portray the faults underpinning their entire intellectual and doctrinal belief structures.

The Words: *and it shall fall, and ye shall be consumed in the midst thereof: and ye shall know that I am the Lord* tells of a great spiritual humbling within all who are willing to finally come to their spiritual senses about the Truth of their Salvation.

The Words: *Thus will I accomplish My wrath upon the wall, and upon them that have daubed it with untempered mortar* describe the Lord overthrowing false arguments about what leads to innermost happiness and genuine fulfillment in life.

The Words: *and will say unto you, The wall is no more, neither they that daubed it* spiritually reveal receiving clarity about the causes of their demise.

> "And every one that heareth these sayings of Mine, and doeth them not, shall be likened unto a foolish man, which built his house upon the sand.
>
> "And the rain descended, and the floods came, and the winds blew, and beat upon that house; and it fell: and great was the fall of it."
>
> Matthew 7:26–27

The easiest way to become harmed by the vanity of your own self-intelligence is to wrestle with the Lord's Message to you about why and how you must live your life.

Christ and the Rich Young Ruler, by Heinrich Hofmann

8
The Seed of Jacob
I have not spoken in secret.

That the Lord even needs to declare that He has "not Spoken in secret" is indicative of our great need to regain spiritual comprehension about the meaning and Purpose of His Testimony to us. And so, He continuously Offers you the spiritual knowledge you need to receive that spiritual comprehension. Should you honestly, sincerely, and humbly accept that Offer, He Promises to make all things True and Right manifest within your mind, heart, and soul.

Your spiritual comprehension about these things is described through the Story of Jacob. "The seed of Jacob" describes what comes forth as you willingly apply that spiritual knowledge to the Way you live your life.

> *I have not spoken in secret, in a dark place of the earth: I said not unto the seed of Jacob, Seek ye Me in vain: I the Lord speak Righteousness, I declare things that are Right.*
>
> Isaiah 45:19

The Words: *I said not unto the seed of Jacob, Seek ye Me in vain* addresses your need to embrace the Opportunity of your lifetime. His Offering you genuine spiritual knowledge about how you may is described by the opening of Jacob's well within Genesis 29:1-3 and again in John 4:1-15.

The Words: *I the Lord speak Righteousness, I declare things that are Right* describe the spiritual knowledge that flows forth from that "Well."

> "*And Jacob awakened out of his sleep, and he said, Surely the Lord is in this Place; and I knew it not.*
>
> "*And he was afraid, and said, How dreadful is this Place! This is none other but the House of God, and this is the Gate of Heaven.*"
>
> Genesis 28:16–17

As you gain spiritual awareness about the Truth of your Salvation, you become "awakened out" of your "sleep." That spiritual awakening is at once wonderful and daunting. Wonderful, because it allows you to recognize that the Opportunity of your lifetime lies just in front of you. Yet daunting, because you will also quickly come to recognize that the work of your spiritual reformation is now at hand.

> "*Then Jacob went on his journey, and came into the land of the people of the East.*
>
> "*And he looked, and behold a Well in the field, and, lo, there were three flocks of sheep lying by it; for out of that Well they Watered the flocks and a great Stone was upon the Well's mouth.*
>
> "*And thither were all the flocks gathered: and they rolled the Stone from the Well's mouth, and Watered the sheep, and put the Stone again upon the Well's mouth in His Place.*"
>
> Genesis 29:1–3

Spiritually, the "East" describes where the Truth about the Way you must live your life first dawns within your mind and heart. That the "wise men" portrayed in Matthew 2:1-2 came "from the East" to worship the return of Divine Truth into our lives describes this same dawning.

To "look" depicts opening yourself up to that comprehension. The "Well" with "flocks of sheep lying on it" describe this spiritual knowledge being made available to all who innocently wish to receive it.

The Words: *for out of that Well they Watered the flocks* describe the genuine spiritual knowledge that refreshes that innocence within your mind and heart.

The Words: *a great Stone was upon the Well's mouth* describe the Principles that Govern spiritual Reality. To roll "the Stone from the Well's mouth" is to open up deep spiritual revelations about the Truth of Love. To "put the Stone again upon the Well's mouth in His Place" describes marking the Place where you may once again find genuine spiritual knowledge about the Lord's Purpose for the Creation of your soul.

> "*Now Jacob's Well was there. Jesus therefore, being wearied with His Journey, sat thus on the Well: and it was about the sixth hour.*"
>
> John 4:6

Everywhere throughout Scripture, the Lord freely Offers you genuine spiritual knowledge about why and how you must live your life. That He has Labored Greatly to Give you that knowledge is depicted by His "being wearied with His Journey." That He "sat thus on the Well" reveals His Resting His Testimony upon things that are eternally True and Right.

The Words: *It was about the sixth hour* describe that the time has now come for each of us to once again to realize and accept what He has been teaching us since the inception of the human race.

> "*And Jacob was left alone; and there wrestled a Man with him until the breaking of the Day.*"
>
> Genesis 32:24

Spiritually, these Words portray a state of personal introspection in the Light of the Lord's Righteousness. In that state of mind, you will be asked to choose what you value most in life. It is then when your remaining self-serving thoughts will "wrestle" with what the Lord is Showing you to be True and Right. And although you may not always be willing to acknowledge that it is the Lord Himself Who is engaging in that struggle within you, it is nevertheless spiritual Reality.

The Words: *until the breaking of the Day* describe the time when you have come to the full extent of your current capacity to receive and accept that spiritual comprehension.

> "*And when He saw that He prevailed not against him, He touched the hollow of his thigh; and the hollow of Jacob's thigh was out of joint, as he wrestled with Him.*"
>
> Genesis 32:25

The freewill choices we make in life are often very far from perfect. Rather, all too often we resist embracing the full extent of the Message the Lord is Offering to all of us. That resistance causes our comprehension about Divine Truth to suffer greatly. That Jacob's "thigh was out of joint" is foretelling about the mental, emotional, and spiritual afflictions we bring upon ourselves as they encumber our ability to walk "upright" in the Light of Righteousness. And yet regardless of our stubbornness, and how lame we may have allowed ourselves to become, the Lord repeatedly bears our imperfections. He does so by continuing to Work within each of us to reform us and transform us into the person that He has Purposed for us to become.

"*And He said, let Me go, for the Day breaketh. And he said, I will not let Thee go except Thou Bless me.*"

Genesis 32:26

The vanity of our self-intelligence can be quite indignant in thinking that it deserves approval and reward about its own correctness. Nevertheless, from His Grace and in His Mercy, the Lord continues to Offer us additional Opportunities to learn from Him, and to inquire about His Purpose for coming into our lives. He will never make that Purpose a secret to you.

"*And He said unto him, What is thy name? And he said, Jacob.*

"*And He said, Thy name shall be called no more Jacob, but Israel: for as a prince hast thou power with God and with men, and hast prevailed.*"

Genesis 32:27–28

Jacob's name being changed to "Israel" describes your spiritual comprehension recognizing that there is something much Greater and much more Perfect in Life than you had ever before acknowledged. And although your comprehension may still be imperfect, these Words describe a new beginning, whereby the Lord will continue to Enlighten you with understanding about why and how you must live your life.

The Words: *for as a prince hast thou power with God and with men, and hast prevailed* express His Entrusting you with the Gift of your own free will … even the fate of your own soul.

"*And Jacob asked Him, and said, Tell me, I pray Thee, Thy Name? And He said, Wherefore is it that thou dost ask after My Name? And He Blessed him there.*"

Genesis 32:29

Through your willingness to continue to honestly, sincerely, and humbly inquire about the Lord's Qualities and Virtues, He begins to heal you from the afflictions caused by the pride of your own self-intelligence. In that state of openness, He teaches you about Himself, Gifting you with a Marvelous new spiritual understanding about His Plan for your salvation and deliverance into the Joys of True Life from His Life.

> "*And Jacob called the name of the place Peniel: for I have seen God face to face, and my Life is preserved.*"
>
> Genesis 32:30

> "*The Righteousness of Thy Testimonies is everlasting: Give me understanding, and I shall Live.*"
>
> Psalms 119:144

> "*Behold, I stand at the door, and knock: if any man hear My Voice, and open the door, I will come in to him, and will sup with him, and he with Me.*"
>
> Revelation 3:20

~

You will surely experience many levels of resistance when facing the realization that you must seek Righteousness first in all you think, feel, and do. And because no one in this world is perfect, remembering why and how you must is vital for the success of your spiritual journey ahead. To place alternative thoughts in front of that remembrance is to take the Opportunity of your lifetime in vain,

> "*Jesus answered and said unto her, Whosoever drinketh of this water shall thirst again:*

"*But whosoever drinketh of the Water that I shall Give him shall never thirst; but the Water that I shall Give him shall be in him a Well of Water springing up into everlasting Life.*"

John 4:13–14

~

From your willingness to abide by the Lord's Commandments, you become spiritually rational in the Way you think, feel, and act in life. That rationality brings forth a new spiritual comprehension about things that are True and Right. Through that new comprehension the Lord Offers you a much deeper spiritual understanding about the Qualities and Virtues of His

Christ and the Woman of Samaria, by Guercino (Giovanni Francesco Barbieri)

Love for you. As you live your life accordingly, He leads you through your spiritual journey in this world, spiritually reforming you and transforming you into becoming the person that He has Purposed for you to become.

This spiritual progression describes the generations of Abraham, Isaac, and Jacob within all who are wise enough, brave enough, and humble enough to look to the Lord for their salvation and deliverance into the Joys of Heavenly Love. Abraham portrays your willingness to rise to the Occasion. Isaac portrays the rational submission needed to do so. And Jacob portrays the new spiritual comprehension that results as you open yourself to accept genuine spiritual knowledge about things that are True and Right.

Taken together. they are described as the "fathers" of Israel, with Israel portraying your new spiritual understanding about the Truth of the Lord's Testimony to you. Receiving True Life from the Lord's Life consists of this progression internally coming into fruition within your life.

> *Behold, the former things are come to pass, and new things do I declare: before they Spring forth I tell you of them.*
>
> Isaiah 42:9

> *And it shall be to Me a Name of Joy, a praise and an honor before all the nations of the earth, which shall hear all the Good that I do unto them: and they shall fear and tremble for all the Goodness and for all the Prosperity that I Procure unto it.*
>
> Jeremiah 33:9

Reflections

The Third Commandment, "Thou shalt not take the Name of the Lord thy God in vain: for the Lord will not hold him guiltless that taketh His Name in vain" has been Given to you by the Lord for your Good and for the Good of all around you. Yet He leaves it up to you, of your own free will, to reverence this Commandment by remembering why and how you must apply it to each and every aspect of your life.

> *Then they that feared the Lord spake often one to another: and the Lord Hearkened, and Heard it, and a Book of Remembrance was Written before Him for them that feared the Lord, and that thought upon His Name.*
>
> Malachi 3:16

> *To Him the porter openeth; and the sheep hear His Voice: and He calleth His Own sheep by Name, and leadeth them out.*
>
> John 10:3

> *Hitherto have ye asked nothing in My Name: ask, and ye shall receive, that your Joy may be full.*
>
> John 16:24

YOU SHALL KEEP THE SABBATH DAY HOLY.

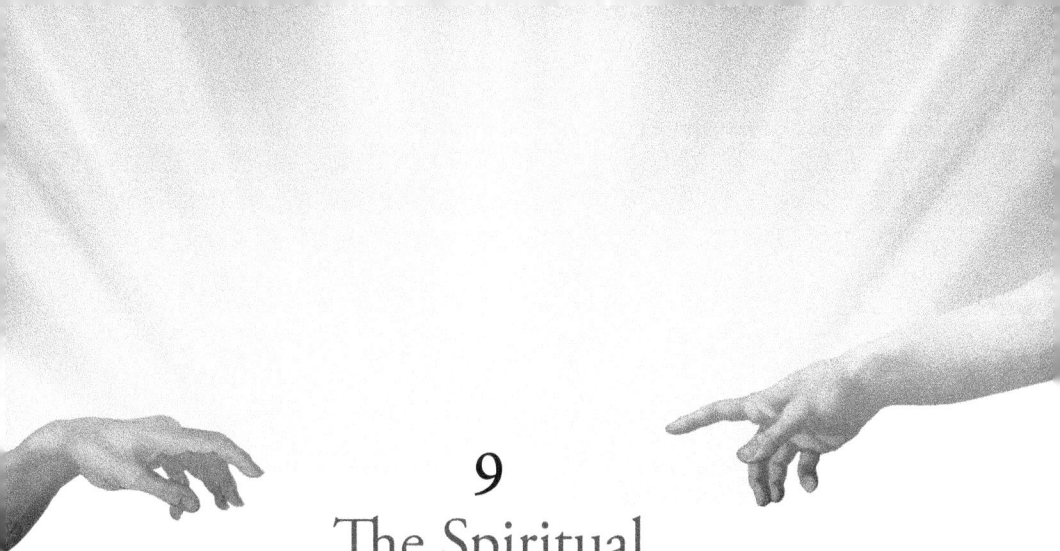

9
The Spiritual
Meaning of *Rest*

You have been Given the ability to allow
the Lord's Love to come to Rest within your soul.

The first verse of the fourth Commandment:

"*Remember the Sabbath Day, to keep it Holy.*"

Exodus 20:8

The Lord has Given you this Fourth Commandment so that you might
always remember what He is Purposing to accomplish within your life. He
has Given you this Commandment in four extraordinary verses, more verses
than any of His other Commandments, with each verse having profound
implications for your Good and for the Good of all around you. You keep
this Commandment Holy through your willingness to live your life according
to the Principles of His Righteousness, nothing withheld. Throughout the
Bible, He teaches you that you cannot keep this Commandment Holy
without keeping His other Commandments Holy as well.

"*Remember the Sabbath Day, to keep it Holy.*

"*Six Days shalt thou labor, and do all thy work:*

"But the Seventh Day is the Sabbath of the Lord thy God: in it thou shalt not do any work, thou, nor thy son, nor thy daughter, not thy manservant, nor thy maidservant, nor thy cattle, nor thy Stranger that is within thy gates.

"For in six Days the Lord made Heaven and earth, the sea, and all that in them is, and Rested the Seventh Day: wherefore the Lord Blessed the Sabbath Day, and Hallowed it."

Exodus 20:8–11

The Sabbath Day describes the fulfillment of the Lord's Promise to deliver you into a state of eternal Heavenly Joy. It is the culmination of all the "Work" He accomplishes within you as you allow Him to reform you and transform you into becoming the person that He has Purposed for you to become.

No one is born into this world already spiritually perfected.

"After this manner therefore pray ye; Our Father which art in Heaven, Hallowed be Thy Name.

"Thy Kingdom come, Thy Will be done in earth, as it is in Heaven."

Matthew 6:9–10

"Peace I leave with you, My Peace I Give unto you: not as the world giveth, Give I unto you. Let not your heart be troubled, neither let it be afraid."

John 14:27

Honor and Rest

Throughout the Bible, the Lord teaches about your need to work with Him through the spiritual development of your mind, heart, and soul. He Promises that as you willingly do so, the Blessings that will come forth within you will amaze you. He Promises that in the life to come, those incomparable Blessings will astound you. Keeping that remembrance Holy through the Way you live your life is the greatest Opportunity of your lifetime. The "work" He requires of you is not complicated or difficult to understand.

> *Then thou shalt prosper, if thou takest heed to fulfill the Statutes and Judgments which the Lord charged Moses with concerning Israel: be strong, and of Good courage; dread not, nor be dismayed.*
>
> 1 Chronicles 22:13

> *Light is Sown for the righteous, and Gladness for the upright in heart.*
>
> Psalms 97:11

> *If ye know that He is Righteous, ye know that everyone that doeth Righteousness is born of Him.*
>
> 1 John 2:29

The Second Verse of the Fourth Commandment:

> *Six Days shalt thou labor; and do all thy work.*
>
> Exodus 20:9

The "six Days" of "labor" preceding the Sabbath Day pertain to the stages of your spiritual reformation in the Light of Righteousness. They are descriptive of the work that allows the Lord to spiritually form you and shape you into becoming an image of His Truth and as a likeness to the Goodness of His Love for you. Through each "Day" He refines you and perfects you until you become reborn in mind, heart, and soul.

> "*Jesus answered and said unto him, Verily, verily, I say unto you, Except a man be born again, he cannot see the Kingdom of God.*"
>
> John 3:3

No one is born into this world already spiritually perfected, and no one is capable of being spiritually perfected by the Lord all at once. And so, no matter where you start in life, He openly welcomes you with Compassion and Forgiveness, freely and continuously Offering you all the spiritual knowledge you need for your spiritual journey ahead. As you willingly accept that Offer and apply that knowledge to the Way you live your life, step by step and stage by stage, you will find the transforming Power of this Divine Truth Marvelous to behold.

> "*Who hath believed our report? And to whom is the arm of the Lord revealed?*"
>
> Isaiah 53:1

Your efforts to work with the Lord to overcome all your spiritual faults and weaknesses are described in the Bible as your "labors." They are the "works" of Righteousness, and they are made through your free will offerings to live your life in the Way that He has Shown you that you must. Those efforts will require you to turn away from your self-serving thoughts, selfish affections, and their corresponding behaviors, and leave them behind. All the while He will Call upon you to turn towards Him for Guidance and understanding as He leads you forward, in the Paths of Righteousness.

Abide by that Holy understanding with all your mind, heart, and strength.

Abiding by this Holy understanding with all your mind, heart, and strength constitutes your "works" of Love. They are the offerings and sacrifices which are acceptable to the Lord for your salvation and deliverance into His Embrace. From those *labors* He stretches forth the Heavens and fills them from people on earth, like you.

"*Ye shall diligently keep the Commandments of the Lord your God, and His Testimonies, and His Statutes, which He has Commanded thee.*

And thou shalt do what is Right and Good in the Sight of the Lord: that it may be well with thee, and that thou mayest go in and possess the Good Land which the Lord sware unto thy fathers.

To cast out all of thine enemies from before thee, as the Lord hath spoken."

Deuteronomy 6:17–19

To "diligently keep the Commandments of the Lord your God, and His Testimonies, and His Statutes" is to willingly live your life according to the Principles of His Righteousness, nothing withheld. To "do what is Right and Good in the Sight of the Lord" is to do so with all your mind, heart, and strength. As you do so to the very best of your ability He Promises that all will "be well with thee."

The Words: *and that thou mayest go in and possess the Good Land which the Lord sware unto thy fathers* describe the incomparable Blessings of Goodness and Peace He has Prepared for you to inherit in mind, heart, and soul since the beginning of time. He Wills to Gift you with those incomparable Blessings "on earth, as it is in Heaven."

Throughout Scripture the causes of your spiritual faults and weaknesses are described as your "enemies." These are the true enemies of your mental, emotional, and spiritual wellbeing. Instead of Peace, they will attempt to wreak havoc within your life.

Everywhere in the Bible the Lord teaches you that you must fight with Him against the causes of your spiritual faults and weaknesses. As you do so, He Promises to Fight with you *To cast out all of thine enemies from before thee, as the Lord hath spoken.*

> "*The Lord said unto My Lord, Sit at My Right Hand, until I make Thine enemies thy footstool.*"
>
> Psalms 110:1

These Words describe the Lord's Divine Truth reassuring His Divine Love for you about the Power of His Righteousness to overcome all your spiritual faults and weaknesses. They are meant to reassure you about the Way He subdues your spiritual enemies as He brings the Joy of His Goodness to Rest within your soul. They portray the Way He puts everything into their Rightful Order within your life.

> "*Then came the disciples to Jesus apart, and said, Why could not we cast him out.*
>
> "*And Jesus said unto them, Because of your unbelief: for verily I say unto you, If ye have faith as a grain of mustard seed, ye shall say unto this mountain, Remove hence to yonder place; and it shall remove; and nothing shall be impossible unto you.*"
>
> Matthew 17:19–20

The Truth of the Lord's Testimony is Powerful, as expressed in Psalms 33:6. Applying it properly Gives you the ability to move *mountains* within your life.

> "*Jesus answered and said unto him, If a man love Me, he will keep My Words: and My Father will Love him, and We will come unto him, and make our Abode with him.*
>
> "*He that loveth Me not keepeth not My Sayings: and the Word which ye hear is not Mine, but the Father's which sent Me.*
>
> "*These things have I Spoken unto you, being yet present with you.*
>
> "*But the Comforter, which is the Holy Ghost, Whom the Father will send in My Name, He shall teach you all things, and shall bring all things to your remembrance, whatsoever I have said to you.*"
>
> John 14:23–26

If you claim to love the Lord, it becomes your responsibility to remember to live your life in the Way He has, is, and will forever be teaching you about why and how you must. Claiming to understand His "Words" and His "Sayings" and the things He has "Spoken" to you, yet inventing reasons not to keep them as your First Works, is spiritual hypocrisy.

> "Behold, happy is the man whom God correcteth: therefore despise not thou the chastening of the Almighty:
>
> "For He maketh sore, and bindeth up: He woundeth, and His Hands make whole.
>
> "He shall deliver thee in six troubles: yea, in Seven there shall no evil touch thee."
>
> Job 5:17–19

The spiritual trials and tribulations you will be asked to face, endure, and overcome during your spiritual reformation in this world are described as the Lord "correcting" you. Those corrections will often make you feel as if you are being "chastened" by "the Almighty." And as child being corrected by a Loving Father those chastisements may hurt your thoughts and feelings, spiritually described as the Lord making you "sore" and "wounding us." Yet it is your pride being wounded, and for all the Right Reasons. You should never become offended, reject or despise the Lord for correcting you, but rather cherish and rejoice in what He is Endeavoring to accomplish within your life. To do so is to have faith in His Testimony to you about His Purpose for the Creation of your soul.

The Third Verse of the Fourth Commandment:

> "But the Seventh Day is the Sabbath of the Lord thy God: in it thou shalt not do any work, thou, nor thy son, nor thy daughter, nor thy manservant, nor thy maidservant, nor thy cattle, nor thy stranger that is within thy gates."
>
> Exodus 20:10

Throughout the Bible the Lord teaches you that when your spiritual reformation in this life has been completed, all the work you have put forth to overcome your spiritual faults and weaknesses will be able to cease. In that "Day," which is a Heavenly spiritual state of being, you will have been wholly liberated from the effects of their lures and entrapments.

That liberation is like no other, for not only has the Lord then healed you from the mental, emotional, and spiritual afflictions they have caused you, but you will have become fully enabled to experience the Peace, Joy, and Goodwill that flow forth from His Love for you. That experience is like none other, making all the "work" you have put forth to abide by His Testimony to you seem as if it were but an instant.

> "*And God shall wipe away all tears from their eyes; and there shall be no more death, neither sorrow, nor crying, neither shall there be any more pain: for the former things are passed away.*
>
> "*And He that sat upon the Throne said, Behold, I make all things new. And He said unto me, Write: for these Words are True and faithful.*
>
> "*And He said unto me, It is done. I am the Alpha and Omega, the Beginning and the End. I will Give unto him that is athirst of the fountain of the Water of Life freely.*"
>
> Revelation 21:4–6

Although it may seem as if your life in this world is long, in the end it will seem to have gone by very quickly. Carrying that awareness with you in your everyday life is crucial because it affords you a sense of urgency about the importance of remembering why and how you must live your life. That remembrance is a Gift.

Receiving spiritual understanding about your need to "Remember the Sabbath Day, to keep it Holy" should be your greatest time of rejoicing.

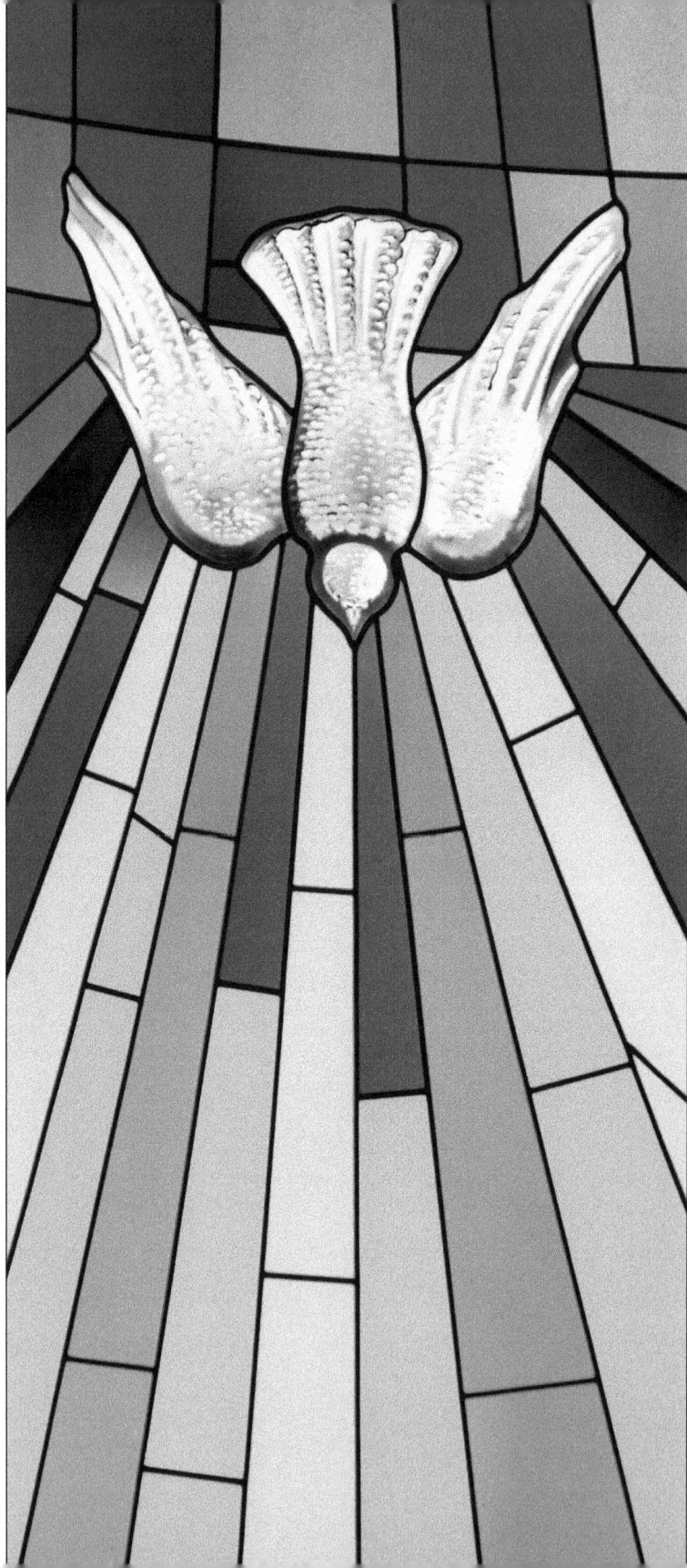

The Words: *And He that sat upon the Throne said, Behold, I make all things new. And He said unto me, Write: for these Words are True and faithful* underscore that spiritual Reality.

> "*Incline your ear, and come unto Me: hear, and your soul shall Live; and I will make an everlasting Covenant with you, even the sure Mercies of David.*
>
> "*Behold, I have Given Him for a Witness to the people, as a Leader and Commander to the people.*
>
> "*Behold, Thou shalt call a nation that Thou knowest not, and nations that knew not Thee shall run unto Thee because of the Lord Thy God, and for the Holy One of Israel; for He hath Glorified Thee.*
>
> "*Seek ye the Lord while He may be found, call ye upon Him while He is near.*"
>
> Isaiah 55:3–6

You "incline" your "ear," and "come to hear" what the Lord is Purposing to bring into your mind and heart as you willingly live your life according to the Way He is Showing you that you must. You do so whenever you resist harboring enmity toward others and instead offer them heartfelt forgiveness. You do so each time you turn away from adulterating the union between Divine Truth and the Doctrine of His Righteousness within your life.

You do so each time you cease from substituting errant and misleading thoughts of your own making in Place of what He has Shown you to be True and Right.

You do so each time you discontinue being a false witness to His Testimony to you about why and how you must live your life.

You do so every time you stop coveting control over what must always be your First Love, and remain as your First Works.

> *And thou shalt write them upon the door posts of thine house, and upon thy gates.*

> *That your days may be multiplied, and the days of your children, in the Land which the Lord sware unto your fathers to Give them, as the days of Heaven upon the earth.*
>
> Deuteronomy 11:20–21

> *And, behold, I come quickly; and My Reward is with Me, to Give every man according as his work shall be.*
>
> Revelation 22:12

10

The Spiritual Meaning of Words

Self-serving thoughts and selfish affections are
what must be overcome, and then left behind.

*I*n Scripture, your ruling love is spiritually described as your "father." Wisdom, or what is being substituted for it, united with that ruling love is described as your "mother." What they bring forth within your mind and heart are spiritually described as your "sons" and "daughters."

As you love the Lord above all else, He becomes your Father. United with spiritual Wisdom, they bring forth Truth and Good Doctrine into your life. The thoughts and affections that come forth from their becoming joined within your soul are spiritually described as the children of the Lord. When that relationship becomes adulterated, what comes forth are spiritually described as the children of perdition.

> *While I was with in the world, I kept them in Thy Name. Those that Thou Gavest Me I have kept; and none of them is lost, but the son of perdition; that the Scripture might be fulfilled.*
>
> John 17:12

"In this the children of God are manifest, and the children of the devil: whosoever doeth not Righteousness is not of God, neither he that loveth not his brother."

1 John 3:10

As thoughts and affections mature, they become attracted to like kind. As they become joined together in Righteousness they are spiritually described as virtuous husbands and wives.

"What therefore God hath joined together, let not man put asunder."

Mark 10:9

Brothers and sisters describe that which comes forth from a common spiritual lineage. In a positive sense your brother is related to you through True thoughts about the Lord's Testimony to you. In a negative sense your brother is related to you through self-serving thoughts. In a positive sense your sister is related to you through your affection for Righteousness. In a negative sense your sister is related to you through selfishness.

"And there went great multitudes with Him and He turned, and said unto them,

"If any man come to Me, and hate not his father, and mother, and wife, and children, and brethren, and sisters, yea, and his own life also, he cannot be My disciple."

Luke 14:25–26

Spiritually, the Lord teaches you to hate thoughts and affections that love themselves above what He has, is, and will forever be teaching you about what is True and Right. He teaches you to hate your own attachments to them, and the self-serving and selfish behaviors they strive to provoke within you.

- He teaches you to hate their attempts to corrupt your understanding about the Way you must live your life.

- He teaches you to hate their insidious efforts to convince you to think otherwise.

- He teaches you that you must learn to recognize them for what they really are.

> Spiritually, the terms disciple and discipline are very closely related.

- He teaches you to reject them for your Good and for the Good of all around you.

- He teaches you to do so in reverence to His Love for you.

- He teaches you that unless you find the internal discipline to do so you risk forfeiting the Opportunity of your lifetime.

" *The fear of the Lord is to hate evil: pride, and arrogancy, and the evil way, and the forward mouth, do I hate.* "

Proverbs 8:13

" *And whosoever doth not bear his Cross, and come after Me, cannot be My disciple.* "

Luke 14:27

As the Lord is Divine Love Himself, He would never ask anyone to hate their *physical father, mother, wife, children, brethren, sisters, and their own life also.* To believe otherwise is mental, emotional, and spiritual insanity.

Likewise, believing that simply ceasing from all bodily work, along with your physical sons and daughters, your manservant, maidservant, cattle, and the stranger that is within your gates will somehow keep the Sabbath Day Holy within your life is very misleading.

Such literal misconceptions about Scripture act as pitfalls and stumbling blocks to your spiritual sensibilities. It is therefore imperative that you gain genuine spiritual understanding about the meaning of the Lord's Testimony to you. That The Lord made a Promise. understanding will keep you from making rash judgments derived solely from the letter of the Word. Paul, of all people, came to that realization the hard way.

> "Now we have received, not the spirit of the world, but the Spirit which is of God; that we might know the things that are freely Given to us of God.

> "Which things also we speak, not in the words which man's wisdom teacheth, but which the Holy Spirit Teacheth; comparing Spiritual things with Spiritual."
>
> 1 Corinthians 2:12–13

> "Who also hath made us able ministers of the New Testament; not of the letter, but of the Spirit: for the letter killeth, but the Spirit Giveth Life."
>
> 2 Corinthians 3:6

Understanding Spiritual Things Spiritually

At the time of the Lord's advent into our world, all genuine spiritual understanding about His Testimony to humanity was fast coming to an end. Religious thought and practice had become inundated by literal mis-interpretations of Scripture. Proclamations based upon those misinterpreta-tions were once again putting all of us in danger of being swept away into an irreversible spiritual darkness and coldness of our own making. In Genesis 9:11, the Lord made a Promise that He would prevent that spiritual catastrophe from ever happening again. In Truth, from His Love for all He came into our world to fulfill that Sacred Promise to all.

"At that time Jesus went on the Sabbath Day through the corn; and His disciples were an hungered, and began to pluck the ears of corn, and to eat.

"But when the Pharisees saw it, they said unto Him, Behold, thy disciples do that which is not lawful to do upon the Sabbath day.

"But He said unto them, Have you not read what David did, when he was hungered, and they that were with him;

"How he entered into the House of God, and did eat the showbread, which was not lawful for him to eat, neither for them which were with Him, but only for the priests?"

Matthew 12:1–4

Here, the Lord explains the differences between man's "laws" and God's "Laws." He does so by contrasting a literal observance of a Sabbath "day" with the spiritual observance of that Hallowed "Day."

The Word "corn," much like the Words "Wheat" and "Bread," describes His spiritual Goodness. Being "an hungered" is descriptive of your internal need to receive that Goodness within your life. And so here the Lord teaches you that your quest for such spiritual nourishment on a physical "Sabbath Day" is both dutiful and Rightful.

The Lord's Love for our minds, hearts, and souls.

Literal misinterpretations about Scripture draw you away from understanding that He Offers you His Goodness, regardless of what calendar "day" of the week it may be, or of who may need it.

Exodus 25:30, 1 Kings 7:48, and John 6:35 all clarify the meaning of the Words "Showbread" and the "Bread of Life" as each describes the spiritual Goodness that comes forth from partaking in the Lord's Love for us all. Relying solely on the literal misinterpretations about Scripture to comprehend these things causes a gathering of the "chaff" rather than the "Wheat" into the storehouse of your mind, heart, and soul.

"And when He was departed thence, He went into their synagogue:

"And behold, there was a man which had his hand withered. And they asked Him, saying, Is it lawful to heal on the Sabbath days? that they might accuse Him.

"And He said unto them, what man shall there be among you, that shall have one sheep, and if it fall into a pit on the Sabbath Day, will he not lay hold on it, and lift it out?

"How much then is a man better than a sheep? Wherefore it is Lawful to do well on the Sabbath Days. "

Matthew 12:9-12

The Lord's Love for you is never passive, especially during your greatest times of need. Therefore, He always looks to restore your ability to grasp why and how you must live your life. If you have innocently fallen into misconceptions derived from the letter of the Word, there is nothing more important to Him than taking hold of that innocence and lifting it out of that "religious" pitfall again. There is no day of the week where your efforts to work with Him to do so will go unrewarded, and this certainly applies to a calendar "Sabbath day."

"Then saith He to the man, Stretch forth thine hand. And he stretched it forth; and it was restored whole, like as the other.

"Then the Pharisees went out, and held a council against Him, how they might destroy Him. "

Matthew 12:13-14

Throughout history, literal misinterpretations of Scripture have been used by self-declared "religious authorities" to mislead the innocent and unsuspecting. They unjustly use them to rule over the minds and hearts of others. And so, at His Own great peril, the Lord came into our world to address the dangers they were posing to our mental, emotional, and spiritual well-being. He has, is, and will forever be reminding us to be aware of those dangers, calling upon each of us to remember the "things" that He has been teaching us since the beginning of human existence.

> *Remember the Days of Old, consider the years of many generations: ask thy Father, and He will Show thee; thy elders, and they will tell thee.*
>
> Deuteronomy 32:7

> *In those Days, and at that time, will I cause the Branch of Righteousness to grow up unto David; and he shall execute Judgment and Righteousness in the Land.*
>
> Jeremiah 33:15

True Life from the Lord's Life comes forth from within you as you allow Him to spiritually reform you in the Light of His Righteousness. The infinite Blessings of Joy and Goodwill towards others that spring forth from that transformation defy description, as they are Pure experience. And so, He Wills to Commune with you about these things in terms that will Enlighten your understanding about the Way you may receive, retain, and forever share in those Experiences.

> *And as they were eating, Jesus took Bread, and Blessed it, and brake it, and Gave it to the disciples, and said, Take, eat; this is My Body.*

> *And he took the Cup, and Gave thanks, and Gave it to them, saying, Drink ye all of it;*

> *"For this is My Blood of the New Testament, which is shed for many for the remission of sins.*
>
> Matthew 26:26–28

The Lord describes His Divine Love for you as His Body, and His Divine Truth as His Blood. His Truth flows through His Body with Love for you as He reaches out to you with understanding about the Way to your salvation and deliverance into an eternal Heavenly state of being. And so, He teaches you about these spiritual things spiritually, and about your need to apply that understanding to each and every aspect of your life.

> "*But I say unto you, I will not drink henceforth of this Fruit of the Vine, until that Day when I drink it new with you in my Father's Kingdom.* "
>
> Matthew 26:29

In that "Day" the newly-conceived thoughts and affections portrayed in this Commandment as "your sons and daughters" will be able to cease from all the labor they have put forth within your life. In that Hallowed Day the Lord will have brought them to Rest in Peace and Goodwill within your soul.

The Spiritual Meaning of the Words *Manservants* and *Maidservants*

The Words: *But the Seventh Day is the Sabbath of the Lord thy God: in it thou shalt not do any work, thou, nor… thy manservant, nor thy maidservant* continues within the third verse of this Fourth Commandment.

During your spiritual reformation, you will be challenged many, many times.

In a positive sense, concerns that minister to your understanding about the Truth of Love are spiritually described as "manservants." "Maidservants" are descriptive of their ministering to your heart about these most important things of all.

> "*If I did despise the cause of my manservant or of my maid-servant, when they contended with me;*

> "What then shall I do when God riseth up? and when He
> visiteth, what shall I answer Him?"
>
> Job 31:13–14

The Words: *the cause of my manservant* spiritually describe your need to understand the importance of living your life in the Way the Lord is Showing you that you must. The "cause" of *my maidservant* describes your need to heed that understanding with all your heart.

During your spiritual reformation in this world you will be challenged many, many times to acknowledge that the Principles of Righteousness must always be, and remain Primary for the Way you live your life.

The Words: *If I did despise the cause of my manservant or of my maidservant when they contended with me* describe harboring disdain for accepting that acknowledgment.

The Words: *What then shall I do when God riseth up? and when He visiteth, what shall I answer Him?* express the shame experienced when your resistance to that vital acceptance becomes exposed in the Light of Righteousness. Unfortunately, it often takes much longer than it should to accept the contentions of your manservant and maidservant when they challenge you to accept their Righteous "cause" within your life.

> "Now Peter sat without in the palace: and a damsel came unto
> him, saying, thou also wast with Jesus of Galilee.
>
> "But he denied before them all, saying, I know not what thou
> sayest.
>
> "And when he was gone out unto the porch, another maid saw
> him, and said unto them that were there, this fellow was also
> with Jesus of Nazareth.

"*And again he denied with an oath, I do not know the Man.*

"*And after a while came unto him they that stood by, and said to Peter, Surely thou also art one of them; for thy speech betrayeth thee.*

"*Then began he to curse and to swear, saying, I know not the Man. And immediately the cock "crew."*

"*And Peter remembered the Word of Jesus, which said unto him, Before the cock crow, thou shall deny Me thrice. And he went out, and wept bitterly.*"

Matthew 26:69–75

In the New Testament, Peter represents your faith in the Lord's Testimony to you. In this heart-wrenching passage, the "damsel" and the "maid" are descriptive of heartfelt concerns that minister to your faith about what must always be, and remain, your First Love. Here, for your Good and for the Good of all around, they are confronting your refusal to acknowledge this Divine Truth. They are attempting to cause you to look within yourself while you are still present in the Light of His Righteousness. That they "came," "saw," and "said" to Peter describe their addressing your need to recognize and accept the Rightful Place that the Principles of His Righteousness must always occupy in your life.

The Words: *But he denied before them all, saying, I know not what thou sayest* express Peter's first rejection to their Call for that acknowledgment.

For his own Good, Peter was reminded in the "palace," and again upon "the porch" about what constitutes True and saving faith in the Lord's Testimony to us, and what does not. That he was reminded in both places describes your need to acknowledge Divine Truth in both the internal and external matters of your life. In those "places" Peter was Called upon "twice" to reconcile himself with the Truth of Love.

The Words: *And again he denied with an oath, I do not know the Man* reveals Peter's faith in the Lord quickly turning into faithlessness.

The Words: *And after a while came unto him they that stood by, and said to Peter, surely thou also art one of them* spiritually describe those heartfelt concerns serving the cause of Divine Truth within your life, as they once again challenge your faith to acknowledge the most important things of all.

The Words: *for thy speech betrayeth thee* reflect their exposing the hypocrisy of faith that has been Given to know better, yet refuses to make that acknowledgment under duress.

The Words: *Then began he to curse and to swear, saying, I know not the Man* reveal the vicious response of hypocrisy when challenged to admit its own shortcomings.

The Words: *And immediately the cock crew* spiritually illustrate your need to realize that any chance of reconciliation with the Righteousness of the Lord will hinge upon your willingness to heed the warnings that will then sound very loudly within your soul.

The Words: *And Peter remembered the Word of Jesus* highlight your faith in the Lord regaining spiritual sensibility about what leads to your salvation and deliverance into an eternal Heavenly state of being, and what does not.

The Words: *which said unto him, Before the cock crow, thou shall deny Me thrice* reveal what the Lord told Peter about the frailty of human faith to abide by His Testimony to us.

The Words: *And he went out, and wept bitterly* painfully show Peter realizing just how weak faith alone in the Lord can be, especially during times of temptation.

> *So when they had dined, Jesus saith to Simon Peter, Simon, son of Jonas, loveth thou me than these? He saith unto Him, Yea, Lord; Thou knowest that I love Thee. He saith unto him, Feed My lambs.*
>
> *He saith to him again the Second time, Simon, son of Jonas, lovest thou Me? He saith unto Him, Yea, Lord; Thou knowest that I love Thee. He saith unto him, Feed My sheep.*
>
> *He saith unto him a Third time, Simon, son of Jonas, lovest thou Me? Peter was grieved because He said unto him a third time, Lovest thou Me? And he said unto Him, Lord, Thou knowest all things; Thou knowest that I love Thee. Jesus said unto him, Feed My sheep.*
>
> John 21:15–17

Living your life in the Way the Lord has Shown you that you must is your most important responsibility in life. Taking that responsibility to mind, heart, and soul serves the Truth of His Love for you. Professing to value that understanding, yet not acknowledging your need to live your life accordingly is faithlessness. The innocence required of you to recognize and apply that Divine Truth to your life is described by the Words "Feed My sheep."

It is then when you become like a little child, innocently trusting and obeying in what the Lord has, is, and will forever be teaching you about what leads to innermost happiness and genuine fulfillment in life. It is only then, when the concerns of the "manservants and maidservants" that minister to the Lord's Purpose for the Creation of your soul may rest from all the "work" they have done to remind you about the most important things of all. Some might even call them your "better Angels" in this life.

"Bless ye the Lord, all ye His hosts; ye ministers of His, that do His pleasure."

Psalms 103:21

"But be ye doers of the Word, and not hearers only, deceiving your own selves.

"For if any one be a hearer of the Word, and not a doer, he is like unto a man beholding his natural face in a glass:

"For he beholdeth himself, and goeth his way, and straightway forgetteth what manner of man he was."

James 1:22–24

The Spiritual Meaning of the Word "Cattle"

The third verse of the Fourth Commandment continues:

The Words, "But the Seventh Day is the Sabbath of the Lord thy God, thou shalt not do any work, thou, nor… thy cattle." Spiritually, "cattle" describes your capacity to receive nourishment about the Joy and Goodness of the Lord's incomparable Love for you.

"But unto you that fear My Name shall the Sun of Righteousness arise with healing in His Wings; and ye shall go forth, and grow up as calves of the Stall."

Malachi 4:2

Spiritually, the Word "fear" describes reverence. To "fear" the "Name" of the Lord is to revere His Qualities and Virtues, which are Righteous in all their Ways. When honest, sincere, and humble, that reverence opens you Up into welcoming spiritual Enlightenment about the most important things of all, spiritually described by the Words: *unto you that fear My Name shall the Sun of Righteousness arise.*

The Words: *with healing in His Wings* address the Lord Inspiring you with the Truth of His Love for you as He makes you whole from all prior mental, emotional, and spiritual afflictions.

The Words: *and ye shall go forth, and grow up as calves* describe your mind and heart, then growing and strengthening in capacity to receive spiritual nourishment about the incomparable Blessings that the Lord Purposes to bring forth within your soul.

The Words *of the Stall* depict the Principles of His Righteousness, acting on all sides to protect you from falsities and evils of all sort as you mature in thought, feeling, and behavior.

As you grow and mature in your capacity to host the Joy and Goodness of the Lord's Love for you, you will emerge in confidence and assurance about the Way you must live your life. Those experiences will lead you into receiving all the spiritual nourishment you will ever need to complete your spiritual journey ahead.

> *The Lord is my Shepherd, I shall not want.*
>
> *He maketh me to lie down in green Pastures: He leadeth me beside the still Waters.*
>
> *He restoreth my soul: He leadeth me in the Paths of Righteousness for His Name's sake.*
>
> Psalms 23:1–3

Throughout Scripture, your capacity to host various spiritual characteristics is described in both a positive and negative sense. In a positive sense, it is described as the capacity to host the Joy and Goodness of the Lord's Love within your soul. In a negative sense, that capacity is described as hosting errant philosophies and misleading religious doctrines that misinform you about what brings innermost happiness and genuine fulfillment into your life.

Being on the wrong side of what the Lord has Shown you to be True and Right is self-defeating.

As depicted in Exodus 9:4 and 9:19-26, those two diametrically opposed capacities act to separate themselves in this life, while fully consummating that separation in the life to come.

> "And when the people saw that Moses delayed to come down out of the Mount, the people gathered themselves together unto Aaron, and said unto him, Up, make us gods, which shall go before us; for as for this Moses, the man that brought us up out of the land of Egypt, we wot not what is become of him.
>
> "And Aaron said unto them, Break off the Golden earrings, which are in the ears of your wives, of your sons, and of your daughters, and bring them unto me.
>
> "And all the people brake off the Golden earrings which were in their ears, and brought them unto Aaron.
>
> "And he received them at their hand, and fashioned it with a graving tool, after he had made it a golden calf, and they said, These be thy gods, O Israel, which brought thee up out of the land of Egypt.
>
> "And when Aaron saw it, he built an altar before it; and Aaron made proclamation, and said, Tomorrow is a feast to the Lord."
>
> Exodus 32:1-5

Spiritually, Moses is descriptive of your reception of the Lord's Commandments. Those Commandments embody all the Principles of Righteousness.

The Words: *And when the people saw that Moses delayed to come down out of the Mount, the people gathered themselves together unto Aaron* reveal a lack of patience and discipline to wait on the reforming Power of those Sacred Principles to transform your life.

The Words: *and said unto him, Up, make us gods, which shall go before us* depict that impatient lack of discipline, imprudently looking for "lofty" alternatives to replace the Truth of Love with errant philosophies and misleading doctrines of their own making.

The Words: *for as for this Moses, the man that brought us up out of the land of Egypt, we wot not what is become of him,* exposes a lack of willingness to keep remembrance about what the Lord has been teaching us since the beginning of our existence.

Breaking off *Golden earrings* from *their ears* is spiritually descriptive of betraying the Goodness of Divine Truth within your life.

The Words: *which are in the ears of your wives* describe breaking your commitment to honor the fidelity of that affection within your life.

The Words: *and sons, and of your daughters* depict depriving all true thoughts and unselfish affections of the Goodness that comes forth from keeping that fidelity Sacred within your life.

The Words: *and bring them unto me* describe placing your trust in misguided intentions about what constitutes saving faith in the Lord's Testimony to you.

The Words: *And all the people brake off the Golden earrings which were in their ears, and brought them unto Aaron* explain the act of foolishly allowing yourself to forget what it means to "Remember the Sabbath Day, to Keep it Holy."

The Words: *And he received them at their hand, and fashioned it with a graving tool, after he had made it a golden calf, and they said, These be thy gods, O Israel, that brought thee up out of the land of Egypt* spiritually describe placing the destiny of your soul in the hands of those who have fashioned spiritual half-truths to stand in the Place of what must always be, and remain, your First Love, regardless of their "best" intentions.

Refashioning *Golden earrings* with a *graving tool* depicts changing the Lord's Testimony to you into something utterly worthless to provide you with the capacity to nourish the Joy and Goodness of His Love within your soul.

The Words: *after he had made it a golden calf* illustrate creating spiritual half-truths to resemble what is worthy of your salvation and deliverance into a Heavenly state of being, when they are not.

The Words: *and they said, These be thy gods, O Israel, which brought thee up out of the land of Egypt* express the insanity of thinking that lofty proclamations made from those spiritual half-truths have the ability to liberate you from your responsibility to live your life in the Way the Lord has Shown you that you must.

The Words: *And when Aaron saw it, he built an altar before it; and Aaron made proclamation, and said, Tomorrow is a feast to the Lord* describe rebuilding the "Tower of Babel" within your own life, just as depicted in Genesis 11:1-9.

Many times during your spiritual journey in this world the Lord will seemingly leave you alone to reflect upon what constitutes True and saving faith in His Testimony to you, and what does not. In that state of self-reflection He will ask you to remember what He has taught you about why and how you must live your life. He will also ask you to remember what constitutes "keeping the Sabbath Day Holy," and what does not.

It is your responsibility to remember these answers while they may still be found within your capacity to recognize, acknowledge, and honor them with all your mind, heart, and strength.

> *I had fainted, unless I had believed to see the Goodness of the Lord in the Land of the Living.*
>
> *Wait on the Lord, be of Good courage, and He shall strengthen thine heart: wait, I say, on the Lord.*
>
> Psalms 27:13–14

> *And I will wait upon the Lord, that hideth His face from the house of Jacob, and I will look for Him.*
>
> Isaiah 8:17

Seeking remembrance about what allows you to host the incomparable Joy and Goodness of True Life from the Lord's Life affords you the Opportunity of your lifetime. Applying that remembrance to the Way you live your life enables the Lord to fulfill His Purpose for the Creation of your soul. At that time, and in that "Day" He will have fully developed your capacity to "lie down in green pastures," "besides the still Waters." In that "Day" He will be able to Rest from all the Work He has done to lead you into the "Promised Land," and so will you.

> *Therefore will I save My flock, and they shall no more be a prey: and I will Judge between cattle and cattle.*
>
> Ezekiel 34:22

> *If ye keep My Commandments, ye shall abide in My Love; even as I have kept My Father's Commandments, and abide in His Love.*
>
> John 15:10

"Here is the patience of the saints here are they that keep the Commandments of God, and the faith of Jesus."

Revelation 14:12

The Spiritual Meaning of the Word "Stranger"

The final phase of the third verse of the Lord's Fourth Commandment instructs you: "But the Seventh Day is the Sabbath of the Lord thy God: in it thou shalt not do any work, thou, nor…thy Stranger that is within thy gates."

No one is born into this world with a mind and heart that is fully familiar with the Lord's Thoughts and Affections. As such, He is initially described as "thy Stranger that is within" your "gates." Getting to know your Creator is both Wonderful and humbling. As you gain genuine spiritual understanding about Him and willingly apply it to the Way you live your life you befriend His Will to deliver you into "a Land of Plenty."

"For My Thoughts are not your thoughts, neither are your ways My Ways, saith the Lord.

"For as the Heavens are Higher than the earth, so are My Ways Higher than your ways, and My Thoughts than your thoughts."

Isaiah 55:8–9

Throughout the Bible, the Lord invites you to learn of Him. That Invitation Calls upon you to put on new thoughts based upon His Thoughts about why and how you must.

> "*Take my yoke upon you, and learn of Me; for I am meek and lowly in Heart: and ye shall find Rest unto your souls.*"
>
> Matthew 11:29

The Divine Humility the Lord puts forth as He Calls upon you to learn about Him is quite astounding. With that Humility, He teaches you about the things that will lead you to your salvation and deliverance into an eternal Heavenly state of being. He teaches you about the Way you may receive, retain, and forever share in these things regardless of your background, ethnicity, nationality, race, gender, or religious orientation. And He Promises that as you willingly abide by what He is teaching you, the Truth of His Love for you will soon be a Stranger within you no longer.

> "*Then shall the King say to them on His Right hand, Come, ye Blessed of My Father, inherit the Kingdom prepared for you from the foundation of the world:*
>
> "*For I was an hungered, and ye gave Me meat: I was thirsty, and ye gave Me drink: I was a Stranger and ye took Me in.*"
>
> Matthew 25:34–35

That the Lord is Righteousness Himself is declared throughout the entire Bible, from Beginning to End. As you allow the Righteousness of His Commandments to Govern your thoughts, affections, and behaviors He becomes your King and Savior. As you abide by that understanding, He Promises to spiritually reform you and transform you until you become enabled to inherit the Rewards that He has prepared in advance for you since your inception.

False thoughts and wayward affections will always strive to entrap you in a very dark and cold place of their own making.

> "*O the Hope of Israel, the Savior thereof in time of trouble, why shouldest Thou be as a Stranger in the land, and as a wayfaring Man that turneth aside to tarry for a night?*

> *"Why shouldest Thou be as a Man astonied, as a Mighty Man that cannot save? Yet thou, O Lord, art in the midst of us, and we are Called by Thy Name; leave us not."*
>
> Jeremiah 14:8–9

The most important things you can offer the Lord is to willingly love Him above all else and love others by abiding by the Principles of His Righteousness, nothing withheld. Doing so allows Him to come into your life and Sup with you, and you with Him, sharing in the Truth and Goodness that brings the Joy of His Love to Rest within your soul.

> *"He that hath My Commndments, and keepeth them, he it is that loveth Me: and he that loveth Me shall be Loved of My Father, and I will Love him, and will manifest Myself to him."*
>
> John 14:21

> *"These things have I spoken unto you, that My Joy might remain in you, and that your Joy might be full.*
>
> *This is My Commandment, That ye love one another, as I have Loved you."*
>
> John 15:11–12

It is important to remember that most terms in Scripture are used in both a positive and in a negative sense. When the term "Stranger" is used in a positive sense, it describes the Lord making all things new through His advent into your life. When used in a negative sense, the term "stranger" depicts thoughts and affections that are the opposite to what He is Showing you to be True and Right.

> *"And when He putteth forth His own sheep, He goeth before them, and the sheep follow Him for they know His Voice.*

> *"And a stranger will they not follow, but will flee from him for they know not the voice of strangers."*
>
> John 10:4–5

False thoughts and wayward affections will always strive to lead you and entrap you into a very dark and cold place of their own making. Regardless of their seemingly "correct" and "attractive" appeal, it is your responsibility to remain steadfast in recognizing them for what they really are, and then to keep them at bay.

> *"Behold, I send you forth as sheep in the midst of wolves: be ye therefore wise as serpents, and harmless as doves."*
>
> Matthew 10:16

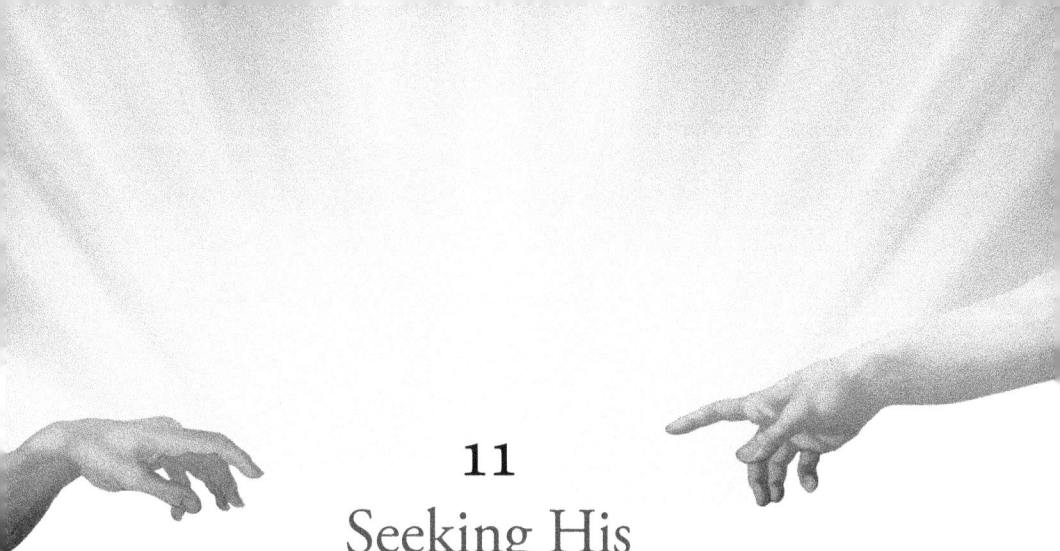

11

Seeking His Righteousness First

He Promises that He will be a Stranger within you
no longer, and that you will no longer be a stranger to Him.

*H*uman history is filled with examples of people who have chosen
to defend the pride of their own self-intelligence rather than to honestly,
sincerely, and humbly submit themselves to seeking Righteousness First,
in all they think, feel, and do. The Lord has Given you many lessons and
examples about the dire effects of doing so.

> *When once the Master of the house is risen up, and hath shut*
> *to the door, and ye begin to stand without, and to knock at the*
> *door, saying Lord, Lord, open unto us; and He shall answer*
> *and say unto you, I know not whence ye are.*
>
> Luke 13:25

Being on the wrong side of what the Lord has Shown you to be True
and Right is self-defeating. And although it may seem as if the Lord has
shut you out from being able to enter into the Joys of Heavenly Love, it
is you who will have caused that inability within yourself. By maintaining
stiff-necked judgments and hardheaded proclamations about your own
correctness, even when you have been Given to know better, you risk
forfeiting the Opportunity of your lifetime.

"As many as I Love, I rebuke and chasten: be zealous therefore, and repent.

"Behold, I stand at the door, and knock: if any man hear My Voice, and open the door, I will come in to him, and will Sup with him, and he with Me.

"To him that overcometh will I grant to sit with Me in My Throne, even as I also overcame, and am set down with My Father in His Throne."

Revelation 3:19–21

Throughout Scripture, the Lord calls upon you to place your trust and faith in His Testimony about your need to seek His Righteousness First in all you think, feel, and do. Everywhere He Promises that as you willingly do the "labor" required, He will Work within you to subdue and overcome every one of your spiritual faults and weaknesses. As you do so, He teaches you that each of them will die off, and new thoughts and affections filled with Truth and Goodness will become born anew with your mind, heart, and soul. That is His Holy Covenant with you, and with all of us. For our Good and for the Good of all around us, it is our responsibility to befriend His Purpose for asking us to keep that Covenant Holy with Him.

"Greater love hath no man than this, that a man lay down his life for his friends.

"Ye are My friends, if ye do whatever I Command you.

"Henceforth I call you not servants: for the servant knoweth not what his Lord doeth: but I have called you friends; for all things that I have heard from My Father I have made known unto you."

John 15:13–15

The fulfillment of the Lord's Covenant is spiritually described in the Bible as the Sabbath Day. In that Blessed "Day," He Promises that He will be a Stranger within you no longer, and that you will no longer be a stranger to Him. In that Blessed "Day," He teaches you that the "Stranger within" your "gates" will be able to Rest from all the Work that He has accomplished within you, and so will you. In that Blessed "Sabbath Day," He teaches you that you will have made the transition from having been His obedient servant, to having become a friend to the Truth and Goodness of His Love within your life, and within the lives of all those around you.

The Fourth and Final Verse of the Lord's Fourth Commandment:

> "*For in six Days the Lord made Heaven and earth, the sea, and all that in them is, and Rested the Seventh Day: wherefore the Lord Blessed the Sabbath Day, and Hallowed it.*"
>
> Exodus 20:11

The Words: *six Days* describe the stages of your spiritual development as the Lord leads you in the Paths of His Righteousness. Each new "Day" depicts the Lord bringing you out from what before was obscure in spiritual understanding and limited in capacity to love others unselfishly, as He reforms you and transforms you into becoming a Better and much more perfect human being.

With each new Day, He spiritually reforms you until your self-serving thoughts and selfish desires die off, with new generations of True thoughts and Unselfish affections then springing forth within your life. As you work Him through the steps and stages of each new Day, He spiritually turns each preceding night into a new morning within your life until He fulfills His Promise to deliver you into an eternal state of Heavenly Joy.

Throughout the Bible, that fulfillment is referred to as your deliverance into *a Land flowing with Milk and Honey*, also and most especially described as *the Promised Land.*

> " *Thus saith the Lord God; The Gate of the inner court that looketh toward the East shall be shut the six working Days; but on the Sabbath it shall be opened, and in the Day of the new moon it shall be opened.* "
>
> Ezekiel 46:1

The Words: *The gate of the inner court that looketh toward the East shall be shut the six working Days* depict the times of your spiritual reformation preceding the fulfillment of the Lord's Promise to transform you into the person you are capable of becoming.

The Words: *but on the Sabbath it shall be opened, and in the Day of the new moon it shall be opened* explain the consummation of that age within you, as the Lord fulfill His Purpose for the Creation of your soul.

> " *Thus the Heavens and the earth were finished, and all the host of them.*
>
> " *And on the Seventh Day God ended His Work which He had Made; and He Rested on the Seventh Day from all His Work which He had Made.*
>
> " *And God Blessed the Seventh Day, and Sanctified it: because that in it He had Rested from all His Work which God Created and Made.* "
>
> Genesis 2:1–3

> " *This is the Lord's doing; it is Marvelous in our eyes.*
>
> " *This is the Day which the Lord hath Made; we will rejoice and be glad in it.* "
>
> Psalms 118:23–24

"And I heard a Voice from Heaven saying unto me, Write,
Blessed are the dead which die in the Lord from henceforth:
Yea, saith the Spirit, that they may Rest from their labors;
and their works do follow them."

Revelation 14:13

Charity of St Elizabeth Feeding the Poor Giving Bread, by Edmund Bliar Leighton

Reflections

> "He that hath an ear, let him hear what the Spirit saith unto
> the churches; To him that overcometh will I Give to him to
> eat of the Tree of Life, which is in the midst of the Paradise of
> God."
>
> Revelation 2:7

When the Lord has completed the spiritual reformation of your mind, heart, and soul, Unselfish love towards others will have become the center of your life. The "Fruit" that come forth from that "Tree" is filled in Joy and Goodness, perpetuating itself in Truth with Goodwill towards others for endless generations to come.

In that *Day*, He Promises to bring forth incomparable Blessings of innermost happiness and genuine fulfillment within your life in degrees that can only be described as "Marvelous" in your eyes. In that "Day," you will have become an image, and as a likeness of His Qualities and Virtues, having then been delivered into "the Paradise of God."

> "Behold, the former things are come to pass, and new things
> do I declare: before they Spring forth I tell you of them."
>
> Isaiah 42:9

> "Think not that I am come to destroy tthe Law, or the
> prophets: I am not come to destroy, but to fulfill."
>
> Matthew 5:17

HONOR THY FATHER AND THY MOTHER

*that thy Days may be long upon the Land
that the Lord thy God Giveth thee.*

Exodus 20:12

12
Love and Wisdom

He has been delivering this Sacred Message
to you since your inception.

*S*piritually, the Lord's Love for you is the Father of all Goodness conceived within your soul. Your Mother is the Wisdom that brings those conceptions forth within your life. "Days" are descriptive of the stages required to bring them to full term within your mind, heart, and soul.

The Words: *The Land which the Lord thy God Giveth thee* illuminate His Promise to fulfill your potential to receive, retain, and forever share in the incomparable Joy of True Life from His Life.

> *Hear, Ye children, the Instruction of a Father, and attend to know understanding.*
>
> *For I Give you Good Doctrine, forsake ye not My Law.*
>
> Proverbs 4:1–2

Honor thy Father and thy Mother

With a Father's Love, the Lord sends you Divine Truth about the Way you must live your life. With a Mother's Love, Wisdom Offers you understanding about why and how you must. The Doctrine that unites that understanding together with Divine Truth is described in the Bible as coming "out of Heaven as a Bride prepared for Her Husband."

> "*Jesus answered them and said, My Doctrine is not Mine, but His that sent Me.*"
>
> John 7:16

Divine Truth Loves the Doctrine of Righteousness as a Bridegroom Loves His Bride, and the Doctrine of Righteousness Loves Divine Truth as a Bride Loves Her Bridegroom. Their Wedding is descriptive of their becoming joined together within you through your understanding about the Way you must live your life.

> "*I will greatly rejoice in the Lord, my soul shall be joyful in my God; for He hath clothed me with the Garments of salvation, He hath covered me with the Robe of Righteousness, as a Bridegroom decketh Himself with ornaments, and as a Bride adorneth Herself with her Jewels.*"
>
> Isaiah 61:10

The Name "Jesus Christ" means the Salvation of Truth. He comes into your life teaching you to honor His Love and Wisdom by seeking His Righteousness First in all you think, feel, and do. He teaches you about your need to cherish and respect that understanding by applying it to every aspect of your life. He does so with Divine Humility, Compassion, and Goodwill, having only your Best interests at Heart.

> "*For I was My Father's Son, tender and only Beloved in the sight of My Mother.*

> "*He Taught Me also, and said unto Me, Let Thine Heart retain My Words: keep My Commandments, and Live.*

> "*Get Wisdom, get understanding: forget it not; neither decline from the Words of My mouth.*

" *Forsake Her not, and She shall preserve thee: love Her, and She shall keep thee.*

" *Wisdom is the Principal thing; therefore get Wisdom: and with all thy getting, get understanding.* "

Proverbs 4:3-7

And so, the Lord implores you to "Get Wisdom" and beseeches you to "Forsake Her not." He teaches you everywhere that this understanding is the "Principal thing" that will lead you into your salvation and deliverance into the Joys of Heavenly Love. He has been delivering this Sacred Message to us since our inceptions.

" *Exalt Her, and She shall promote thee: she shall bring thee to honor, when thou dost embrace Her.*

" *She shall Give to thine head an ornament of Grace: a crown of Glory shall She deliver to thee.* "

Proverbs 4:8-9

Divine Truth honors Divine Wisdom by teaching you about the Opportunity of your lifetime.

The Words: *She shall Give to thine head an ornament of Grace* describe receiving that invaluable understanding.

The Words: *a crown of Glory shall She deliver to thee* describe the inmost gladness of mind and heart that await you as you live your life in the Way the Lord is Showing that you must.

" *Hear, O My Son, and receive My Sayings; and the years of Thy Life shall be many.*

" *I have Taught Thee in the Way of Wisdom; I have led Thee in Right Paths.*

"*When Thou goest, Thy steps shall not be straitened; and when Thou runnest, Thou shalt not stumble.*

"*Take fast hold of Instruction, let Her not go; keep Her, for She is Thy Life.*"

Proverbs 4:10–13

"*For whosoever shall do the Will of My Father which is in Heaven, the same is my brother, and sister, and Mother.*"

Matthew 12:50

The Lord Wills for you to share in the incomparable Goodness that comes forth from His Divine Love for you. To that End, Wisdom invites you to come into the wedding celebration between Divine Truth and the Doctrine of Righteousness within your life.

And yet, even though humanity has been Given to know better, many times we have cast aside that invitation, then going about our own way, to our great detriment.

"*Doth not Wisdom cry? And understanding put forth Her Voice?*

"*She standeth in the top of High Places, by the Way in the Places of the Paths.*

"*She crieth at the Gates, at the entry of the City, at the coming in at the doors.*

"*Unto you, O men, I call; and My Voice is to the sons of man.*

"*O ye simple, understand Wisdom: and ye fools, be ye of an understanding heart.*

"*Hear; for I will speak of Excellent things; and the opening of My lips shall be Right things.*

> "For My mouth shall speak Truth; and wickedness is an
> abomination to My lips.
>
> "All the Words of My mouth are in Righteousness; there is
> nothing forward or perverse in them.
>
> "They are plain to all that understandeth, and Right to them
> that find knowledge."
>
> Proverbs 8:1–9

Your need to recognize and acknowledge what constitutes the most important things of all, and what does not, cannot be overstated. Willfully receiving and applying that understanding to your life is vital for the prosperity of your mental, emotional, and spiritual wellbeing. And although that understanding is vital for your wellbeing in this life, it is essential for your continued prosperity in the life to come.

> "After this manner therefore pray ye: Our Father which art in
> Heaven, Hallowed be Thy Name.
>
> "Thy Kingdom come, Thy Will be done in earth, as it is in
> Heaven."
>
> Matthew 6:9–10

This Fifth Commandment, "Honor thy Father and Mother: that thy Days may be long upon the Land which the Lord thy God Giveth thee" has been Given to you for your Good and for the Good of all around you. This Commandment is seamlessly woven into all the other of the Lord's Commandments. Honoring these Commandments with all your mind, heart, soul, and strength is the Opportunity of your lifetime.

> "But Wisdom is justified of all Her children."
>
> Luke 7:35

"But the Wisdom that is from Above is first Pure, then peaceable, gentle, and easy to be intreated, full of Mercy and Good fruits, without partiality, and without hypocrisy.

"And the fruit of Righteousness is sown in Peace of them that make Peace."

James 3:17–18

One God

Lest you begin to think that there is more than One God, consider that Wisdom, Divine Truth, spiritual understanding, and the Doctrine of Righteousness all come forth from the Mind and Heart of One Loving Being, even the Lord Himself.

> He describes your understanding about these things as coming from His Holy Spirit.

Treating them as *separate persons* only creates unnecessary confusion. Given the age-old Clarity of the Lord's Testimony about His being One God, there should be no confusion about these things.

"Hear, O Israel, The Lord our God is One Lord.

"And thou shalt love the Lord thy God with all thine heart, and with all thy soul, and with all thy might.

"And these Words, which I Command thee this Day, shall be in thine heart.

"And thou shalt teach them diligently unto thy children, and thou shalt talk of them when thou sittest in thine house, and when thou walkest by the Way, and when thou liest down, and when thou risest up."

Deuteronomy 6:4–7

"*Phillip saith unto Him, Lord, show us the Father, and it sufficeth us.*

"*Jesus saith unto him, Have I been so long time with you, and yet hast thou not known Me, Phillip? He that hath seen Me hath seen the Father; and how sayest thou then, Show us the Father?*"

John 14:8–9

Throughout the Bible, the Lord describes Himself in terms that address His Qualities and Virtues. Those terms manifest Who He is while revealing His Purpose for coming into your life. He portrays His Divine Love as your Father and His Wisdom as your Mother. He describes His Divine Truth as His Son, coming forth from His Love for you to save you from mental, emotional, and spiritual harm as He delivers you into "the Kingdom of Heaven." He describes the Doctrine of Righteousness as the "Holy City, New Jerusalem, coming down from God out of Heaven, as a Bride prepared for Her Husband." He describes that Doctrine as a Holy City because it is filled with Thoughts and Affections that are much Higher, and much more Perfect than anything we could ever conceive on our own.

He describes your understanding about these things as coming forth from His Holy Spirit, Given to teach you about His Purpose for coming into your life. What better way is there for Him to inform you about the most important things of all?

"*I said, Days should speak, and multitude of years should teach Wisdom.*

"*But there is a Spirit in man: and the Inspiration of the Almighty Giveth them understanding.*"

Job 32:7–8

The Sermon of the Beatitudes, by James Tissot

> " *You are the Light of the world. A City that is set on a Hill cannot be hid.*
>
> " *Neither do men light a candle and place it under a bushel, but on a Candlestick; and it Giveth Light to all that are in the house.*
>
> " *Let your Light so shine before men, that they may see your Good works, and Glorify your Father which is in Heaven.* "
>
> Matthew 5:14–16

The Spiritual Meaning of the Terms *Fatherless* and *Widow*

> " *When the ear heard Me, then it Blessed Me; and when the eye saw Me, it Gave witness to Me.*
>
> " *Because I delivered the poor that cried, and the Fatherless, and him that had none to help him.*
>
> " *The Blessing of Him that was ready to perish came upon Me and I caused the Widow's heart to sing for Joy.*
>
> " *I put on Righteousness, and it clothed Me: My Judgment was as a robe and a Diadem.* "
>
> Job 29:11–14

The Lord uses physical terms to teach you about spiritual things, always speaking to you about your need to seek Righteousness First in all aspects of your life.

The Words: *When the ear heard Me* describe your willingness to attend and obey that Divine Truth.

The Words: *when the eye saw Me* express your realization about why and how you must. Willingly abiding by that "hearing" and "seeing" honors your Father and Mother in mind, heart, and soul.

A lack of understanding about these things causes you to become spiritually "poor" and "needy." Without that understanding you will soon become unable to recognize the Way you may share in the Goodness of the Lord's Love for you. That deprived state of being is spiritually descriptive of becoming "Fatherless."

The Words: *him that had none to help Him* refer to the lack of genuine spiritual Truth within your life.

The Words: *The Blessing of Him that was ready to perish came upon Me* describe the Lord making His advent into your life. Before His advent His Wisdom is spiritually described as a "Widow" within you.

The Words: *and I caused the Widow's heart to sing for Joy* portray the fulfillment of His Promise to restore your spiritual understanding about the most important things of all.

The Words: *I put on Righteousness, and it clothed Me* spiritually describe the Lord Offering you True Thoughts about what will lead you into your salvation and deliverance into the Goodness of His Embrace.

The Words: *My Judgment was as a Robe and a Diadem* communicate being Given Good Judgment to discern things that are True and Right.

> "*Come ye near unto Me, hear ye this; I have not spoken in secret from the Beginning; from the time that it was, there am I: and now the Lord God, and his Spirit, hath sent Me.*
>
> "*Thus saith the Lord, thy Redeemer, the Holy One of Israel; I am the Lord thy God which teacheth thee to profit, which leadeth thee by the Way that thou shouldest go.*"
>
> Isaiah 48:16–17

Turning Water to Wine (the Wedding at Cana), by Bloch Carl Heinrich

> *"Thus saith the Lord, Keep ye Judgment, and do Justice: for My salvation is near to come, and My Righteousness to be revealed."*

Isaiah 56:1

He will no longer be a Stranger to you. Exercising Good Judgment about the Way you must live your life does Justice to the Lord's Quest for your salvation and deliverance into His Embrace. Everywhere He teaches you that you exercise Good Judgment as you apply the Principles of His Righteousness to each and every aspect of your life, nothing withheld. As you willingly do so, He Promises that the Joy and Goodness that will evolve within your mind, heart, and soul will far exceed your greatest expectations.

> *"Thus saith the Lord; Execute ye Judgment and Righteousness, and deliver the spoiled out of the hand of the oppressor: and do no wrong, do no violence to the Stranger, the Fatherless, nor the Widow, neither shed innocent Blood in this Place."*

Jeremiah 22:3

> *"If ye love Me, keep My Commandments.*
>
> *"And I will pray the Father, and He shall Give you another Comforter, that He may abide with you forever;"*

John 14:15–16

You allow the Lord to deliver you "out of the hand of the oppressor" as you willingly live your life in the Way He is Showing you that you must. In that manner, you "do no wrong" to His Purpose for the Creation of your soul. In that manner, you "do no **He especially warns those who have been Given to know better.** violence to the Stranger, the Fatherless, nor the Widow." Otherwise, you risk wasting the many Sacrifices that He has made to bring the Spirit of that Sacred understanding back into your life, depicted as shedding "innocent Blood in this Place."

"*They that hate Me without a cause are more than the hairs of Mine Head: they that would destroy Me, being Mine enemies wrongfully, are mighty: then I Restored that which I took not away.*"

Psalms 69:4

~

As Righteousness Himself, the Lord warns you about the dangers of adding or subtracting to His Testimony to you. Everywhere He warns you about the self-inflicted harm you will bring upon yourself by doing so. He especially warns those who have been Given to know better, yet persist in promoting their own errant philosophies and misleading religious doctrines to stand in place of that Holy understanding.

"*And I will come near to you to Judgment; and I will be a swift Witness against the sorcerers, and against the adulterers, and against false swearers, and against those that oppress the hireling in his wages, the Widow, and the Fatherless, and that turn aside the Stranger from His Right, and fear not Me, saith the Lord of hosts.*"

Malachi 3:5

"*Wherefore I say unto you, All manner of sin and blasphemy shall be forgiven unto men: but the blasphemy against the Holy Ghost shall not be forgiven unto men.*"

Matthew 12:31

> "*But woe unto you, scribes and Pharisees, hypocrites! For ye shut up the Kingdom of Heaven against men: for ye neither go in or yourselves, neither suffer ye them that are entering in to go in.*
>
> "*Woe unto you, scribes and Pharisees, hypocrites! For ye devour Widows' houses, and for a pretense make long prayer: therefore you shall receive the greater damnation.*"

Matthew 23:13–14

Your Need to Honor Spiritual Wisdom in All You Think, Feel, and Do

Given the long history of the human race, it is reasonable to think that we should have come to a common understanding about what supports our mental, emotional and spiritual wellbeing. Yet that consensus has been fleeting. Too often it has become rejected and replaced by "thoughts formed from the imaginations" of our own hearts. Instead of bringing forth understanding about what brings innermost happiness and genuine fulfillment into fruition within our lives, they bring forth what is spiritually stillborn.

> "*For I have heard a Voice as of a Woman in travail, and the anguish as of Her that bringeth forth Her first Child, the Voice of the daughter of Zion, that bewaileth Herself, that speadeth Her hands, saying, Woe is Me now! For my Soul is wearied because of the murderers.*"

Jeremiah 4:31

Whenever you deny that abiding by the Principles of Righteousness must always be, and remain, your First Works, spiritual Wisdom cries out "in travail." She laments the resulting loss of that understanding within your life with a Mother's grief. She bewails the "murderers" of the Truth that Divine Love Wills to bring into your life as a Mother pleading for Mercy for Her Firstborn Child, Who is Righteousness Himself.

She cries out to your spiritual sensibilities, asking you to stop and reconsider the dire consequences you are causing to yourself and to those around you. Her "Soul" is described as "wearied" because Her "Cry" so often goes unheeded. And yet the Lord continues to defend Her Honor, teaching you to value Her Guidance about the Way you must live your life. That spiritual knowledge is Life-Giving.

> *Thy Mother is like a Vine in thy blood, planted by the Waters:*
> *she was fruitful and full of branches by Reason of many Waters.*
>
> Ezekiel 19:10

Throughout the Bible, the Lord teaches you that receiving genuine spiritual knowledge about the Truth of His Love for you is not restricted to a particular bloodline, culture, gender, or religious denomination. Rather, He teaches you that He freely Offers that knowledge to all who are willing to live their life accordingly. He teaches you that trying to justify philosophies or doctrines that teach otherwise is self-defeating.

> *Plead with your mother, plead: for she is not My Wife, neither*
> *am I her Husband: let her therefore put away her whoredoms*
> *out of her sight, and her adulteries from between her breasts;*
>
> *Lest I strip her naked, and set her as in the day that she was*
> *born, and make her as a wilderness, and set her like a dry*
> *land, and slay her with thirst.*
>
> *And I will not have Mercy on her children: for they be the*
> *children of whoredoms.*
>
> Hosea 2:2–4

Throughout the Bible, the Lord teaches you about the causes and effects that will determine the state of your mental, emotional, and spiritual wellbeing. He teaches you that the qualities and virtues you choose to host within you in this life will determine your state of being in the life to come. And so, He beseeches you to honestly, sincerely, and humbly reflect upon what brings innermost happiness and genuine fulfillment into fruition within your life, and what does not.

He implores you to use Good Judgment in making those discernments, warning you many times about the dangers of doing otherwise.

He "pleads" with you to reverence His Testimony to you about these things in all you think, feel, and do. He forewarns you about the dire effects of refusing to do so, and about the dishonor you do to His Love and Wisdom by being, and remaining, "wise in your own eyes."

> *And the Light of a Candle shall Shine no more at all in thee; and the Voice of the Bridegroom and of the Bride shall be heard no more at all in thee: for thy merchants were the great men of the earth; for by thy sorceries were all nations deceived.*
>
> Revelation 18:23

The pride of self-intelligence dealing in spiritual half-truths is depicted by the Words; *for thy merchants were the great men of the earth; for by thy sorceries were all nations deceived.* Those "merchants" do great disservice to your ability to understand the most important things of all.

13
The Wisdom of Solomon

The Divine Truth is to be found where the Lord
dwells in the Glory of His Love for you.

The lessons the Lord presents to you through the story of Solomon are timeless examples about Divine Wisdom. They Offer you Truth and Good Doctrine about the Way you must live your life. They also warn you about the dangers of adulterating that Sacred union within your life.

"Give therefore Thy servant an understanding heart to judge
Thy people, that I may discern between Good and bad: for who
is able to Judge this Thy so great a people?

"And the speech pleased the Lord, that Solomon had asked this
thing.

"And God said unto him, Because thou has asked this thing,
and hast not asked for thyself long life; neither hast asked riches
for thyself, nor hast asked the life of thine enemies; but hast
asked for thyself understanding to discern Judgment.

"Behold, I have done according to thy words: lo, I have Given
thee a wise and understanding heart; so that there was none like
thee before thee, neither after thee shall any arise like unto thee."

1 Kings 3:9–12

Your thoughts and affections make you the person you are. As you willingly receive and apply True thoughts and Unselfish affections conceived from the Lord's Thoughts and Affections, spiritually you become as His children, then described as being *a part* of His "people." In this manner you become interrelated with all others who share in the Truth and Glory of His Love for you.

Whenever you honestly and sincerely seek His Thoughts and Affections to discern between "Good and bad," your "speech" pleases Him, for it Guides you into making Just decisions based upon His Testimony to you.

The Words: *for who is able to Judge this Thy so great a people?* illuminate the humility of realizing that you are not fully capable of making those Judgments on your own. Abiding by that recognition is all-important to your mental, emotional, and spiritual wellbeing. Without it, you are prone to making many wrong and harmful decisions during your spiritual journey in this world. Before his Enlightenment on the road to Damascus, Paul was certainly one who lacked Good Judgment about these most important things of all.

Asking the Lord for "long life," for "riches," and for "the life of your enemies" without understanding their spiritual meaning and implications results in a long list of vain prayers. And because Solomon first asked the Lord for the ability to "discern between Good and bad," he became an example to all about what it means to ask for "a wise and understanding heart."

> "*And God Gave Solomon Wisdom and understanding exceeding much, and largeness of heart, even as the sand that is on the seashore.*"
>
> 1 Kings 4:29

Everywhere the Lord invites you to seek understanding from Him about what leads to "long Life" and "Riches." He Promises you that if you willingly do so with trust and faith in His Testimony to you, He will Give you all the spiritual knowledge you need to receive that understanding. He Promises to Show you what is required of you to receive the most valuable things of all. He also Promises to Give you the spiritual understanding you need to realize what it means to overcome the "life of your enemies."

It allows you to make Good Judgments about why and how you must live your life.

> " *Thy Testimonies are Wonderful: therefore doth my soul keep them.*
>
> " *The entrance of Thy Words Giveth Light; it Giveth understanding unto the simple.* "
>
> Psalms 119:129–130

> " *And of Thy Mercy cut off mine enemies, and destroy all them that afflict my soul: for I am Thy servant.* "
>
> Psalms 143:12

> " *He that followeth after Righteousness and Mercy findeth Life, Righteousness, and Honor.* "
>
> Proverbs 21:21

The Word: *simple* does not mean being unintelligent or uneducated. Rather, it describes being unconfused about what leads to lasting happiness and genuine fulfillment in life. That spiritual "simplicity" brings a childlike innocence into your mind and heart, allowing you to immediately discern the differences between Good and bad without debate or ambiguity. It allows you to make Good Judgments about why and how you must live your life. And it Gives you the spiritual sensibility to realize what it means to "honor thy Father and thy Mother" in all that you think, feel, and do.

"The Law of the Lord is perfect, converting the soul: the Testimony of the Lord is sure, making wise the simple."

Psalms 19:7

"Happy is the man that findeth Wisdom, and the man that getteth understanding.

"For the Merchandise of it is better than the merchandise of silver, and the gain thereof than fine gold.

"She is more precious than rubies: and all the things thou canst desire are not to be compared unto Her.

"Length of Days is in Her Right hand; and in Her left hand Riches and Honor."

Proverbs 3:13–16

"And why take ye thought for raiment? Consider the lilies of the field, how they grow; they toil not, neither do they spin:

"And yet I say unto you, That even Solomon in all his glory was not arrayed like one of these."

Matthew 6:28–29

The Song of Solomon

One of the most beautiful examples in the Bible about seeking, finding, and gaining spiritual understanding from the Lord is found in Solomon's Song. With these Lyrics, Solomon recalls what the Lord has Given you to know about where you might find His Truth, dwelling in the Glory of His Love for you:

"Whither is thy Beloved gone, O fairest among Women? Whither is thy Beloved turned aside, that we may seek Him with thee?

"My Beloved is gone down into His Garden, to the beds of spices, to feed in the Gardens, and to gather lilies.

"I am my Beloved's and my Beloved is Mine: He feedeth among the lilies."

Song of Solomon 6:1–3

In this Wonderful Song, Solomon recalls the spiritual understanding he gained when honestly, sincerely, and humbly searching for answers about where he might find the Truth of Love. The Lord's Bride answers him by explaining that Divine Truth is to be found where the Lord dwells in the Glory of His Love for you.

As the "fairest among" all Affections for Divine Truth, She explains that in that Garden of Love the Lord Communes with you about the Way you you must live your life. She makes clear that this is where He gathers all your pure thoughts and pleasing affections into His Embrace.

The Words: *My Beloved is gone down into His Garden, to the beds of spices, to feed in the Gardens, and to gather lilies* are Glorious indeed. They describe the Lord's Bride, as the Doctrine of His Righteousness, Offering you a Beautiful glimpse about how He brings the minds and hearts of all who are willing to live their lives according to the Principles of His Righteousness into the Goodness of His Love's Embrace.

"Behold, I stand at the door, and knock: if any man hear My Voice, and open the door, I will come in and will Sup with him, and he with Me.

"To him that overcometh will I grant to sit with Me in My Throne, even as I also overcame, and am set down with My Father in His Throne.

> *"He that hath an ear, let him hear what the Spirit saith unto the churches."*
>
> Revelation 3:20–22

To innocently seek answers about where you may find the Truth of Love is wise indeed. And such was the initial innocence of Solomon, for his inquiry was simple and unencumbered by any "thoughts formed from the imaginations" of his own heart. In turn, the Lord Blessed Solomon with Wisdom, understanding, and vast spiritual knowledge about the Way we must live our lives.

The Words: *so that there was none like thee before thee, neither after thee shall any arise like unto thee* portray the timelessness of that understanding.

At first, these invaluable Treasures were all that Solomon ever requested from the Lord. They are illustrated as Solomon's *glory* because they are a reflection and a likeness of the Lord's Love for you in their importance and value to your mental, emotional, and spiritual wellbeing.

> *"But seek ye first the Kingdom of God, and His Righteousness; and all these things shall be added unto you."*
>
> Matthew 6:33

~

From beginning to the ending in the Bible and everywhere in between, the Lord invites you to seek spiritual understanding from Him. He invites you to discover what brings innermost happiness and genuine fulfillment into fruition within your life. Yet so many times, we have squandered that priceless Opportunity in favor of our own errant philosophies and misleading religious doctrines. Instead of honoring Love and Wisdom, we have honored the pride of our own self-intelligence, often derived from letter-of-the-Word misconceptions about Scripture. The worst of these have produced unimaginable offenses to the most rudimentary levels of common sense and human decency among the peoples of the world.

> "*Then the Lord said unto me, The prophets prophesy lies in My name: I sent them not, neither have I Commanded them, neither spake unto them: they prophesy unto you a false vision and divination, and a thing of nought, and the deceit of their heart.*"
>
> Jeremiah 14:14

The Fall of Solomon

The danger of being seduced by the pride of your own self-intelligence is described in many stories and examples throughout the Bible. Falling for that seduction caused Adam and Eve's exile from the Garden of Eden.

- It caused the flood of falsities and evils that inundated and swept away the spiritual sensibilities of the people of Noah's time.

- It caused the eventual demise of Noah's descendents' ability to communicate with each other about the True meaning of the Lord's Testimony to us.

- It caused the rise and fall of the lofty proclamations depicted by the Tower of Babel.

He needed to know about what brings innermost happiness and genuine fulfillment into his life.

- It caused the spiritual perverseness that resulted in the destruction of Sodom and Gomorrah.

- It caused the Israelites to become subjugated to the mental, emotional, and spiritual cruelties they suffered in the land of Egypt.

- It caused the fall of their first temple, and their consequent harsh servitude to the corrupt religious doctrines described by their captivity in the city of Babylon.

- It caused the religious hypocrisy that resulted in the utter destruction of their second temple.

Solomon Sacrificing to His Wives Idols, by Jacopo Amigoni

The dire effects those seductions have caused to humanity have been repeated countless times throughout history. All of those tragedies befell people who were Given to know better, who were Given a second chance to change their ways, but refused to do so. And even though Solomon was Given all the invaluable answers he needed to realize what brings innermost happiness and genuine fulfillment into fruition within our lives, he also fell victim to wayward affections that fanned the pride of his own self-intelligence. Remembering those Lessons serves you in understanding what must always be, and remain your First Love.

> "And likewise did he for all his strange wives, which burnt incense and sacrificed unto their gods.
>
> "And the Lord was angry with Solomon, because his heart was turned from the Lord God of Israel, which had appeared unto him Twice.
>
> "And had Commanded him concerning this thing, that he should not go after other gods: but he kept not that which the Lord Commanded.
>
> "Wherefore the Lord said unto Solomon, Forasmuch as this is done of thee, and thou hast not kept My Covenant and My Statutes, which I have Commanded thee, I will surely rend the Kingdom from thee, and will Give it to thy servant."
>
> 1 Kings 11:8–11

The Words: *likewise, did he for all his strange wives, which burnt incense and sacrificed unto their gods* reference falling for the seductions that wayward affections use to flatter the pride of your own self-intelligence. Sacrificing "unto their gods" describes placing "thoughts formed from the imagination" of your own heart in front of what the Lord has, is, and forever will be Showing you to be True and Right.

By doing so, Solomon adulterated the bonds that had united Divine Truth with the Doctrine of Righteousness within his own life. The mental, emotional, and spiritual harm he caused to himself appeared to him as if it was "anger" coming forth from the Lord, yet that harm was solely self-inflicted.

~

> "Therefore, thou Son of Man, say unto the children of Thy people,
> The righteousness of the righteous shall not deliver him in the
> day of his transgression: as for the wickedness of the wicked,
> he shall not fall thereby in the Day that he turneth from his
> wickedness; neither shall the righteous be able to Live for his
> righteousness in the day that he sinneth."
>
> Ezekiel 33:12

The spiritual causes and effects that will determine your internal state of being are described by the Lord throughout the Bible, from Beginning to End. They are the result of the spiritual Laws that He has established to Guide you in the Way you may enter into, and remain, in the Joys and Goodness of His Heavenly Love for you. And so, just as breaking the laws of physics by jumping off the roof of a three-story house will harm you physically, it is imperative to realize that breaking the Laws of Righteousness will cause equal or greater harm to befall the wellbeing of your mind, heart, and soul.

To have been Given to know better, yet blame the Lord for either form of harm is very shortsighted. Unfortunately, it sometimes takes a very hard fall for you to prove the validity of that Reality to yourself.

> "Behold therefore the Goodness and severity of God: on them
> which fell, severity; but toward thee, Goodness, if thou continue
> in His Goodness: otherwise thou also shalt be cut off."
>
> Romans 11:22

The Lord continually approaches your thoughts and affections in Truth from His Love for you. Once received, if you lose your willingness to live your life in the Way He has Shown you that you must, what remnants of Goodness shall you expect to remain within your soul before it becomes too late? And so, if Solomon in all his "glory" could not maintain his will to live his life in the Way the Lord had Showed him that he must, how shall you? The answers to those questions are Offered to you freely by the Lord. They are not far off, difficult, or complicated to understand.

> "For unto every one that hath shall be Given, and he shall have Abundance: but from him that hath not shall be taken away even that which he hath."
>
> Matthew 25:29

Spiritual Sensibilities

> "And He spake a Parable unto them to this end, that men ought always to pray, and not to faint;
>
> "Saying, There was in a city a judge, which feared not God, neither regarded man:
>
> "And there was a Widow in that city; and She came unto him, saying, Avenge Me of Mine adversary.
>
> "And he would not for a while, but afterward he said within himself, though I fear not God, nor regard man;
>
> "Yet, because this Widow troubleth me, I will avenge Her, lest by Her continual coming She weary me."
>
> Luke 18:1–5

King Solomon, by G. Doreh

This Parable describes your need to stay sensible about spiritual causes and effects.

The Words: *And He spake a Parable unto them to this end, that men ought always to pray, and not to faint* address your need to stay awake and aware about what leads to your salvation. If you remain cognizant, and not forgetful, that spiritual sensibility will keep you from making offenses to the Goodness remaining within your soul.

Spiritually, a doctrine is described as a "city" in the Bible. The city you dwell in is built upon the convictions you hold in greatest esteem. You build belief structures based upon those convictions that act to house your thoughts and affections. Those convictions have pathways of assertions that give direction to the way you think, feel, and behave in life.

Arguments based upon those assertions act as walls that defend your belief structures. Those arguments can also be used as weapons to attack the belief structures of others.

When united together with assertions based upon similar convictions, "cities" become formed into nations. The nations described in the Bible depict spiritual doctrines united in Truth, or in falsity. Each nation corresponds to what they value greatest in life.

In this parable, the Lord is describing a religious doctrine that has no reverence for Divine Truth.

The Words: *Saying, There was in a city a judge, which feared not God* describe judgments made with utter disregard to the Truth of the Lord's Testimony to us.

The Words: *neither regarded man* tell of having no regard for the Divine Laws that Govern the mental, emotional or spiritual wellbeing of others.

The Words: *And there was a Widow in that city; and She came unto him, saying, Avenge me of Mine adversary* disclose a cry of anguish, coming out from the remnant of spiritual Wisdom still remaining within the spiritual sensibility of that misguided religious doctrine.

The Words: *And he would not for a while* reveal poor judgment resisting the Call to pause and reconsider what leads to innermost happiness and genuine fulfillment in life.

The Words: *but afterward he said within himself* illuminate sensing that something Greater than the pride of its own self-intelligence was Advocating for the very last remnant of Good remaining within its soul.

The Words: *though I fear not God, nor regard man; Yet, because this Widow troubleth me, I will avenge Her, lest by Her continual coming She weary me* describe reluctantly losing a battle against our own poor judgments, for all the Right Reasons.

> "*And the Lord said, Hear what the unjust judge saith.*"
>
> Luke 18:6

Your willingness to attend the "still, small Voice" within you allows the Lord to restore a semblance of spiritual sensibility about the Truth of Love within your life.

Your need to attend to that Cry cannot be overstated. Surrendering the pride of your own self-intelligence to that *cause* allows the Lord to bring Good Judgment back into your life about the most important things of all.

> "*And shall not God avenge His own elect, which cry day and night unto Him, though He bear long with them?*
>
> "*I tell you that He will avenge them speedily. Nevertheless, when the Son of Man cometh, shall He find faith on the earth?*

> "*And He spake this parable unto certain which trusted in*
> *themselves that they were righteous, and despised others.*"
>
> Luke 18:7–9

You are described as the Lord's "elect" from your willingness to receive
and apply spiritual understanding about Divine Truth to the Way you
live your life. As you do so, He Promises to liberate you from all the poor
judgments that would otherwise keep you
Widowed from receiving the Goodness of
His Love within your soul.

> He beckons you to use
> Good Judgment about
> what He has been teaching
> you since your inception.

The Words: *And shall not God avenge His
own elect, which cry day and night unto Him, though He bear long with
them?* amplify your need to look within yourself with honesty, sincerity,
and humility about the Way that restoration takes place, and about what
sustains it within your life.

The Words: *I tell you that He will avenge them speedily* confirms the Lord's
Promise to liberate you from all mental, emotional, and spiritual affliction.
Yet, knowing all too well the indigence existing within the pride of human
self-intelligence, He asks, "Nevertheless, when the Son of Man cometh,
shall He find faith on the earth?"

The Words: *And He spake this parable unto certain which trusted in themselves that they were righteous, and despised others* describe the Lord asking
you to look within yourself a Second time, and once again reexamine your
spiritual sensibilities in the Light of His Righteousness. In that Light, He
asks you to reconsider your own philosophies and religious doctrines to
see if they accurately discern the Truth about what leads to your salvation
and deliverance into an eternal state of Heavenly Joy, or if they do not.

Through that personal introspection, He beckons you to use Good Judgment
about what He has, is, and will forever be teaching you about the Truth
of His Love for you. He asks you to reflect upon what brings innermost

happiness and genuine fulfillment into fruition within your life, and most especially, what will sustain those incomparable Blessings within you in the life to come.

The Lord came into our world and suffered greatly to restore our individual and collective spiritual understanding about these most important things of all. He did so by teaching all of us about the importance of heeding Wisdom's call to keep the Principles of His Righteousness in their Rightful Place within our lives.

By doing so, He teaches you about what it means to "Honor thy Father and Mother" in all that you think, feel, and do.

> "Trust in the Lord with all thine heart; and lean not unto thine own understanding.

> "In all thy ways, acknowledge Him, and He shall direct thy Paths.

> "Be not wise in thine own eyes: fear the Lord, and depart from evil.

> "It shall be health to thy navel, and marrow to thy bones.

> "Honor the Lord with thy substance, and with the first fruits of all thine increase:

> "So shall thy barns be filled with Plenty, and thy presses shall burst out with new Wine.

> "My son, despise not the chastening of the Lord; neither be weary of His correction:

> "For whom the Lord Loveth He correcteth; even as a Father the son in whom He delighteth.

"Happy is the man that findeth Wisdom, and the man that getteth understanding.

"For the Merchandise of it is better than the merchandise of silver, and the Gain thereof than fine gold.

"She is more Precious than rubies: and all the things thou canst desire are not to be compared unto Her.

"Length of Days are in Her Right hand; and in her Left hand Riches and Honor.

"Her Ways are Ways of Pleasantness, and all Her Paths are Peace.

"She is a Tree of Life to them that lay hold upon Her: and happy is every one that retaineth Her.

"The Lord by Wisdom hath founded the earth; by understanding hath He established the Heavens."

Proverbs 3:5–19

"My son, keep thy Father's Commandment, and forsake not the Law of thy Mother:

"Bind them continually upon thine heart, and tie them about thy neck.

"When thou goest, it shall lead thee; when thou sleepeth, it shall keep thee; when thou awakest, it shall talk with thee.

"For the Commandment is a Lamp; and the Law is Light; and reproofs of Instruction are the Way of Life:"

Proverbs 6:20–23

"Lay not up for yourselves treasures upon earth, where moth and rust doth corrupt, and where thieves break through and steal:

"But lay up for yourselves Treasures in Heaven, where neither moth nor rust doth corrupt, and where thieves do not break through nor steal:

"For where your Treasure is, there will your heart be also.

"The light of the body is the eye: if therefore thine eye be Single, thy whole body shall be full of Light."

Matthew 6:19–22

Portrait of Christ, by Heinrich Hofmann

Reflections

You honor your physical parents' love for you by returning it with the love you have for them. You honor their wisdom by taking their guidance to heart. Likewise, you honor the Lord's Love for you by returning it with the love you have for Him, and you honor His Wisdom by loving others in the Way He Loves you. To do so is to honor His Love and Wisdom in all you think, feel, and do.

> *"And thine ears shall hear a Word behind thee Saying, This is the Way, walk ye in it, when you turn to the Right hand, and when you turn to the left."*
>
> Isaiah 30:21

Woodcut engraving from drawing, by Julius Schnorr von Carolsfeld .

THE SIXTH COMMANDMENT

THOU SHALT NOT KILL.

Exodus 20:13

14
Cause and Effect

He has freely Offered you this spiritual knowledge
since the beginning of your existence.

To take away another person's physical life is a monumental travesty. Doing so deprives the Lord from reforming them and transforming them into the person that He has Purposed for them to become. And although the Lord Commands you not to physically kill another person, He teaches you that there is still a much worse form of killing. That form of killing murders the Goodness of His Love from existing within your own soul. When left unabated, that form of murder can also kill the Goodness within the souls of those around you.

> *"And fear not them which kill the body, but are not able to kill the soul: but rather fear him which is able to destroy both soul and body in hell."*
>
> Matthew 10:28

Throughout the Bible, the Lord teaches you that harboring hatred, committing adultery, stealing, lying, and engaging in covetous acts extinguish the Goodness of His Love from existing within your soul. He teaches you that these cause your mind and heart to turn into what is internally dark and cold, spiritually causing you to become an image and likeness to a physical corpse. He describes this form of killing as the "second death." And because you survive your physical death in this life, what remains when the Goodness of His Love has become extinguished within your soul in the life to come is both pathetic and horrifying.

> "For what shall it profit a man, if he shall gain the whole world, and lose his own soul?"
>
> Mark 8:36

The history of humanity is filled with individual and collective testimonies about our spiritual survival after our physical death on Earth. Every civilization, old and new, large and small, and near and distant has recorded testimonies about that survival. Those testimonies are ongoing, now being reported by many people who have suffered near-death experiences in this age of modern medical resuscitation.

Denying those testimonies simply because you don't believe them, don't understand them, or because they have not been proved in a physical science lab yet is very shortsighted. Yet accepting them as true, and then ignoring their implications about the Way you must live your life is a much more dangerous form of thinking.

> "With the ancient is Wisdom; and in length of Days understanding."
>
> Job 12:12

Modern science has concluded that although physical matter changes form, it never just ceases to exist. Its physical mass might change form, from solid to energy and from energy to solid, but its continued existence, in one form or another, is eternal. And so, to think that your life will simply cease to exist upon your physical death goes against the most advanced implications that modern science has to offer you about the nature of our universe. It also ignores everything the Lord has Given us about the nature of our own lives.

> "*Have ye not known? Have ye not heard? hath it not been Told you from the Beginning? have you not understood from the foundations of the earth?*"
>
> Isaiah 40:21

In both the Old and New Testaments, the Lord teaches you about the importance of recognizing the causes that determine your mental, emotional, and spiritual wellbeing. He teaches you about their effects upon your innermost happiness and genuine fulfillment in this life, and most especially about their effects upon your wellbeing in the life to come. From His Love for you He asks you to trust in the Wisdom of His Testimony to you about these things, Promising that He is teaching you about things that are True and Right. He also teaches that you can "prove" these things for yourself, if you honestly, sincerely, and humbly try.

> "*Bring ye all the tithes into the storehouse, that there may be meat in Mine House, and prove Me now herewith, saith the Lord of hosts, if I will not open you the Windows of Heaven, and pour you out a Blessing, that there shall not be room enough to receive it.*"
>
> Malachi 3:10

Throughout the Bible, the number "ten" pertains to the Lord's Commandments. These embody all the Principles of His Righteousness. "Tithes," or a "tenth," describe your willing efforts to abide by each, and every aspect of those Holy Principles. To do so is to "offer" the Lord the most valuable things of all, for from these *offerings* you allow Him to transform you into

There is really nothing that can be devised or done to circumvent those requirements.

a Living soul. Partaking in that understanding is the Opportunity of your lifetime.

"The Righteousness of Thy Testimonies is everlasting. Give me understanding, and I shall Live."

Psalms 119:144

~

The Lord knows that it takes great courage, diligence, and endurance to abide by the Principles of His Righteousness with all your mind, heart, and strength. He knows that tremendous efforts will be required to turn away from your self-serving thoughts, selfish affections and their corresponding behaviors, and leave them behind. Yet everywhere He asks you to make those efforts, Promising to Guide and Comfort you as you make them in reverence to your love for Him, and in reverence for the Good of those around you. There is really nothing that can be devised or done to circumvent those requirements, try as you may.

"Speak unto the children of Israel, that they bring Me an offering: of every man that giveth willingly with his heart ye shall take My Offering."

Exodus 25:2

"Wait on the Lord, and keep His Way, and He shall exalt thee to inherit the Land: when the wicked are cut off, thou shall see it."

Psalms 37:34

"He that hath an ear, let him hear what the Spirit saith unto the churches; He that overcometh shall not be hurt of the second death."

Revelation 2:11

In Truth from His Love for you, the Lord Offers you this spiritual knowledge to invest in your life for your Good and for the Good of all around you. Nevertheless, He leaves it up to you, from your own free will to live your life accordingly. Applying your faith in this Divine knowledge gives you the Keys to unlock the spiritual potential of your soul.

Who is Your Brother?

"Ye have heard that it was said by them of old time, Thou shalt not kill; and whosoever shall kill shall be in danger of the Judgment.

"But I say unto you, That whosoever is angry with his brother without a cause shall be in danger of the Judgment: and whosoever shall say to his brother, Raca, shall be in danger of the council: but whosoever shall say, Thou fool, shall be in danger of hell fire.

Matthew 5:21–22

In a positive sense, your "brother" is descriptive of all True thoughts you have received from the Lord's Thoughts. Those Thoughts come to you in Peace and Goodwill, encouraging you to trust and have faith in His Guidance to you by living your life in the Way He is teaching you that you must.

They are described throughout the Bible as your brethren because they share a common spiritual lineage, all coming forth from the Lord's Quest for your salvation and deliverance into His Love's Embrace. Those Thoughts have been Given to you to cherish and apply with brotherly love to each and every aspect of your life.

" And the King shall answer and say unto them, Verily I say unto
you, Inasmuch as ye have done it unto one of the least of these
My brethren, ye have done it unto Me. "

Matthew 25:40

To be angry against the Lord for sharing Thoughts filled with Divine
Truth about why and how you must live your life is to be "angry with his
brother without a cause." Yet there is never "cause" great enough to justify
being angry with any of them because even the least of them has your Best
interests at Heart. Should you reject or turn against them, you become
described as coming into the "danger of the Judgment." Spiritually, "the
Judgment" describes the effects you bring upon yourself by "kicking
against the pricks," as portrayed in Numbers 33:55 and Acts 9:5. Question
that understanding as you may, it is nevertheless spiritual Reality.

" Thou shalt not hate thy brother in thine heart: thou shalt in
any wise rebuke thy neighbor, and not suffer sin upon him.

" Thou shalt not avenge, nor bear any grudge against the children
of thy people, but thou shalt love thy neighbor as thyself: I am
the Lord. "

Leviticus 19:17–18

The Words: *and whosoever shall say to his brother Raca, shall be in danger*
of the council describe your fate should you use false and misleading
arguments to try to discredit His
Testimony to you about the Way you
must live your life. And so, the Lord
warns you against arguing against His

Ignoring these Scriptural warnings
will cause you to become your
own worst enemy.

Thoughts, for doing so opens doors for mental, emotional, and spiritual
infirmities of all sorts to enter into your mind and heart.

The Words: *but whosoever shall say, Thou fool, shall be in danger of hell fire*
forewarn you, that if you call those warnings foolish, you will put yourself
in even greater danger of extinguishing the Goodness of His Love from
existing within your soul. Ignoring these Scriptural warnings will cause
you to become your own worst enemy.

> "But they refused to hearken, and pulled away the shoulder,
> and stopped their ears, that they should not hear.
>
> "Yea, they made their hearts as an adamant stone, lest they
> should hear the Law, and the Words which the Lord of hosts
> hath sent in His Spirit by the former prophets: therefore came a
> great wrath from the Lord of hosts."
>
> Zechariah 7:11–12

Whenever you reject acknowledging that abiding by the Principles of
Righteousness is Primary for your salvation, you become guilty of pulling
"away" your "shoulder" from your spiritual task at hand. Instead of accepting
your responsibility to obey the Lord's Commandments with all *your heart,
soul and might*, you become described as one who has "stopped their ears,
that they should not hear."

The Words: *Yea, they made their hearts as an adamant stone, lest they should
hear the Law* express your coldhearted refusal to live your live in the Way
the Lord has Shown you that you must.

The Words: *which the Lord of Hosts hath sent in His Spirit by the former
prophets* express refusing to accept the spiritual knowledge He has Offered
you through the Testimony of the prophets cited in the Old Testament.

The Words: *therefore came a great wrath from the Lord of Hosts* communicate
the dire effects of rejecting the validity of those Divine Laws.

And although that "great wrath" is described as if it had come from the Lord Himself, it just appears that way to those who have indignantly rejected the Truth of that spiritual understanding within their lives.

> "Think not that I am come to destroy the Law, or the prophets: I am not come to destroy, but to fulfill.
>
> "For verily I say unto you, till heaven and earth pass, one jot or one tittle shall in no wise pass from the Law, till all be fulfilled.
>
> "Whosoever shall break one of these least Commandments, and shall teach men so, he shall be called least in the Kingdom of Heaven: but whosoever shall do and teach them, the same shall be called great in the Kingdom of Heaven.
>
> "For I say unto you, That except your righteousness shall exceed the righteousness of the scribes and Pharisees, ye shall in no case enter into the Kingdom of Heaven."
>
> Matthew 5:17–20

Throughout the Bible, the Lord Proclaims that His Thoughts are much Higher and much more Prefect than anything we can conceive on our own. And so, for your Good and for the Good of all around you, He teaches you that you should never refuse to "hearken," or "close" your "ears," or "harden" your "heart" to receiving and embracing His Thoughts. Rather, He teaches you in both Old and New Testaments to realize that your mental, emotional, and spiritual wellbeing will not "Live by Bread alone, but only as you receive and apply "every Word that proceedeth out of the mouth of God." These Words are Given to you in Truth from the Goodness of His Love for you.

> "Hast ye not known? hast thou not heard, that the everlasting God, the Lord, the Creator of the Ends of the earth, fainteth not, neither is weary? There is no searching of His understanding."
>
> Isaiah 40:28

As Righteousness Himself, the Lord has, is, and will always be Giving
you Good Reasons about why and how you must live your life. Yet, it is
quite amazing how many times we have rejected
His Reasoning and substituted "reasons" of our
own. Each substitute does a great injustice to your
ability to host the incomparable Blessings of True
Life from His Life within your soul. Each substitute acts to diminish your
ability to understand the most important things of all.

> *"O, Jerusalem, Jerusalem, thou that killest the prophets and*
> *stonest them which are Sent unto thee, how often would I have*
> *gathered thy children together, even as a hen gathereth her*
> *chickens under her Wings, and ye would not!"*
>
> Matthew 23:37

Claiming to have received True Doctrine from the Lord about the Way
you must live your life, yet changing it to fit "thoughts formed from the
imaginations" of your own heart casts you into a spiritual darkness and
coldness of your own making.

> *"And I say unto you, That many shall come forth from the east*
> *and west, and shall sit down with Abraham, and Issac, and*
> *Jacob, in the Kingdom of Heaven.*
>
> *"But the children of the kingdom shall be cast out into outer*
> *darkness: and there shall be weeping and gnashing of teeth."*
>
> Matthew 8:11–12

Adding or subtracting to what the Lord is teaching you about the Way
you must live your life presents spiritual death traps to your mental,
emotional, and spiritual wellbeing. And although there are many religious

Misleading religious doctrines act as spiritual death traps.

doctrines that make their additions and subtractions appear *educated*, appealing, and even *holy* on the outside, they insidiously act to confuse and divert your ability to recognize the most important things of all.

> "*For My Thoughts are not your thoughts. neither are your ways My Ways, saith the Lord.*
>
> "*For as the Heavens are Higher than the earth, so are My Ways Higher than your ways, and my thoughts than your thoughts.*"
>
> Isaiah 55:8–9

The Effects of Adding or Subtracting to the Doctrine of Righteousness

Religious leaders assume a great responsibility when they attempt to teach others about the Truth of Love. Whether a rabbi, priest, or pastor, their need to minister accurate knowledge about what liberates us from mental, emotional, and spiritual harm and allows us to receive, retain, and forever share in the Goodness of the Lord's Love for us cannot be overstated. Diluting that knowledge with spiritual half-truths "profits" no one. Rather, the effects of causing that loss within others will one day return upon their own lives.

> "*But the fearful, and unbelieving, and the abominable, and the murderers, and whoremongers, and sorcerers, and idolaters, and all liars, shall have their part in the lake which burneth with fire and brimstone: which is the second death.*"
>
> Revelation 21:8

Here "the fearful" describes those who reverence their own self-intelligence over the Lord's Testimony to humanity. The "unbelieving" describes those who have been Given to know better, yet refuse to submit themselves to receiving and abiding by the Truth of His Testimony to us.

The Words: *the abominable, and the murderers, and sorcerers, and idolaters, and all liars* express all forms of spiritual hypocrisy; haters of Divine Truth, proclaimers of spiritual misinformation, and the false witnesses that place their own errant philosophies and misleading religious doctrines in place of what the Lord has Sacrificed so Greatly to teach us about the Truth of our salvation. Spiritually, "the lake that burneth with fire" is descriptive of the consumption they cause to any genuine spiritual understanding remaining within their own lives.

The Words: *and brimstone* describe the harmful arguments they put forth, raining down with stinging ridicule upon anything that differs from their own "witty inventions." Everywhere the Lord warns you about those dangers, always teaching you to stay awake and aware about the separation they can cause between your thoughts and His Thoughts.

> "*Behold, the Lord's hand is not shortened, that it cannot save; neither is His ear heavy, that it cannot hear:*
>
> "*But your iniquities have separated between you and your God, and your sins have hid His face from you, that He will not hear.*"
>
> Isaiah 59:1–2

> "*And beside all this, between us and you there is a great gulf fixed: so that they which would pass from hence to you cannot; neither can they pass to us, that would come from thence.*"
>
> Luke 16:26

> "*Then he said, I pray thee therefore, father, that thou would send him to my father's house:*
>
> "*For I have five brethren; that he may testify unto them, lest they also come into this place of torment.*

"*Abraham saith unto him, They have Moses and the prophets;
let them hear them.*

"*And he said, Nay, father Abraham: but if One went unto them
from the dead, they will repent.*

"*And he said unto him, if they hear not Moses and the prophets,
neither will they be persuaded, though One rose from the dead.*"

Luke 16:27–31

As you pass from this life into the life to come, Righteousness and
unrighteousness will not be able to coexist within you. And because each is
diametrically opposed to the other, one will utterly reject the other until a
complete separation occurs between them within your soul. At that time,
your dominant love will lead you to where it desires to dwell with others
of like kind. Everywhere throughout the Bible, the Lord teaches about the
dangers of believing otherwise.

~

"*The prophet that hath a dream, let him tell a dream; and he
that hath My Word, let him speak My Word faithfully. What is
the chaff to the Wheat? saith the Lord.*

"*Is not My Word like a Fire? saith the Lord; And like a hammer
that breaketh the rock in pieces?*

"*Therefore, behold, I am against the prophets, saith the Lord,
that steal My Words every one from his neighbor.*

"*Behold, I am against the prophets, saith the Lord, that use their
tongues, and say, He saith.*

> "Behold, I am against them that prophesy false dreams, saith the Lord, and do tell them, and cause My people to err by their lies, and by their lightness; yet I sent them not, nor commanded them; therefore they shall not profit this people at all, saith the Lord.

> "And when this people, or the prophet, or a priest, shall ask thee, saying, What is the Burden of the Lord? thou shalt then say unto them, What Burden? I will even forsake you, saith the Lord."
>
> Jeremiah 23:28–33

Errant philosophies and misleading religious doctrines that teach that innermost happiness and genuine fulfillment can be achieved without first undergoing your spiritual reformation in the Light of Righteousness are depicted as *them that prophesy false dreams*. Those that promote these "smooth things" instead of teaching spiritual Reality are further described as they who *cause My people to err by their lies, and by their lightness*.

The Words: *What Burden?* then illustrate your indispensable need to recognize your spiritual task at hand. Believing and teaching otherwise causes a breach to occur between your ability to discern Truth from falsity and Right from wrong within your own life. That *breach* threatens your inmost ability to host the Goodness of the Lord's Love from existing within your soul.

> "Woe be unto the pastors that destroy and scatter the sheep of My pasture! saith the Lord.

> "Therefore thus saith the Lord God of Israel against the pastors that feed My people; Ye have scattered My flock, and driven them away, and have not visited them: behold, I will visit upon you the evil of your doings, saith the Lord."
>
> Jeremiah 23:1–2

Spiritual Reconciliation

> *"Therefore if thou bring thy gift to the Altar, and there remembrest that thy brother hath ought against thee;*
>
> *"Leave there thy gift before the Altar, and go thy Way; first be reconciled to thy brother, and then come and offer thy gift."*
>
> Matthew 5:23–24

To *bring thy gift to the Altar* is to approach the Lord with honesty, sincerity and humility in the Light of His Righteousness, nothing withheld. In that state of mind and heart you will experience an almost immediate remembrance about any Truth you have offended about the Way you must live you life. It is then when you will be Given an Opportunity to reconcile yourself with those offenses before you allow even greater harm to afflict your mental, emotional, and spiritual wellbeing.

Spiritual understanding is described as what Illuminates the Truth of your Salvation.

> *"Agree with thy Adversary quickly, whiles thou art in the Way with Him; lest at any time the Adversary deliver thee to the Judge, and the Judge deliver thee to the Officer, and thou be cast into prison."*
>
> Matthew 5:25

Should you refuse to reconcile yourself with any aspect of the Principles of Righteousness that you have offended, you will have made the Truth of the Lord's Love for you your *Adversary.* You will then find yourself "rowing hard" against a great tempest within your mind, heart, and soul; as portrayed in Jonah 1:13. And so, the Lord Instructs you to recognize the spiritual folly of making Him your *wrestling* opponent while you are still cognizant, and able to surrender to His Will about the Way you must live your life; as portrayed in Genesis 32:24-25. Instead, He teaches you to "Agree with thy Adversary quickly" while you still have the spiritual sensibility to do so.

The Words: *lest at any time the Adversary deliver thee to the Judge, and the Judge deliver thee to the Officer, and thou be cast into prison* describe the spiritual darkness and coldness you will cause within yourself by continuing to refuse to surrender your thoughts to the Lord's Thoughts. Continued refusal to do so will cast you into a spiritual "prison" of your own making. You should take great care not to allow the remaining Goodness within your soul to die there.

> "*Verily I say unto thee, Thou shalt by no means come out thence, till thou hast paid the uttermost farthing.*"
>
> Matthew 5:26

Spiritual reconciliation with the Truth of Love requires you to fully divest yourself of maintaining the pride of your own self-intelligence. It requires you to give up justifications for harboring unrighteous thoughts, feelings, and behaviors of any sort. It requires you to forgive others as you would wish to be forgiven yourself, and to forgive them in the Way the Lord has Forgiven you. It then requires you to wholly invest yourself in living your life in the Way the Lord has Shown you that you must.

> "*Thou oughtest therefore to have put My Money to the exchangers, and then at My coming I should have received Mine Own with usury.*"
>
> Matthew 25:27

The Words: *Thou oughtest therefore to have put My Money to the exchangers* reveal your need to value what the Lord is Showing you to be True and Right above all else. They describe exchanging any "thoughts formed from the imagination" of your own heart for His Thoughts.

The Words: *and at My coming I should have received My Own with usury*
Illustrate the incomparable yield those investments will bring into your life,
for in time they will far exceed your greatest expectations.

~

*" And the King shall answer and say unto them, Verily I say unto
you, Inasmuch as ye have done it unto one of the least of these My
brethren, ye have done it unto Me. "*

Matthew 25:40

~

Your spiritual reformation is accomplished by the Lord in steps and stages
as you apply the refining Power of His Divine Truth to the Way you live
your life. Confessing your need for reformation while surrendering yourself
to the Lord's Will about the Way you must live your life is an indispensable
starting place. Thinking that spiritual reformation can be accomplished
in an instant is very naïve, no matter how much you would like to think
otherwise. And although, in His Grace and through His Mercy He Quickens
the steps and stages of your reformation, your transformation will still
take time and effort, and the time you have been Given to make those
efforts is *"now,"* as exclaimed in Genesis 28:16–18 and Romans 13:11.

The sooner you begin to reconcile yourself with each and every aspect of the
Principles of the Lord's Righteousness within your life, the Better. Having
that sense of urgency is a Righteous cause.

*" Then shall the King say unto them on His Right hand, Come,
Ye Blessed of My Father, inherit the Kingdom prepared for you
from the foundation of the world.*

> *"For I was an hungered and ye gave Me meat, I was thirsty and ye gave Me drink, I was a stranger and ye took Me in,*
>
> *"Naked and ye clothed Me, I was sick and ye visited Me, I was in prison and ye came unto Me."*

Matthew 25:34–36

Each time you honestly, sincerely, and humbly put forth efforts to reconcile yourself with the Principles of His Righteousness, you nourish the Goodness of the Lord's Love within your own soul. Each effort you make aligns your thoughts with His Thoughts, putting everything in their proper Order within your life. Each effort you make allows Him

You should love them in the Way that the Lord Loves you.

to heal you from your mental, emotional, and spiritual afflictions as He liberates you from being entrapped in a prison of your own making.

The Lord came into our world seeking to restore this spiritual understanding within our lives so that He might fulfill His Purpose for the Creation of our souls. Yet, He leaves it up to you—from your own free will to Embrace and apply that understanding to the way you live your life. And it is by far the Greatest Opportunity of your lifetime.

> *"See, I have set before thee this Day Life and Good, and death and evil."*

Deuteronomy 30:15

> *"Then Jesus said unto them, Yet a little while is the Light with you. Walk while ye have the Light, lest darkness come upon you: for he that walketh in darkness knoweth not where he goeth."*

John 12:35

"*To wit, that God, Who was in Christ, reconciling the world unto Himself, not imputing their trespasses unto them; and hath committed unto us the Word of Reconciliation.*"

2 Corinthians 5:19

15
Loving Others

Forgiving others in the Way that the Lord
has Forgiven you is your responsibility.

*T*he Lord never wearies of trying to help you unlock the spiritual potential of your soul. From His Love for you, He continuously provides you with the spiritual knowledge you need to receive innermost happiness and genuine fulfillment within your life. And just as the Lord never wearies of Loving you, neither should you give up on loving others. Rather, instead of "imputing their trespasses unto them," you must wholly apply yourself to loving them in the Way that the Lord Loves you. Doing so befriends His Quest to help redeem, save, and deliver even the very worst among us back into His Embrace. In this manner you become an image of His Truth and a likeness to His Goodness to all around you. The Words: "There is no searching of His understanding" do not imply that you should stop inquiring and learning from the Lord, but rather inform you that you need not to question the validity of His Testimony to you about why and how you must.

> "*A new Commandment I Give unto you, that you love one*
> *another; as I have Loved you, that ye also love one another.*"
>
> John 13:34

Although justly protecting yourself from anyone who would do harm to you or others, you should never physically put anyone to death. Instead, you should offer them mercy and compassion by giving them every means and chance to reconcile themselves with any Principle of Righteousness they have offended while they still have time in this world to do so.

If you look closely within yourself, you will find that you are not perfect. No one is. Rather, you will realize that you also need all the time you are Given to do the same.

You should never take away another person's chance to change for the better.

Recognizing that you are a spiritual Work in progress allows you to realize why you should never take away another person's chance to change for the Better. To do so is to walk that "extra mile," hand in Hand with the Lord in the Paths of His Righteousness.

> "For there is not a just man upon earth, that doeth Good, and sinneth not."
>
> Ecclesiastes 7:20

> "Thus speaketh the Lord of hosts, saying, Execute True Judgment, and show Mercy and Compassions every man to his brother."
>
> Zechariah 7:9

> "For all have sinned, and come short of the Glory of God;"
>
> Romans 3:23

Forgiving Others

Forgiving others in the Way that the Lord has Forgiven you is your responsibility. Only you can do it. Taking on that responsibility allows Him to move mountains of mental, emotional, and spiritual harm out of your Way.

> "For if ye forgive men their trespasses, your heavenly Father will also Forgive you;
>
> "But if ye forgive not men their trespasses, neither will your Father Forgive your trespasses.
>
> Matthew 6:14–15

As Divine Love Himself, the Lord Forgives you for your trespasses, even if you are among the very worst. Yet the spiritual effects of His Forgiveness become fulfilled only as you allow Him to reform you and transform you in the Light of His Righteousness. To think that "faith alone" or "Grace alone" or belonging to a certain religious demonization alone can effectuate the Goodness of His Forgiveness within you is very shortsighted. That shortsightedness deprives you from recognizing your need to abide by the most important things of all.

> "Then came the disciples to Jesus apart, and said, Why could we not cast him out?
>
> "And Jesus said unto them, Because of your unbelief: for verily I say unto you, If you have faith as a grain of mustard seed, ye shall say unto this mountain, Remove hence to yonder place; and it shall remove; and nothing shall be impossible unto you.
>
> Matthew 17:19–20

The Words: *But if ye forgive not men their trespasses, neither will your Father Forgive your trespasses* express the effects of the internal harm you cause to yourself by not fully forgiving others for their trespasses against you. To think otherwise is spiritual folly.

Literal Misconceptions

Throughout history, letter-of-the-Word misinterpretations have misguided many into believing the exact opposite of their spiritual meaning. Instead of informing you about why and how you must live your life, those misleading literal beliefs have been used to grant "biblical" permissions to harbor treacherous thoughts and malicious feelings against others. The worst of them have resulted in justifying unimaginably cruel behaviors among the human race.

> "And if a man cause a blemish in his neighbor; as he hath done, so shall it be done to him;"
>
> Leviticus 24:19

These Words in Leviticus portray the spiritual harm you cause to yourself by harboring hatred for others. Spiritually, a "blemish" is descriptive of the many mental, emotional, and spiritual afflictions you bring upon the innocence, purity, and spiritual integrity of your own soul by not fully forgiving others their trespasses, as the Lord has Forgiven yours.

> "Breach for breach, eye for eye, tooth: for tooth as he hath caused a blemish in a man, so shall it be done to him again."
>
> Leviticus 24:20

When left unrepentant, ill will toward others will cause a "breach" to form between yourself and the Goodness of the Lord's Love within your own soul.

The Words: *an eye for an eye* refer to the loss of spiritual understanding that results from maintaining that *breach* within your life.

The Words: *tooth for tooth* describe the lost ability to process and digest the things that nourish your mental, emotional, and spiritual wellbeing.

The Words: *as he hath caused a blemish in a man, so shall it be done to him again* forewarn how ill will toward others will cause disfiguration to the comeliness of your mind and heart. And so, the Lord warns you about the severity ill will bring upon your spiritual beauty in this life, and most specially what it will cause to the appearance of your soul in the life to come.

> *So shall the King greatly desire thy beauty: for He is thy Lord; and worship thou Him.*
>
> Psalms 45:11

As Divine Truth Himself, the Lord came into our world to liberate us from the horrific mis-conceptions that letter-of-the-Word doctrines were causing to the beauty of Goodness within the human race.

When evil strikes, you must turn away from it.

~

> *Ye have heard that it hath been said, An eye for an eye, and a tooth for a tooth:*
>
> *But I say unto you, That ye resist not evil: but whosoever shall smite thee on thy right cheek, turn to him the other also.*
>
> Matthew 5:38–39

From His earliest advent into our world, the Lord once again began teaching us about why and how we must live our lives. And because so many had fallen into letter-of-the-Word miscon-ceptions about Scripture, He taught all of us to ignore what we had "heard," and instead Implored us to open up our minds and hearts to receive a renewed spiritual under-standing about the Truth of Love. That Message is timeless, presenting you with invaluable spiritual knowledge about the most important things of all.

Returning evil with evil will only bring still greater spiritual harm.

Everywhere the Lord teaches you about your need to embrace understanding about spiritual causes and effects. They teach you about what will determine the state of your mental, emotional, and spiritual wellbeing.

The Words: *But I say unto you, That ye resist not evil,* the Lord is teaching you that of yourself, you are not strong enough to overcome evil, try as you may. Rather, when evil strikes, He is teaching you to turn away from it, and turn toward Him for Guidance about the Way you must deal with it.

The Words: *but whosoever shall smite thee on thy right cheek, turn to him the other also* illustrates that turning. He teaches you never to resist that understanding, but rather to realize that returning evil with evil will only cause still greater harm to return upon your mind, heart, and soul.

> "*He will keep the feet of His saints, and the wicked shall be silent in darkness; for by strength shall no man prevail.*"
>
> 1 Samuel 2:9

> "*All Scripture is Given by Inspiration of God, and is profitable for Doctrine, for reproof, for correction, for Instruction in Righteousness:*
>
> "*That the man of God may be perfect, thoroughly furnished unto all Good works.*"
>
> 2 Timothy 3:16–17

The pride of your own self-intelligence considers itself to be much stronger than it really is. From Beginning to Ending in the Bible, the Lord teaches you about the dangers of thinking that you can overcome falsities and evils on your own. And so, in Truth from His Love for you, He continually reaches out to you to Give you Inspiration and Instruction about the Way you may defeat them. It is your responsibility to submit yourself to keeping that understanding Holy within your life.

> "And if any man will sue thee at the Law, and take away thy coat, let him have thy cloak also."
>
> Matthew 5:40

The Words: *if any man will sue thee at the Law* describe letter-of-the-Word arguments that attempt to justify violating the Spirit of the Word.

The Words: *and take away thy coat* reveal how those arguments can be very convincing as they endeavor to strip away your spiritual sensibilities about what the Lord has Shown you to be True and Right.

The Words: *let him have thy cloak also* express the Lord teaching you to respond to those misleading arguments by offering up the spiritual meaning of His Testimony to you, for it is internal, and closest to His Heart. Doing so will restore seamless clarity, balance, and Good Judgment about the most important things of all.

> "And whosoever shall compel thee to go a mile, go with him twain."
>
> Matthew 5:41

These Words describe the challenges you will be asked to bear during your spiritual journey in this world. The Words: *go with him twain,* Instruct you to walk that "Second mile" in the Path of Righteousness with the Lord Himself.

> "Give to him that asketh thee, and from him that would borrow of thee turn not thou away."
>
> Matthew 5:42

The Words: *Give to him that asketh thee, and from him that would borrow of thee turn not thou away* illustrate the Lord teaching you to willingly offer your thoughts and feelings to anything that is poor and needy for Righteousness within your life. And although you may be severely tempted to withhold that willingness, there is never reason enough to deny lending it to any circumstance that needs it. By doing so you will find that such lending doesn't deplete you, but rather replenishes the Goodness within your soul. The return on that investment is like none other.

> "*Ye have heard that it hath been said, Thou shalt love thy neighbor and hate thine enemy.*
>
> "*But I say unto you, Love your enemies, bless them that curse you, do Good to them that hate you, and pray for them which despitefully use you, and persecute you.*"
>
> Matthew 5:43–44

It is important to realize that the Lord is warning you about the many pitfalls and stumbling blocks caused by letter-of-the-Word misinterpretations about Scripture.

The Words: *love your enemies, bless them that curse you, do Good to those that hate you, and pray for those who despitefully use you, and persecute you,* He is Guiding you to to offer forgiveness and compassion to anyone who acts abusively against you, for doing so will keep you from inviting thoughts and feelings into your life that will strive to extinguish the Goodness of His Love within your soul.

Has not humanity adequately demonstrated the futility and harm caused by returning offense with offense and hate with hate among themselves?

And so the Lord implores you to understand that those who wrong you are not your true enemies. He is teaching you to realize that they are actually causing much more harm to themselves than they are able to comprehend.

The Words: *for they know not what they do* cited within Luke 23:34 exemplify that spiritual Reality.

⟡

While it is certainly just to defend yourself and loved ones from offenses and hatred from others, it is not just to use offenses and hatreds of your own as weapons against them. Rather, we should all look to the Lord for Guidance about how we may put all of these destructive thoughts, feelings, and behaviors to Rest within humanity. And although that may seem impossible when considering the pride, indigence, and coarseness of human nature, where there is a Will, there is a Way!

> "*And He said, The things which are impossible with men are possible with God.*"
>
> Luke 18:27

⟡

Regardless of your present or past offensives against others, the Lord Gives you all the Opportunity you need to reconcile yourself with the Principles of His Righteousness.

> "*That ye may be the children of your Father which is in Heaven: for He maketh His Sun to rise on the evil and on the good, and sendeth rain on the just and the unjust.*"
>
> Matthew 5:45

The Words: *for He maketh His Sun to rise on the evil and on the good, and sendeth rain on the just and the unjust* portray that invaluable Opportunity. Recognizing that you

You should never allow yourself to hate.

are not perfect Gives you the spiritual sensibility to realize that if you are not willing to forgive others for their trespasses against you, how can you expect to be Forgiven for your own?

> *"For if ye love them which love you, what reward do have ye? do not even the publicans the same?"*
>
> Matthew 5:46

~

Heartfelt Forgiveness

Forgiving others requires great humility on your part, and the Lord knows that much more than you realize it yourself. He knows that you are initially much more inclined to harbor animosity against someone who trespasses against you than forgive them. Yet, He warns you against falling to those temptations. Instead, for your Good and for the Good of all around you, He teaches you never to allow yourself to hate "thy brother in thine heart" nor suffer "sin upon him" as He shares with you in Leviticus 19:17.

Rather, being Righteousness Himself, He teaches you that you must forgive them as He has Forgiven you, knowing that doing so is a genuine Labor of Love. Working with Him to do so allows you to overcome anything that would otherwise to destroy His Goodness from remaining within your soul. Those efforts also work to encourage and inspire the spiritual sensibilities in others to do the same.

> *"And when He had called the people unto Him with His disciples also, He said unto them, Whosoever will come after Me, let him deny himself, and take up his Cross, and follow Me."*
>
> Mark 8:34

Everywhere the Lord teaches you that shouldering your responsibility to live your life in the Way that He has Shown you that you must is fundamental for your salvation and deliverance into an eternal Heavenly state of being. Denying that responsibility, for whatever reason, threatens your ability to find innermost happiness and genuine fulfillment in life. It also acts to the great detriment of the Goodness within all those around you.

"Take My yoke upon you, and learn of Me; for I am meek and lowly in heart: and ye shall find Rest unto your souls.

"For My yoke is easy and My Burden is Light."

Matthew 11:29–30

"For all the Law is fulfilled in one Word, even in this; Thou shall love thy neighbor as thyself."

Galatians 5:14

~

A limit to our need for forgivingness?

"Then came Peter to Him, and said, Lord, how oft shall my brother sin against me, and I forgive him? Till seven times?"

Matthew 18:21

The Lord teaches you that forgiving others is a prerequisite for protection against mental, emotional, and spiritual harm. Yet considering the atrocities committed by some against others, Peter's inquiry about how far your forgiveness should go is a reasonable question. And so, the Lord teaches Peter, and you, that there should be no limit to your forgiveness. He teaches you this lesson for this essential reason: not fully forgiving others poses a much greater danger to the wellbeing of your own mind, heart, and soul than you can ever imagine.

"Jesus saith unto him, "I say not unto thee, Until seven times: but, Until seventy times Seven."

Matthew 18:22

The Words: *I say not unto thee, Until seven times: but, Until seventy times Seven* amplify what the Lord is teaching you about the extent of your need to forgive others for any trespasses they have made against you. The number "Seven" describes a state of complete liberation from mental, emotional, and spiritual harm. The number "Ten" describes the Principles of Righteousness. By asking you to multiply them together, and then multiply within your life once again, He is Instructing you to realize the full extent of what it means to forgive others in the same Way that He has Forgiven you.

> "*This is My Commandment, That ye love one another, as I have Loved you.*"
>
> John 15:12

> "*He that saith he abideth in Him ought himself also so to walk, even as He walked.*"
>
> 1 John 2:6

The more complete your reconciliation with the Righteousness of the Lord, the less your Burden remains, the Lighter your soul becomes, and the more enabled you become to enter into the Joys and freedom of Heavenly Love. That is True in this life, and most especially True in the Life to come.

16

Spiritual Persistence

The Battle of the Ages

> "*Then came Peter to Him, and said, Lord, how oft shall my brother sin against me, and I forgive him? Till seven times?*"
>
> Matthew 18:21

The Lord Has Forgiven You First

No adult person can claim they have not committed sin during their lifetime in this world. Yet, feeling guilt and sorrow because of having committed sin is nevertheless a healthy reaction, for they usher in much needed wakeup calls. And although these calls are internally painful, the Lord teaches us never to allow them to paralyze us.

> He teaches you to recognize that He has Forgiven you.

Rather, He teaches us to recognize that He has Forgiven us first, while asking us to realize that these are the Burdens of conscience that He sends to warn us about our need for introspection, correction, and reconciliation in the Light of His Righteousness.

As you heed His warnings and attend those Calls, He Promises to Help you overcome *all* your mental, emotional, and spiritual faults and weaknesses before they ruin your ability to host the Goodness of His Love within your soul.

> *"Come unto Me, all ye that labor and are heavy laden, and I will Give you Rest."*
>
> Matthew 11:28

Bearing the guilt and sorrow caused by our sins is a heavy task. Finding excuses to dismiss our guilt and sorrow by justifying our sins is self-defeating. Rather, liberation from sin requires your willingness to honestly, sincerely, and humbly seek discernment between Truth and falsity and Right from wrong, followed by self-correction to any trespass made to what the Lord has revealed as True and Right within your mind, heart, and soul. It requires reconciliation with the Righteousness of the Lord, nothing withheld.

Bringing your sins before the Lord in that Light requires overcoming self-denial and pride. It requires heartfelt confession about the extent of your need for liberation from sin. It necessitates recognizing what leads to your liberation from sin, and what does not. And it needs a deep commitment to change for the Better. That willing commitment brings you into a "Place" where all true spiritual healing begins. It is there where you will begin to experience the extent of the Lord's Forgiveness and Compassion within your life, and it is there where you will begin to receive the Guidance and Comfort you need as He lifts the weight that your sins, and the sins of others, have caused within your life.

> *"Jesus went unto the Mount of Olives.*
>
> *"And early in the morning He came again into the Temple, and all the people came unto Him, and He sat down, and taught them.*
>
> *"And the scribes and Pharisees brought unto Him a woman taken in adultery; and when they had set her in the midst,*
>
> *"They say unto Him, Master, this woman was taken in adultery, in the very act.*

" *Now Moses in the Law commanded us, that such should be stoned: but what sayest Thou?*

" *This they said, tempting Him, that they might have to accuse Him. But Jesus stooped down, and with His finger wrote on the ground, as though He heard them not.*

" *So when they continued asking Him, He Lifted up Himself, and said unto them, He that is without sin among you, let him first cast a stone at her.*

" *And again He stooped down, and wrote upon the ground.*

" *And they which heard it, being convicted by their own conscience, went one by one, beginning at the eldest, unto the last: and Jesus was left alone, and the woman standing in the midst.*

" *When Jesus has Lifted up Himself, and saw none but the woman, He said unto her, Woman, where are those thine accusers? Hath no man condemned thee?*

" *She said, No man, Lord. And Jesus said unto her, neither do I condemn thee: go, and sin no more.* "

John 8:1–11

It is extremely humiliating to realize that your sins are openly exposed to the Lord. Whenever you adulterate the relationship between what is True and Right within your life you can expect to experience the shame of that exposure. Yet the Lord teaches you that you must never beat yourself up to the point of hopelessness, but rather acknowledge that it is your responsibility to cease from committing those sins. That responsibility requires honest, sincere, and humble discernment in the Light of His Righteousness.

He teaches you not to be afraid or become fainthearted.

To think that His Forgiveness has somehow relieved you of that responsibility is to take His Grace in vain. And so, just as the Lord Instructed this adulteress with His Words: *go, and sin no more*, He likewise Instructs you to do the same. He also warns you that if you do not forgive others for their sins in the Way He has Forgiven you, your sins will remain.

> "*Come now, and let us Reason together, saith the Lord: though your sins be as scarlet, they shall be as white as snow; though they be red like crimson, they shall be as wool.*
>
> "*If ye be willing and obedient, ye shall eat the Good of the Land.*"
>
> Isaiah 1:18–19

> "*And when He was demanded of the Pharisees, when the Kingdom of God should come, He answered them and said, The Kingdom of God cometh not with observation:*
>
> "*Neither shall they say, Lo here! or, lo there! for, behold, the Kingdom of God is within you.*"
>
> Luke: 17:20–21

Overcoming

Everywhere the Lord Calls upon you to understand that abiding by the Principles of His Righteousness is the Way He Conquers all of the mental, emotional, and spiritual afflictions within your life. These also include hopelessness, depression, and loss of self-esteem, regardless of what has caused them to afflict you. He teaches you not to be afraid or become fainthearted as He Works within you to overcome them. Instead, He Implores you to trust and have faith in the Power of His Truth to liberate you from them.

He teaches you to take Comfort in His Promise to renew His Goodness within your soul. Within 2 Corinthians 4:8-18, Paul expresses the Way the Lord fulfills this expansive Promise. Of all people, Paul came to realize that as you live your life according to the Way the Lord is Showing you that you must, that He will do all of the Rest. By trusting, By not losing heart. And by embracing the Truth of this internal spiritual understanding with all your mind, heart, and strength.

Forgiving the Lord (!)

"And Blessed is he, whosoever shall not be offended in Me."

Matthew 11:6

It may sound preposterous to think that the Lord is asking you not to be offended by His advent into your life. Nevertheless, you must remain cognizant of the fact that any falsity or evil residing within you will resent being exposed in the Light of His Righteousness.

- Instead of welcoming Him, they will fight to reject Him.

- Instead of confessing to the mental, emotional, and spiritual harm they cause you, they will never accept blame.

- Instead of surrendering to the Way He liberates you from them, they will despise being called out and exposed for what they really are.

- Instead of rejoicing in His Message to you about why and how you must leave them behind, they will invent arguments of all sorts to preserve and justify their own existence within you.

Your willingness to fight against the many falsities and evils that insidiously seek dominance within you will cause you stress. Defeating them will require you to engage in many spiritual battles during your entire lifetime in this world. Such is the Burden of Light within your life.

> "*Grid Thy Sword upon Thy thigh, O most Mighty, with Thy Glory and Thy Majesty.*
>
> "*And in Thy Majesty ride Prosperously because of Truth and Meekness and Righteousness; and Thy Right hand shall Teach thee terrible things.*"
>
> Psalms 45:3-4

Spiritually, the Lord's "Sword" describes what divides Truth from falsity and Right from wrong within your life. It cuts through any confusion you may have about why and how you must live your life. It allows Him to pierce the veil about what brings innermost happiness and genuine fulfillment into your mind and heart. And it reveals the Way He brings His Love to Rest in Peace, then overflowing with Goodwill toward all others within your soul.

The Words: *And in Thy Majesty ride Prosperously* define how the Lord fulfills His Love's Quest for your salvation and deliverance into His Embrace.

The Words: *because of Truth and Meekness and Righteousness* explain the Way He changes everything within you, and among all of us for the Better.

Recognizing why the Lord is fighting to overcome any falsities or evils striving to remain within you allows you to comprehend why it is in your Best interest to fight with Him.

The Words: *and Thy Right hand shall Teach thee terrible things* illuminate your need to realize the extent of the harm that will result otherwise. Yet realizing the extent of their insidious influence within you, and then understanding the strength and commitment that will be required of you to overcome those falsities and evils will seem very daunting to you at times—even "terrible," as you confront your need to battle against them.

And yet, the Lord asks you to trust in the Power of His Righteousness to overcome over those "terrible things." He Promises you that as you live your life accordingly, He will Help you defeat each and every one of them. That is the internal spiritual Battle of the Ages.

> *Blessed are they which are persecuted for Righteousness' sake: for theirs is the Kingdom of Heaven.*
>
> Matthew 5:10

> *Put on the whole Armor of God that ye may be able to stand against the wiles of the devil.*

> *For we wrestle not against flesh and blood, but against principalities, against powers, against the rulers of the darkness of this world, against spiritual wickedness in high places.*

> *Wherefore take unto you the whole Armor of God that ye may be able to withstand in the evil day, and having done all, to stand.*

> *Stand therefore, having your loins girt about with Truth, and having on the breastplate of Righteousness;*

> *And your feet shod with the preparation of the Gospel of Peace;*

> *Above all, taking the Shield of faith, wherewith ye shall be able to quench all the fiery darts of the wicked.*

> *And take the helmet of salvation, and the Sword of the Spirit, which is the Word of God.*
>
> Ephesians 6:11–17

> "*And I saw, and behold a White horse and He that sat upon him had a Bow; and a Crown was Given unto Him: and He went forth Conquering, and to Conquer.*"
>
> Revelation 6:2

Trust in the Way the Lord Reforms You

> "*And thou shall speak unto the children of Israel, saying, Whosoever curseth his God shall bear his sin.*"
>
> Leviticus 24:15

Allowing yourself to become offended by what the Lord is teaching you about the Way you must live your life causes a "curse" to befall your mental, emotional, and spiritual wellbeing. And so, as Righteousness Himself, He asks you not to dismiss, despise, or reject His Purpose for coming into your life. Rather, He asks you to trust in the understanding He is Giving you about your need to confront and overcome all falsity and evil within your life.

> "*He that hateth Me hateth My Father also.*

> "*If I had not done among them the Works which none other man did, they had not had sin: but now have they both seen and hated both Me and My Father.*

> "*But this cometh to pass, that the Word might be fulfilled that is written in their Law, They hated Me without a cause.*"
>
> John 15:23–25

If humanity fully realized the mental, emotional, and spiritual harm they bring upon themselves by rejecting their need to abide by what the Lord has Shown them to be True and Right, they would be shocked.

Yet, instead of accepting that understanding, we have so many times ignored, dismissed, and rejected it, to our own great detriment. Those who have been Given to know better but continue to follow "thoughts formed from the imaginations" of their own hearts, and teach them to others risk the greatest harm of all. And yet through all this, the Lord still extends His Hand to you, to all of us, Offering His Divine Message about the Way He saves us from our own rash judgments and grievous missteps.

> *Then said Jesus, Father, Forgive them; for they know not what they do. And they parted His Raiment, and cast lots.*
>
> Luke 23:34

> *These things have I spoken unto you, that ye should not be offended.*
>
> John 16:1

> *If ye be reproached for the Name of Christ, happy are ye; for the Spirit of Glory and of God resteth upon you: on their part He is evil spoken of, but on your part He is Glorified.*
>
> 1 Peter 4:14

A Righteous Hatred

The Lord warns you to always refrain from hating others, yet He teaches you to hate falsity and evil. Everywhere He teaches you to look deeply within yourself to discern the difference between these two forms of hatred. Once understood, He Instructs you to forgive others fully, but to hate any form of falsity or evil that attempts to destroy the Goodness of His Love from existing within your life, or within the lives of those around you.

> *Stand in awe, and sin not: commune within your heart upon your bed, and be still. Selah.*
>
> Psalms 4:4

The Words: *Stand in awe, and sin not* describe your need to recognize and detest the harmful effects that falsities and evils inflict upon your mind, heart, and soul. To hold these in utmost contempt is a Righteous anger.

The Words: *Commune within your heart upon your bed, and be still* express your need to look deeply within yourself to discern their presence within your life. In that state of personal introspection, the Lord exposes your true spiritual enemies for what they really are, exemplified by the Word *Selah*.

> "*Ye that love the Lord, hate evil: He preserveth the souls of His saints; He delivereth them out of the hand of the wicked.*"
>
> Psalms 97:10

The Words: *Ye that love the Lord, hate evil* highlight the defensive mindset that allows you to recognize the nature of your true spiritual enemies. Keeping that mindset in focus allows the Lord to supply you with the wakefulness, strength, and weapons you need to fight and overcome each and every one of them. Look directly to Him within your mind, heart, and soul for that discernment, letting no others lead you astray.

The Words: *He preserveth the souls of His saints; He delivereth them out of the hand of the wicked* describe His Promise to Help you achieve that discernment and those victories within your life.

> "*The fear of the Lord is to hate evil: pride, and arrogancy, and the evil way, and the forward mouth, do I hate.*"
>
> Proverbs 8:13

Reverencing your need to hate falsity and evil is your responsibility. Arguments to the contrary are described as coming forth from a "forward mouth." Those arguments all originate from the pride of self-intelligence. Covering yourself with self-selected fig leaves to justify those arguments is self-defeating.

> *"I will set no wicked thing before Mine eyes: I hate the work of them that turn aside; it shall not cleave to Me.*
>
> *"A forward heart shall depart from Me: I will not know a wicked person."*
>
> Psalms 101:3–4

The Lord "hates" the ensuing misery and suffering that falsities and evils cause within your life.

The Words: *I hate the work of them that turn aside* reveal how He "hates" the arguments that divert you from understanding what it means to love others as you wish to be loved yourself.

The Words: *it shall not cleave to Me* expose their effects upon your ability to retain the Goodness of His Love within your soul.

> *"Do I not hate them, O Lord, that hate Thee? and am I not grieved with those that rise up against Thee?*
>
> *"I hate them with perfect hatred: I count them mine enemies."*
>
> Psalms 139:21–22

The Words: *Do I not hate them, O Lord, that hate Thee?* communicate your need to maintain your defensive mindset against any errant philosophy or misleading religious doctrine that attempts to dilute, corrupt, or stand in the Place of understanding your spiritual task at hand.

The Words: *and am I not grieved with those that rise up against Thee?* describe your willingness to keep your focus upon what must always be, and remain, your First Works. Your commitment to reject arguments to the contrary is described as a "perfect hatred." It is called "perfect" because of the acute Clarity that focus brings into your life about the most important things of all.

"These six things doth the Lord hate: yea, seven are an abomination to him:

"A proud look, a lying tongue, and hands that shed innocent Blood.

"A heart that deviseth wicked imaginations, feet that be swift in running to mischief.

"A false witness that speaketh lies, and he that soweth discord among brethren."

Proverbs 6:16–19

"Behold, I send you forth as sheep in the midst of wolves,: be ye therefore wise as serpents, and harmless as doves."

Matthew 10:16

Paul also understood that being angry against any form of falsity or evil within your life is a Righteous anger. He understood that it is your responsibility to fight against those enemies, having Singular focus about your spiritual task at hand. He recognized that keeping the Light of the Lord's Righteousness burning Brightly within your life leaves no quarters for allowing substitutes of any kind to stand in the Place of what must always be, and remain, your First Love.

"Be ye angry, and sin not; let not the Sun go down on your wrath:"

Ephesians 4:26

Reflections

With His Sixth Commandment, *Thou shalt not kill*, the Lord is warning you to refrain from indulging in any thoughts, feelings, or behaviors that will destroy the Goodness of His Love from existing within your life, or within the lives of others. This Message is simple to understand to all who are willing to place their faith and trust in His Guidance about the Way you must live you life and treat others around you, nothing withheld.

That Guidance is internal, Given to all who are willing to bend their knees and bow their heads in the Light of Righteousness, and then listen to what "the still small Voice" within them is teaching them about the most important things of all.

> "And after the earthquake a fire; but the Lord was not in the fire: and after the fire a still small Voice.

> "And it was so, when Elijah heard it, that he wrapped his face in his mantle, and went out, and stood in the entrance of the cave. and behold, there came a Voice unto him, and said, What doest here, Elijah?"
>
> 1 Kings 19:12–13

> "Verily, verily, I say unto you, He that heareth My Word, and believeth on Him that sent Me, hath everlasting Life, and shall not come into condemnation; but is passed from death unto Life."
>
> John 5:24

> "If ye love Me, keep My Commandments."
>
> John 14:15

THOU SHALT NOT COMMIT ADULTERY.

Exodus 20:14

17
Physical and Spiritual Marriage

There is something internally transcending
about the vows of fidelity.

*T*he Seventh Commandment sets the stage for a whale of a tale. One that is woven around broken promises and denial. One that can destroy lives, families, and the underpinnings of moral societies. One that leaves a trail of misery in its wake. And one that can lead to redemption, salvation, and deliverance into the Joys of Heavenly Love.

~

The "I do" in a physical wedding constitutes a promise by two people to love their marriage partner above themselves. It corresponds to the promise you make to the Lord to love Him above yourself. Both sets of promises constitute a Covenant, uniting both husband and wife together with one another in Righteousness on earth, and in Heaven with the Lord Himself.

> *Mercy and Truth are met together; Righteousness and Peace have kissed each other.*

Psalms 85:10

As anyone who has been married on earth may attest, marriage is both an event and a journey. There are many steps and stages of joy and difficulties.

Times of emotional closeness and of emotional distance. Times of need for dedicated self-sacrifice while overcoming personal pride and selfishness. And times of need for reconciliation. Yet, as both husband and wife persist in honoring their wedding vows, their love will grow with inmost happiness and genuine fulfillment from a life well lived.

> "What therefore God hath joined together, let not man put asunder."
>
> Mark 10:9

As husbands and wives keep the fidelity of their marriage vows Sacred, those vows will Guide them in the way they think, feel, and treat each other. And although challenges to their vows will certainly arise, every effort made to overcome them will act to refine each of them for the Better.

Each honest, sincere, and humble effort to do so is an offering of Love. Each offering nurtures the development of Goodness within their thoughts and affections. And as all Goodness Originates from the Lord Himself, as each person honors their wedding vows on earth, their reception of the Goodness of God's Love for them becomes ever more perfected within their souls.

For that Reason, the fidelity of physical marriage is Holy to the Lord. Through it, He Prepares a very special Place in Heaven for those who have kept their wedding vows Sacred on earth. Could that be you? Your wedding ring represents your dedicated aspiration to complete your spiritual journey into that beautiful "Place," wherein "Mercy and Truth are met together" and "Righteousness and Peace have kissed each other."

> "And I will betroth thee unto Me for ever; yea, I will betroth thee unto Me in Righteousness, and in Judgment, and in Loving kindness, and in Mercies.
>
> "I will even betroth ye unto Me in faithfulness: and thou shalt know the Lord."
>
> Hosea 2:19–20

Turning Water into Wine

The first Miracle the Lord performed during His physical advent into our world was at a wedding ceremony "in Cana of Galilee." There He sustained a wedding celebration by turning water into Wine. Through this first Miracle, He began to Gift humanity with a renewed spiritual understanding about the Way He unites us together with one another, and with Him in Truth about the eternal Blessings of Heavenly Love.

> "And the Third Day there was a marriage in Cana of Galilee;
> and the Mother of Jesus was there:"
>
> John 2:1

The Word: *Day* portrays a spiritual state of being. And as evening turns into morning, and morning turns into daytime, as you continue to walk in the Light of the Lord's Righteousness, Day by Day you progress into a more perfect spiritual state of being.

Spiritually, a "Third Day" describes a state of fullness, wherein you have been prepared to evolve into an entirely new, and greatly elevated mental, emotional, and spiritual state of being. And as Cana in Galilee was located at the far outskirts of the nation of Israel, it describes a "place" that was remote from spiritual understanding about that Divine Truth.

Intentions and emotions containing the truth and goodness of mutual love run high.

The Words: *and the Mother of Jesus was there* reveal Wisdom, calling upon the Lord to bring a renewed spiritual understanding about Divine Truth into our lives.

> "And both Jesus was called, and His disciples, to the marriage."
>
> John 2:2

As a Son coming forth from His Father's Love for you, the Lord comes into your life to save you from self-inflicted mental, emotional, and spiritual harm as He leads you into the Joys of Heavenly Love. The love that exists between people on earth needs that same protection and Guidance.

The Words: *And both Jesus was called, and His disciples, to the marriage* describe that realization.

> "*And when they wanted Wine, the Mother of Jesus said unto Him, They have no Wine.*"
>
> John 2:3

At the beginning of any marriage celebration, initial intentions and emotions containing mutual love run high. In that beginning you are spiritually surrounded by thoughts and affections that act as your welcome wedding "guests." As they gather in that celebration, it is easy to recognize that there is something special about what is being experienced and shared. It is also easy to perceive there is something internally transcending about the vows of fidelity that are being made.

The Words: *And when they wanted Wine, the mother of Jesus said unto Him, They have no Wine* express how, in time, a deeper sense of spiritual understanding will be required to sustain the very special Qualities and Virtues that are being shared in that internal wedding celebration.

Sustaining the union of mutual love between two people requires more than just good intentions. It requires a very deep spiritual understanding about why and how they must live their lives.

> "*Jesus said unto her, Woman, what have I to do with thee? Mine hour is not yet come.*"
>
> John 2:4

At the time of the Lord's advent into our world, genuine spiritual understanding about the Way we must live our lives had become nearly nonexistent. The rituals, traditions, and ceremonies that remained were lovely on the outside, but offered very limited sustenance to sustain the reforming and transforming Power of Divine Truth on the inside.

Because the Lord had not yet rent the veil that had come to cover over our understanding about what brings innermost happiness and genuine fulfillment into our lives, He replied to Wisdom's plea by saying "Mine hour is not yet come." Nevertheless, from that point forward, the Lord's "Time" did indeed begin.

> *"His Mother saith unto the servants, Whatsoever He saith unto you, do it.*
>
> *"And there were set six waterpots of Stone, after the manner of the purifying of the Jews, containing two or three firkins apiece."*
>
> John 2:5–6

Without having the spiritual knowledge to help you recognize the presence of Divine Truth within your life, what sustains the internal Goodness of Heavenly Love within your mind and heart will soon run dry. And so, the Lord comes into your life to Offer you that knowledge, asking you to willingly receive it, and then apply it to each and every aspect of your life.

> *"Jesus said unto them, Fill the waterpots with Water. And they filled them up to the brim."*
>
> John 2:7

In a positive sense, "Water" represents genuine spiritual knowledge about the things that affect your mental, emotional, and spiritual wellbeing. When willfully applied to the Way you live your life, that knowledge acts to internally cleanse and refresh your thoughts and affections. For these reasons, water is symbolically used in religious purifications through physical washings and baptisms. Here, "waterpots" correspond to your capacity to act as vessels capable of receiving that spiritual knowledge.

As you apply yourself to filling those "waterpots with Water," you act as "servants" who willingly accept that personal responsibility within your life. Filling "them up to the brim" is descriptive of exercising your full capacity to do so. As you do so in reverence to your love for the Lord and in reverence for the Good of all around you, that spiritual knowledge becomes transformed into a *Living Water* within your soul.

As revealed in John, 4:10 and throughout the entire Bible, the Lord freely Offers you genuine spiritual knowledge about how you may forever share in the Joy and Goodness of His Love for you.

> "*And He said unto them, Draw out now, and bear unto the governor of the Feast. And they bare it.*"
>
> John 2:8

The Words: *Draw out now* declare that once you accept genuine spiritual knowledge, the Lord will ask you to reach deeply within yourself and apply it to the Way you live your life. At times those efforts will need to be considerable. Your commitment to "bare it" describes your willing efforts to do so. As you make those efforts with honesty, sincerity, and humility, the Lord turns that all-important knowledge into a new spiritual understanding within you that is much deeper, much more rewarding, and much more fulfilling than anything you could have ever brought forth on your own.

The Lord turning *Water into Wine at the Wedding Feast in Cana of Galilee* reveals the beginning of your receiving that spiritual understanding.

> "*When the ruler of the Feast had tasted the Water that was made Wine, and knew not whence it was: (but the servants which drew the Water knew;) the governor of the Feast called the Bridegroom.*

"And saith unto him, Every man at the beginning doth set forth good wine; and when men have well drunk, then that which is worse: but Thou hast kept the Good Wine until now."
John 2:9–10

Through His first Miracle at the wedding celebration in Cana of Galilee, the Lord began to restore our spiritual understanding about the Truth of Love.

The "ruler of the Feast" represents your prior dominant thoughts, beginning to realize that there is something much Greater, Richer, and much more fulfilling within the meaning of your "marriage vows" than you had ever before recognized or accepted. The "governor" of the Feast is descriptive of your free will, then gratefully acknowledging the Source of that realization, Namely the Lord, Who is Righteousness Himself.

"This beginning of Miracles did Jesus in Cana of Galilee, and manifested forth His Glory; and His disciples believed on Him."
John 2:11

The Words: *This beginning of Miracles did Jesus in Cana of Galilee, and manifested forth His Glory* set the stage, as the Lord began His Quest to restore our understanding about why and how we must live our lives. Through your willingness to receive and apply that Holy understanding to the Way you live your life, He changes everything within you for the Better. At that time, and in that Day, it may Truly be said that your Last state of being is much, much Better than your first.

"The Kingdom of Heaven is like unto a certain King, which made a marriage for His Son."
Matthew 22:2

Throughout Scripture, Divine Truth from the Lord is called the "Bridegroom." The Doctrine of His Righteousness is called "His Bride." Contained in the Words of Psalms 19:5 and Isaiah 61:10 are spiritual descriptions of the Strength and Joy they bring forth within your life as you honor the fidelity of their Union in all you think, feel, and do.

Matthew 22:3-14 describes your invitation to their "Wedding" celebration. How you prepare yourself to come into that celebration is all-important to your future happiness and fulfillment in this life. And it will most certainly determine the extent of your happiness and fulfillment in the life to come.

> "The Voice of Joy, and the Voice of Gladness, the Voice of the Bridegroom, and the Voice of the Bride, the Voice of them that shall say, Praise the Lord of hosts: for the Lord is Good; for His Mercy endureth for ever: and of them that shall bring the sacrifice of Praise into the House of the Lord. For I will cause to return the captivity of the Land, as at the First, saith the Lord."
>
> Jeremiah 33:11

Bringing a "sacrifice of Praise into the House of the Lord" is spiritually descriptive of your willingness to live your life in the Way the Lord has Shown you that you must, nothing withheld. Your dedicated efforts to work with Him to overcome any challenges that would have you do otherwise prepare you to enter into the internal Paradise that He has Prepared for you to inherit, and share with Him and with one another since the Beginning of time. Such is the Power of Divine Truth as He Redeems your ability to host the Goodness of His Love within your soul.

> "And, behold, I come quickly; and My Reward is with Me, to Give every man according as his work shall be.
>
> "I am the Alpha and Omega, the Beginning and the End, the First and the Last."
>
> Revelation 22:12–13

~

Physical Adultery

At any level of indulgence, physical adulterers destroy the internal Goodness of Love existing within themselves, between themselves and their spouse, and between themselves and the Lord. That destruction grievously harms their minds, hearts, and souls, regardless of what justifications they may use to argue otherwise.

Physical adulterers most especially risk harming the mental, emotional, and spiritual wellbeing of

> When lust prevails, it is cruel and destructive beyond depiction.

their children. They risk wounding what is innocent and most susceptible within them, causing lasting distress, turmoil, and confusion. The unjust guilt and prolonged inner suffering that results often turns itself into depression, insecurity, and resentment. All those afflictions can lead to various forms of internal and external violence, further harming the soundness of their minds, hearts, and souls. Those many forms of afflictions often create a repetitive cycle that adversely affect the individual and collective mental, emotional, and spiritual wellbeing of people for generations to come.

And although adulterers may not care about the harm they cause to others, they should take great to consider consider that all the internal harm they cause to others will eventually return upon themselves.

And so, the Lord warns us in no uncertain terms, if adultery is a path you have been on, alter your direction. For yourself. For others. For God's sake.

> *Ye have heard that it was said by them of old time, Thou shalt not commit adultery.*

> *But I say unto you, That whosoever looketh on a woman to lust after her hath committed adultery with her already in his heart.*
>
> Matthew 5:27–28

The Damage of Lust

When lust prevails, it is destructive and cruel beyond depiction. Any and all forms of lust strive to break the fidelity between Divine Truth and the Doctrine of Righteousness within your life solely for their own self-gratification. They are deceptive, bold, and relentless, lying in wait to exploit any weakness within your resolve to live your life in the Way that the Lord is Showing you that you must.

> "The eye also of the adulterer waiteth for the twilight, saying, No eye shall see me and disguiseth his face."
>
> Job 24:15

Lusts seeks domination over your mind and heart, and through that domination they seek to dominate the minds and hearts of others. They are the adulterers of all the Blessings the Lord Purposes to bring forth within you, between you and others, and between His Righteousness and Peace within your life.

> "And I will Walk among you, and will be your God, and ye shall be My people.
>
> "I am the Lord your God, which Brought you forth from the land of Egypt, that ye should not be their bondmen; and I have Broken the bands of your yoke, and made you go Upright.
>
> "But if ye will not hearken unto Me, and will not do all these Commandments;
>
> "And if ye shall despise My Statutes, or if your soul abhor My Judgments, so that ye will not do all My Commandments, but that ye break My Covenant:

> "*I will also do this unto you; I will even appoint over you terror, consumption, and the burning ague, that shall consume the eyes, and cause sorrow of heart: and ye shall sow your seed in vain, for your enemies shall eat it.*"
>
> Leviticus 26:12–16

Spiritually, "terror" results when lust is allowed to destroy the Joy and Goodness of the Lord's Love within your soul. That terror is also described throughout the Bible as a "burning," ignited by selfish desires that fuel that destruction. These act to consume your understanding about why and how you must live your life, spiritually described as "the burning ague, that shall consume the eyes."

They are insatiable, never finding lasting happiness or peace.

The Words: *cause sorrow of heart* describe that consumption resulting in a loss of innermost happiness and genuine fulfillment in life.

The Words: *and ye shall sow your seed in vain, for your enemies shall eat it* illuminate your wasted Opportunity to evolve into a Better and more perfect human being.

Lusts seek to indulge in their own self-serving thoughts, selfish desires, and corresponding behaviors. They insidiously manifest themselves through ill will toward others, through adultery, through embezzlement, through deceit, and through want of control over the minds and hearts of others. They are insatiable, never finding lasting contentment or peace, yet claiming that they do so in the most fulfilling *ways*.

"And they came over unto the other side of the sea, into the county of Gadarenes.

"And when He was come out of the ship, immediately there met Him out of the tombs a man with an unclean spirit.

"Who had his dwelling among the tombs; and no man could bind him, no, not with chains:

"Because that he had been often bound with fetters and chains, and the chains had been plucked asunder by him, and the fetters broken in pieces: neither could any man tame him.

"And always, night and day, he was in the mountains, and in the tombs, crying, and cutting himself with stones.

"But when he saw Jesus afar off, he ran and worshiped Him.

"And cried with a loud voice, and said, What have I to do with thee, Jesus, Thou Son of the Most High God? I adjure Thee by God, that Thou torment me not."

Mark 5:1–7

On the surface, all forms of lust are quite capable of making themselves appear submissive to the Truth of Love. Yet, when exposed in the Light of Righteousness, their selfish motives become quite transparent. And so, the Lord calls them out within you, so that you may recognize them for what they really are. Through that recognition He asks you to confront them, and then to turn to Him for Guidance and Strength as He helps you overcome each and every one of them.

> *"For He said unto him, Come out of the man, thou unclean*
> *spirit.*
>
> *"And He asked him, What is thy name? And he answered, saying,*
> *My name is Legion, for we are many.*
>
> *"And he besought Him much that He would not send them*
> *away out of the country."*
>
> Mark 5:8–10

There is nothing inconsequential about allowing lusts to remain uncontested within your life. If you give them permission to remain, they will continuously infest your mind and heart until they have undermined the integrity of your soul. Therefore, the Lord warns you about their dangers, and about the severity of the internal harm they pose to your mental, emotional, and spiritual wellbeing. I will have more to share with you about what is depicted in this example from Mark about the fate of the man with the "unclean spirit" within the chapter on *The Tenth Commandment.*

~

Both Paul and John recognized the grave dangers that lusts pose to your internal wellbeing. Everywhere they teach you about your need to combat them, imploring you to gain the spiritual understanding you need to become victorious over them.

> *"That ye put off concerning the former conversation the old man,*
> *which is corrupt according to the deceitful lusts;*
>
> *"And be renewed in the Spirit of your mind.*
>
> *"And that ye put on the new man, which after God is Created*
> *in Righteousness and True Holiness."*
>
> Ephesians 4:22–24

"For the Grace of God that bringeth Salvation hath appeared unto all men,

"Teaching us that, denying ungodliness and worldly lusts, we should live soberly, Righteously, and Godly, in this present world."

Titus 2:11–12

"And the world passeth away, and the lust thereof: but he that doeth the Will of God abideth forever."

1 John 2:17

Positive and Negative Spiritual Meanings

Most terms in the Bible are used in both a positive and a negative sense.

In a positive sense, the Word "fire" is used to describe the spiritual Light and Warmth that comes forth from the Lord's Divine Love for the human race. In that sense it depicts the Lord as a Divine Sun, Illuminating your thoughts and Inspiring your affections with spiritual understanding about why and how you must live your life.

In a negative sense, the Word "fire" is used to describe falsities and evils consuming any spiritual understanding from remaining within your mind, heart, and soul.

"Now Moses kept the flock of Jethro his father-in-law, the priest of Midian: and he led the flock to the backside of the desert, and came to the Mountain of God, even to Horeb."

Exodus 3:1

Here, Moses represents your thoughts open to receiving a new understanding about the spiritual meaning and implications of the Lord's Testimony to you. His keeping and leading "the flock of Jethro his father-in-law" describes maintaining and bringing forth the innocent quest required for that reception. Jethro, being "the priest of Midian" is descriptive of those honest, sincere, and humble intentions. Moses, leading "his flock to the backside of the desert" describes avoiding the dangers existing within the philosophical and religious wasteland that existed among the people of the world at that time. Can you see similar perils within the world we live in today?

The Words: *and came to the "Mountain of God, even to Horeb* are spiritually descriptive of where the magnitude of Lord's Divine Love for you … for all of us, begins to be experienced in a Way that transcends all that came before it.

> "*And the Angel of the Lord appeared unto him in a Flame of Fire out of the midst of a Bush and he looked, and behold, the Bush burned with Fire, and the Bush was not consumed.*"
>
> Exodus 3:2

The "the Angel of the Lord" that appeared to Moses "in a Flame of Fire out of the midst of a Bush" is descriptive of the Truth of Love being Illuminated within you. Spiritually, an "Angel" acts to bring the Goodness of that realization into your comprehension. The Word "Bush" is very similar in meaning to a "Vine" and a "Branch of Righteousness." These all relate to the Way the Lord reaches out to you, extending Himself with the Sole Intent to teach you about the Way He brings the Joy of His Love into fruition within your life.

The Words: *and he looked, and, behold, the Bush burned with Fire, and the Bush was not consumed* depict His never-ceasing Reaching out to Give you the understanding needed to Guide you into His Embrace.

> "*And Moses said, I will now turn aside, and see this Great Sight, why the Bush is not burnt.*"
>
> Exodus 3:3

The Words: *And Moses said, I will now turn aside* express a change in pre-conceived thinking about what brings innermost happiness and genuine fulfillment into your life.

The Words: *and see this Great Sight, why the Bush is not burnt* tell of your amazement when realizing that the Principles of Righteousness are timeless in their ability to fulfill the Lord's Purpose for the Creation of your soul.

> "*And when the Lord saw that he turned aside to see, God Called unto him out of the midst of the Bush, and said, Moses, Moses. And he said, Here am I.*"
>
> Exodus 3:4

Whenever you honestly, sincerely, and humbly open yourself up to receiving a new spiritual understanding from the Lord about the Truth of Love, He Provides you with all you need to know for success during your spiritual journey ahead.

> "*The Voice of the Lord divideth the flames of Fire.*"
>
> Psalms 29:7

> "*And all of thy children shall be taught of the Lord; and great shall be the Peace of thy children.*
>
> "*In Righteousness shalt thou be established: thou shalt be far from oppression; for thou shalt not fear: and from terror; for it shall not come near thee.*"
>
> Isaiah 54:13–14

The icon of Jesus among the apostles on the canvas in church Brigitta Kirche
by unknown artist

"*Abide in Me, and I in you. As a branch cannot bear fruit of itself, except it abide in the vine; no more can ye, except ye abide in Me.*

"*I am the vine, ye are the branches: He that abideth in Me, and I in him, the same bringeth forth much fruit: for without Me ye can do nothing.*"

John 15:4–5

"And I turned to see the Voice that Spake with me. And being turned, I saw Seven Golden Candlesticks;

"And in the Midst of the Seven Candlesticks One like unto the Son of Man, clothed with a Garment down to the foot, and girt about the paps with a Golden Girdle.

"His head and His hairs were White like Wool, as White as snow; and His eyes were as a Flame of Fire;

"And His feet like unto fine Brass, as if they Burned in a furnace; and His Voice as the sound of many Waters.

"And He had in His Right hand Seven Stars: and out of His mouth went a sharp two-edged Sword: and His Countenance was as the Sun Shineth in His Strength. "

Revelation 1:12–16

18
Temptations

The Lord leads no one into temptation.
Yet He knows all too well that you will be tempted
by falsities and evils innumerable times during
your spiritual journey in this world.

*T*emptations offer many reasons to convince you that violating the union between Divine Truth and the Doctrine of Righteousness is somehow inconsequential to your mental, emotional, and spiritual wellbeing. And although you are not immune to being tempted by their lures, it is how you respond to them that matters.

> "*Then was Jesus led up of the Spirit into the wilderness to be tempted of the devil.*
>
> "*And when He had fasted forty Days and forty nights, He was afterward an hungered.*
>
> "*And when the tempter came to Him, he said, If thou be the Son of God, Command that these stones be made Bread.*
>
> "*But He answered and said, It is Written, Man shall not Live by Bread alone, but by every Word that proceedeth out of the mouth of God.*"
>
> Matthew 4:1–4

The Lord allowed Himself to be brought into many temptations during His advent into our world. By doing so, He made Himself an Example to you...to all of us about how we must respond to them.

The Words: *Then was Jesus led up of the Spirit into the wilderness to be tempted of the devil* portray the Lord coming to where genuine spiritual understanding about the Truth of Love had become desolate among the human race.

The Words: *And when He had fasted forty Days and forty nights* reveal the lack of spiritual nourishment that existed among people at that time. Are we in dire need of that spiritual nourishment yet once again?

The Words: *He was afterward an hungered* express the Lord's need to Commune with us about the Way to our salvation and deliverance into the Joy and Goodness of Heavenly Love.

The Words: *And when the tempter came to Him, he said, If thou be the Son of God, Command that these stones be made Bread* describe falsities attempting to convince you that your salvation and deliverance can be achieved without first undergoing your spiritual reformation in the Light of Righteousness.

The proponents of those falsities would even have the Lord Himself confess that "faith alone" or "Grace alone" or "confessions of the mouth alone" or many like erroneous notions will suffice to justify your transformation into the Goodness of that incomparable Blessed spiritual state of being.

They would also have you believe that simply because you come from a particular physical or historical lineage, or belong to a certain religious domination, or because you have been baptized, or have diligently followed certain letter-of-the-Word-based dictates, that these alone will suffice to fulfill His Purpose for coming into your life.

These false arguments, and many more like them are described as being "truths," when they are nothing besides counterfeit substitutes. Rather, they present spiritual stumbling blocks placed in front of your need to realize what constitutes the most important things of all.

Those false arguments have been used throughout history to give the innocent and unsuspecting a false sense of security about what brings Goodness into fruition within their lives. Teachers of those false notions have led many astray.

> "When said He unto the disciples, It is impossible but that offences will come: but woe unto him, through whom they come!
>
> "It were better for him that a millstone were hanged about his neck, and he cast into the sea, than that he should offend one of these little ones."
>
> Luke 17:1–2

There are many variations of philosophies and religious beliefs spread throughout the people of the world. There are also variations of races, ethnicity, cultures, and genders existing among us. Yet there is only One set of Standards that the Lord has established to Give us Good Judgment about the Way we must live our lives and treat all others around us. That Standard is founded upon our willingness to abide by His Righteousness First, in all we think, feel, and do.

You will be tempted by falsities many times during your spiritual journey.

What "standards" do you use to make judgments about the Goodness exiting within the minds, hearts, and souls of others?

> "Judge not, that ye be not judged.
>
> "For with what judgment ye judge, ye shall be judged: And with what measure ye mete, it shall again be measured to you again."
>
> Matthew 7:1–2

Throughout the Bible, the Lord teaches you to use Good Judgment in the Way you live your life and about the Way you think, feel, and behave towards others. He teaches you that your judgment will one day return upon yourself. Using letter-of-the-Word misinterpretations about Scripture to justify making unjust judgments about others leaves you treading upon very treacherous ground.

> "*Go through, go through the Gates; prepare ye the Way of the people; cast Up, cast Up the Highway; gather out the stones; lift Up a Standard for the people.*"
>
> Isaiah 62:10

The Words: *But He answered and said, It is Written, Man shall not Live by Bread alone, but by every Word that proceedeth out of the mouth of God* proclaim the Reasons why you must always seek to live your life, according to the Standards that the Lord has established for us to live by, nothing added or subtracted. Abiding by that understanding keeps you from adulterating the relationship between Divine Truth and the Doctrine of His Righteousness within your own life.

> "*All the Commandments which I Command thee this Day shall ye observe to do, that ye may Live, and multiply, and go in and possess the Land which the Lord sware unto your fathers.*

> "*And thou shalt remember all the Way which the Lord thy God led thee these forty years in the wilderness, to humble thee, and to prove thee, to know what was in thine heart, and whether thou wouldest keep His Commandments, or no.*

"*And He humbled thee, and suffered thee to hunger, and fed thee with Manna, which thou knewest not, neither did thy fathers know; that He might make thee know that man doth not live by Bread only, but by every Word that proceedeth out of the mouth of the Lord doth man Live.*"

Deuteronomy 8:1–3

"*Incline your ear, and come unto Me: hear, and your soul shall Live; and I will make an everlasting Covenant with you, even the sure Mercies of David.*

"*Behold, I have Given Him for a Witness to the people, a Leader and Commander to the people.*"

Isaiah 55:3–4

"*If ye keep My Commandments, ye shall abide in My Love; even as I have kept My Father's Commandments, and abide in His Love.*

"*These things have I spoken unto you, that My Joy might remain in you, and that your Joy might be full.*

"*This is My Commandment, That you love one another as I have Loved you.*"

John 15: 10–12

19

The Sign of the Prophet Jonas

He teaches you to look deeply within yourself and
confront anything that differs from that Holy understanding.

> "Then certain of the scribes and of the Pharisees answered,
> saying, Master, we would see a sign from thee.
>
> "But He answered, and said unto them, An evil and adulterous
> generation seeketh after a sign; and there shall no sign be Given
> unto it, but the Sign of the prophet Jonas."
>
> Matthew 12:38–39

The Lord has put forth all the lessons, stories, and examples in the Bible
to act as "Signs" to Guide you in the Way to live your life. Nevertheless,
many prefer to look for some other type of "sign," not willing to acknowledge
or accept that the Lord has already Given us all the Signs we will ever need
to find innermost happiness and genuine fulfillment within our lives.

> "And God said, Let there be Lights in the firmament of the
> Heaven to divide the Day from the night; and let them be for
> Signs, and for Seasons, and for Days, and Years:"
>
> Genesis 1:14

The "Lights in the firmament of Heaven" illuminate your understanding about the Way you must live your life, and about the Way you must think, feel, and treat others. Your willingness to follow and abide by those Signs allows you to discern Truth from falsity and Right from wrong. Those Signs are Given to you for your Good and for the Good of all around you.

> Look deeply within yourself and confront anything that differs.

> "And Moses told Aaron all the Words of the Lord who had sent him, and all the Signs which He had Commanded him."
>
> Exodus 4:28

> "How Great are His Signs! and how Mighty are His Wonders! His Kingdom is an everlasting Kingdom, and His Dominion is from generation to generation."
>
> Daniel 4:3

Through the story of Jonas, who is also called Jonah in the Bible, the Lord teaches you about your need to keep the fidelity between Divine Truth and the Doctrine of His Righteousness Sacred in all you think, feel, and do. He teaches you to look deeply within yourself and confront anything that differs from that Holy understanding. He teaches you about the futility of attempting to flee away from your responsibility to do so. He warns you that falling back into any errant philosophy or misleading religious doctrine that professes otherwise adulterates all that He has been Showing you to be True and Right since your inception.

> "Now the Word of the Lord came unto Jonah the son of Amittai, saying,
>
> "Arise, go to Nineveh, that great city, and cry against it; for their wickedness is come up before Me."
>
> Jonah 1:1-2

Spiritually, all "cities" in the Bible depict doctrines that give shelter and comfort to your thoughts and affections. In a positive sense, the "Holy City" is spiritually descriptive of the Doctrine wherein affection for Divine Truth reigns Supreme. It is therefore the Rightful "Capital" of all genuine spiritual understanding, described by John in Revelation 21:2 as "the Holy City, new Jerusalem, coming down from God out of Heaven, prepared as a Bride adorned for Her Husband."

~

The city of Nineveh was located outside the Holy Land. It is thereby descriptive of a doctrine distanced in beliefs from the Doctrine of Righteousness. And so, the Lord begins "the Sign of the prophet Jonas" by asking Jonah to visit that doctrine, for it was corrupting humanity's ability to understand what must always be, and remain, our First Love. And just as the Lord asked Jonah to internally visit and confront any misguided doctrine that distorts, dilutes, or corrupts our need to receive that spiritual understanding, He asks you to do the same.

The Words: *Arise, go to Nineveh, that great city, and cry against it; for their wickedness is come before Me* describe His asking you to visit and confront any doctrine within your life that differs from what He has Given for you to know and cherish as True and Right.

> "*But Jonah rose up to flee unto Tarshish from the Presence of the Lord, and went down to Joppa; and he found a ship going to Tarshish: so he paid the fare thereof, and went down into it, to go with them unto Tarshish from the Presence of the Lord.*"
>
> Jonah 1:3

Spiritually, "to flee unto Tarshish from the Presence of the Lord" describes trying to escape your responsibility to confront any misguided doctrinal belief that conflicts with what He has Shown You to be True and Right.

It is descriptive of attempting to run away from honest personal self-reflection in the Light of His Righteousness. That fleeing away employs excuses of every sort to dismiss your need to submit yourself to that introspection, spiritually described by Jonah, first fleeing to Joppa, and then finding "a ship going to Tarshish."

The Words: *so he paid the fare thereof, and went down into it, to go with them unto Tarshish from the Presence of the Lord* describe Jonah, using the currency of *thoughts formed from the imagination* of his own heart to avoid confronting his own misconceptions about what constitutes True and saving faith in the Lord's Testimony to us, and what does not.

❧

"*But the Lord sent out a Great Wind into the sea, and there was a Mighty tempest in the sea, so that the ship was like to be broken.*"

Jonah 1:4

Everywhere the Lord teaches you that trying to flee away from your need to confront misguided beliefs in your life is futile in securing internal Peace within your soul. Throughout history, many have tried and failed. The fortunate ones attend the remnant of "the still small Voice" remaining in their life, and thereby regain the spiritual sensibility to reconsider their false notions about the Truth of Love before it becomes too late.

The Words: *there was a Mighty tempest in the sea, so that the ship was like to be broken* refer to the futility of resisting that need. The futility of that denial is depicted by the Lord many, many times throughout the Bible.

"*Wherefore kick ye at My Sacrifice and at Mine Offering, which I have Commanded in My Habitation; and honorest thy sons above Me, to make yourselves fat with the chiefest of all the offerings of Israel My people?*"

1 Samuel 2:29

"Gird up thy lions now like a man: I will Demand of thee, and Declare thou unto Me.

"Wilt thou also disannul My Judgment? Wilt thou condemn Me, that thou mayest be righteous?

"Hast thou an arm like God? or canst thou thunder with a Voice like Him?"

Job 40:7-9

"And he fell to the earth, and heard a Voice saying unto him, Saul, Saul, why persecutest thou Me?

"And he said, Who art thou, Lord? And the Lord said, I am Jesus whom thou persecutest: it is hard for thee to kick against the pricks.

"And he trembling and astonished said, Lord, what wilt Thou have me to do? And the Lord said unto him, Arise, and go into the City, and it shall be told thee what thou must do."

Acts 9:4–6

Whenever you choose to defend thoughts formed from the imagination of your own heart instead of realizing what must always be, and remain, your First Works, you persecute the Truth of your Salvation. The Story of Jonah underscores the dangers of thinking otherwise. And so, during His advent into our world the Lord raised up the Story of Jonas as a "Sign" to once again Gift all of humanity with the Spiritual understanding needed to regain that spiritual sensibility. The Lord's Instructions to Samuel, Job, and Paul each offer you spiritual examples about this same timeless lesson.

~

> *"Nevertheless the men rowed hard to bring it to the land; but they could not: for the sea wrought, and was tempestuous against them."*
>
> Jonah 1:13

The Words: *Nevertheless the men rowed hard to bring it to the land; but they could not* further explain the futility of trying to escape your need to confront and correct any misguided belief that differs from what the Lord has Shown you to be True and Right.

The Words: *the sea wrought, and was tempestuous against them* reflect the same conditions described within Matthew 14:22-36, depicting the danger of trying to chart your own course rather than trusting in the Message that the Lord has been Offering us since our inceptions.

> *"Wherefore they cried unto the Lord, and said, We beseech Thee, O Lord, we beseech Thee, let us not perish for this man's life, and lay not upon us innocent Blood: for Thou, O Lord, hast done as it pleased Thee."*
>
> Jonah 1:14

The remnant of your spiritual sensibilities will always cry out when perceiving the impending demise of your willingness to seek Righteousness First within your life.

The Words: *Wherefore they cried unto the Lord, and said, we beseech Thee, let us not perish for this man's life* describe the internal perception about what is causing that impending demise.

The Words: *and lay not upon us innocent Blood* portray recognizing the danger of allowing your Opportunity to apply the Truth about the most important things of all to go to waste within your life.

The Words: *for Thou, O Lord, hast done as it pleased Thee* refer to having the spiritual sensibility to heed that internal wakeup Call within your life.

> " *So they took up Jonah, and cast him forth into the sea: and the sea ceased from her raging.*
>
> " *Then the men feared the Lord exceedingly, and offered a sacrifice unto the Lord, and made vows.* "
>
> Jonah 1:15–16

The Words: *So they took up Jonah, and cast him forth into the sea* reveal your regaining the common sense needed to reject false notions about

A "Great fish" depicts the Greatest Principle of all.

what must always be, and remain, your First Love.

The Words: *and the sea ceased from her raging* describe the resulting calm and surety that results from acknowledging the Truth about why and how you must.

The Words: *Then the men feared the Lord exceedingly* express the internal reverence and gratitude felt for the Mercy, Peace, and confidence that results.

The Words: *and offered a sacrifice unto the Lord, and made vows* refer to giving the Lord His Just Due through your promise to seek the Principles of His Righteousness as Primary for the Way you live you life.

⁓

"*Now the Lord had prepared a Great fish to swallow up Jonah. And Jonah was in the belly of the fish three Days and three nights.*"

Jonah 1:17

When used in a positive sense, the Words "seas" and "waters" describe genuine spiritual knowledge about Divine Truth. Spiritually, a "fish" is descriptive of principles that dwell within that knowledge. A "Great fish" depicts the Greatest Principle of all.

The Words: *Now the Lord had prepared a Great fish to swallow up Jonah* tell of the Lord having prepared that "Great fish" to swallow Jonah's pride-filled, hardheaded, and stiff-necked misconceptions about what constitutes True and saving faith in His Testimony to us.

The Words: *And Jonah was in the belly of the fish three Days and three nights* describe a time of inescapable internal reflection, whereby Jonah was once again Given the Opportunity to come to full-term with the folly of rejecting his responsibility to confront the misguided doctrinal beliefs that were misleading him, and others, in life.

"*Then Jonah prayed unto the Lord his God out of the fish's belly,*

"*And said, I cried by Reason of mine affliction unto the Lord, and He heard me; out of the belly of hell cried I, and Thou heardest my voice.*

"*For Thou hadst cast me into the deep, in the midst of the seas; and the floods compassed me about: all Thy billows and Thy waves passed over me.*

"*Then I said, I am cast out of Thy sight; yet I will look again toward Thy Holy Temple.*

"*The waters compassed me about, even to the soul: the depth closed me round about, the weeds were wrapped around my head.*

"*I went down to the bottoms of the mountains; the earth with her bars was about me for ever: yet hast Thou brought up my Life from corruption, O Lord my God.*

"*When my soul fainted within me I remembered the Lord: and my prayer came in unto Thee, into Thine Holy Temple.*

"*They that observe lying vanities forsake their own Mercy.*

"*But I will sacrifice unto Thee with the voice of thanksgiving; I will pay that that I have vowed. Salvation is of the Lord.*"

Jonah 2:1–9

Throughout Scripture, the Lord teaches you that there will be many times in your life when you will find the need to come to your senses about what constitutes True and saving faith in His Testimony to you … and what does not. Some of those times will feel very uncomfortable to you. And yet, as any remnant of spiritual humility remaining within you comes to its senses, you will be most inclined to seek His Forgiveness for fleeing away from accepting your spiritual task at hand.

The Words: *Then Jonah prayed unto the Lord his God out of the fish's belly* describe that state of spiritual humility.

The Words: *And said, I cried by Reason of mine affliction unto the Lord, and He heard me; out of the belly of hell cried I, and Thou heardest my voice* reveal that it is then when you will soon rediscover a lost sense of Reason about why and how you must.

The Words: *For Thou hadst cast me into the deep, in the midst of the seas* describe acknowledging that your spiritual afflictions have been caused by your lack of willingness to confront the flaws of your own misguided religious doctrinal beliefs.

The Words: *the floods compassed me about* depict realizing that such continued resistance will only result in still greater internal torments of your own making.

The Words: *all Thy billows and Thy waves passed over me* describe recognizing the overwhelming strength of that spiritual Reality.

The Words: *Then I said, I am cast out of Thy sight; yet I will look again toward Thy Holy Temple* welcome a renewed state of personal introspection, wherein with confession and hope, you honestly and sincerely accept your need to surrender yourself to the Truth of Love.

The Words: *The waters compassed me about, even to the soul: the depth closed me round about, the weeds were wrapped around my head* describe the spiritual turmoil and entrapments that you bring upon yourself by resisting to come to terms about what must always be, and remain, your First Works.

As unpleasant as all these torments may seem, they cause you to bend your knees, bow your head, and seek answers about why you are experiencing them, and about how you may find relief from them. It is then when you will become most inclined to drop the pride of your self-intelligence and surrender yourself to the Lord, then honestly, sincerely, and humbly seeking His Forgiveness, Help and Guidance in mind, heart, and soul.

The Words: *I went down to the bottom of the mountains; the earth with her bars was about me for ever: yet hast Thou brought up my life from corruption* portray a new sense of liberation found when you experience the Lord Lifting you up out of the bowels of despair.

The Words: *O Lord my God* describe the heartfelt gratitude felt through that liberation, as you are brought into a state of remembrance about all things True and Right.

The Words: *When my soul fainted within me I remembered the Lord: and my prayer came in unto Thee, into Thy Holy Temple* amplify the extent of that gratitude, as you recall the Message and Promise the Lord has been Giving you since your inception.

The Words: *They that observe lying vanities forsake their own Mercy* are Truthful and insightful. They openly *acknowledge and confess* the grave dangers of placing your own beliefs in front of the Doctrine the Lord has sent down from Heaven from His Love for you, for your Good and for the Good of all around you.

The Words: *But I will sacrifice unto Thee* reveal your offering to leave your prior thoughts about what brings innermost happiness and genuine fulfillment behind you, then gladly accepting what the Lord has been teaching you about the most important things of all.

The Words *with the voice of thanksgiving* express your hope in the Forgiveness of the Lord fulfilled.

The Words: *I will pay that that I have vowed* verify your commitment to then refocus upon your responsibility to complete your spiritual task at hand.

The Words: *Salvation is of the Lord* illuminate professing to having received a new internal understanding about the Truth of Love.

> "*And the Lord Spake unto the fish, and it vomited out Jonah upon the dry land.*"
>
> Jonah 2:10

There will be times in your life when you find yourself making mistakes about acknowledging what must always be, and remain, your First Works.

There will be times when the Lord will ask you to recognize the harm those mistakes are causing to the Goodness of His Love within your own soul.

It is during those times when you will most clearly perceive the Truth of Love.

There will be times when you will regain the spiritual sensibility to repent and turn away from your misguided beliefs about what brings innermost happiness and genuine fulfillment into your life.

And there will be times when you will find the honesty, sincerity, and humility to reconcile yourself with the Truth of your Salvation.

Through your willingness, those invaluable tithes and offerings to give to what is poor and needy within you, will find His Mercy, allowing you to become liberated from what had so greatly afflicted your ability to think clearly about what must always be, and remain, your First Love.

Those will be the times to acknowledge the most important things of all. It is during those times when you will most clearly remember His Testimony to you, then resonating deeply within your mind, heart, and soul.

> *And the Word of the Lord came unto Jonah the Second time, saying,*

> *Arise, go unto Nineveh, that great city, and preach unto it the preaching that I bid thee.*

> *So Jonah arose, and went unto Nineveh, according to the Word of the Lord. Now Nineveh was an exceeding great city of three Days' journey.*

> *And Jonah began to enter into the city a day's journey, and he cried, and said, Yet forty days, and Nineveh shall be overthrown.*

> *So the people of Nineveh believed God, and proclaimed a fast, and put on sackcloth, from the greatest of them even to the least of them.*

> *For Word came unto the king of Nineveh, and he arose from his throne, and he laid his robe from him, and covered him with sackcloth, and sat in ashes.*

> *And he caused it to be proclaimed and published through Nineveh by the decree of the king and his nobles, saying, Let neither man nor beast, herd nor flock, taste any thing: let them not feed, nor drink water:*

> *But let man and beast be covered with sackcloth, and cry mightily unto God: yea, let them turn every one from his evil way, and from the violence that is in their hands.*

> *"Who can tell if God will turn and repent, and turn away from His fierce anger, that we perish not?*
>
> *"And God saw their works, that they turned from their evil way; and God repented of the evil, that He had said that He would do unto them; and He did it not."*
>
> Jonah 3:1–10

The Words: *And the Word of the Lord came unto Jonah the Second time, saying* confirm that Jonah had finally come to acknowledge the Truth about what must always be, and remain his First Love.

Receiving that Truth allows you to comprehend the overriding importance of confronting and addressing any misguided beliefs in your life.

He teaches you to realize that He will never forsake you.

The Words: *saying, Arise, go unto Nineveh, that great city, and preach unto it the preaching that I bid thee* describe heeding the Lord's Call for you to do so.

The Words: *So Jonah arose, and went unto Nineveh, according to the Word of the Lord* refer to elevating your mind and heart to fulfill your spiritual task at hand.

The Words: *Now Nineveh was an exceeding great city of three Days' journey* define your need to walk the "extra mile" required to overcome any doubt about the Reasons why you must.

The Words: *And Jonah began to enter into the city a day's journey* describe approaching the tenants of your prior misleading beliefs with newfound confidence in what the Lord has Shown you to be True and Right.

The Words: *and he cried, and said, Yet forty days, and Nineveh shall be overthrown* demonstrate your willingness to call out why course corrections are necessary to the doctrine that had been misguiding you in the past.

The Words: *So the people of Nineveh believed God* reveal a conversion taking place within your thoughts and affections with confession about your inmost need to do so.

The Words: *and proclaimed a fast, and put on sackcloth, from the greatest of them even to the least of them* explain gaining the humility to leave your prior misleading doctrinal beliefs behind.

The Words: *For Word came unto the king of Nineveh, and he arose from his throne, and he laid his robe from him* describe willfully offering your faith and trust in the Guidance that the Lord is now bringing into your life.

The Words: *and covered him with sackcloth, and sat in ashes* reveal the remorse felt when realizing just how far you had allowed yourself to stray from the Truth of Love.

Jonah becomes an example to you of your irrefutable need to acknowledge the Truth of your Salvation.

The Words: *And he caused it to be proclaimed and published through Nineveh by the decree of the king and his nobles, saying, Let neither man nor beast, herd nor flock, taste any thing: let them not feed, nor drink water* explain turning away from all of the false notions that misled you from comprehending that Divine Truth.

The Words: *But let man and beast be covered with sackcloth, and cry mightily unto God: yea, let them turn every one from his evil way, and from the violence that is in their hands* portray the sober and unwavering recognition about your spiritual task at hand.

The Words: *Who can tell if God will turn and repent, and turn away from His fierce anger, that we perish not?* describe not feeling worthy to receive the Lord's Grace, Forgiveness, and Mercy within your life. And although that lack of self-worth is a natural reaction when realizing how far you had gone astray, He teaches you to realize that He will never forsake you in your journey back into His Embrace. Paul, on the road to Damascus, was Given this very same Message, and experienced this very same revelation.

The Words: *And God saw their works, that they turned from their evil way; and God repented of the evil, that He had said that He would do unto them; and He did it not* communicate your perception of receiving the Lord's Forgivingness for your prior missteps. And although it is said that "God repented of the evil," that is just the spiritual appearance of your becoming liberated from the mental, emotional, and spiritual harm you have caused to yourself, and to those around you.

As Divine Love Himself, the Lord brings evil on no one. Rather, He Guides you away from the internal harm you cause to yourself and to others by placing your faith in your own errant philosophies and misleading religious doctrines instead of the "Signs" that He has Established for you to recognize as True and Right.

~

"*But it displeased Jonah exceedingly, and he was very angry.*"

Jonah 4:1

This very next verse in the Story of Jonah describes the perplexity of the ages. When considering how many times the Lord has Offered humanity genuine spiritual knowledge about our need to trust in His Testimony to us about why and how we must live our lives, it is amazing how many times we have rejected it, without a "Just" cause. And so here, Jonah becomes an example to you ... to all of us about the spiritual insanity of that rejection. And even though Jonah had been Given to know better, he now begins to adulterate his relationship with Divine Truth and the Doctrine of His Righteousness by backsliding into his prior misguided doctrinal beliefs.

> *"And he prayed unto the Lord, and said, I pray thee, O Lord, was not this my saying, when I was yet in my country? Therefore I fled before unto Tarshish: for I knew that thou art a Gracious God, and Merciful, slow to anger, and of Great Kindness, and repentest Thee of the evil."*
>
> Jonah 4:2

Throughout the Bible the Lord warns you about backsliding into "thoughts formed from the imaginations" of your own heart. He teaches that doing so will leave the last state of your thinking much more irrational than your first. And so, even though the Lord has Reasoned with us many times about the dangers of such backsliding, we have repeatedly rebelled against Him, instead choosing to remain "wise in our own eyes." The Story of Jonas depicts the quandary of why so many times we have insisted on doing so, even to our dying breath.

> *"Therefore now, O Lord, take, I beseech thee, my Life from me; for it is better for me to die than to Live."*
>
> Jonah 4:3

There is never "reason" enough to be angry against understanding what the Lord has, is, and will forever be teaching you about your need to keep the Righteousness of His Commandments as your First Love. And so, the Lord addresses Jonah's irrational thinking yet again, asking him to take pause and reconsider why he keeps insisting that his thoughts are superior to His Thoughts.

> *"Then said the Lord, Doest thou well to be angry?"*
>
> Jonah 4:4

The Lord Gives us many Opportunities to reflect upon what constitutes Divine Truth about the Way we must live our lives and treat others, and what does not, even during the times of our greatest spiritual irrationality.

> "So Jonah went out of the City, and sat on the East side of the City, and there made him a booth, and sat under it in the shadow, till he might see what would become of the City."
>
> Jonah 4:5

The City Nineveh now describes thoughts and affections that have gladly embraced the Principles of the Lord's Righteousness as Primary for the Way we must think, feel, and treat others. And so now, Jonah is Given yet another chance to reconsider the errors of once again placing his own prior misguided beliefs in front of that acceptance.

Throughout the Bible, the Word "East" spiritually describes where genuine spiritual Enlightenment about Divine Truth comes into your life. And just as the physical sun on earth rises in the east, that spiritual Light also appears as a Sun, rising up out of a prior lack of spiritual comprehension Illuminating the Principles of Righteousness for all to see and understand for application to life. Jonah, now coming to sit "on the East side of the City" and there making himself "a booth" describes finding the humility to reconsider the validity of your own thinking in that Light yet once again, before it becomes too late.

> "And the Lord God prepared a Gourd, and made it to come up over Jonah, that it might be a shadow over his head, to deliver him from his grief. So Jonah was exceeding glad of the Gourd."
>
> Jonah 4:6

The Words: *And the Lord God prepared a Gourd, and made it to come up over Jonah* describe being Given a refuge by the Lord to yet once again enter into a state of honest reflection about what constitutes Good

Doctrine about the Way you must live your life and treat others, and what does not.

The Words: *So Jonah was exceeding glad of the Gourd* reveal the "place" where the Lord once again Offers you Truth-filled Compassion about your need to accept what He has, is, and forever will be Showing you to be True and Right.

It is there, in that internal state of stillness of mind and heart, where the Lord affords you yet another Opportunity to reconsider what constitutes the most important things of all.

~

> "*But God prepared a worm when the morning rose the next day, and it smote the Gourd that it withered.*"
>
> Jonah 4:7

The indignance of the pride of your own self-intelligence is spiritually described here as the "worm" that "rose the next day." That "it smote the Gourd" so "that it withered" is descriptive of the way that indignance strips away your remaining spiritual sensibilities about what leads to your inner-most happiness and genuine fulfillment in life. Left unabated, that invasive *worm* will eventually consume your ability to think clearly about what leads to your salvation and deliverance into an eternal state of Heavenly Joy. Yet the pride of self-intelligence will never accept blame for that loss. Instead, it will blame that loss on the Lord Himself rather than on its own irrational obstinance. Your need to recognize and guard against falling prey to that "worm" cannot be overstated.

> "*That which the palmerworm hath left hath the locust eaten; and that which the locust hath left hath the cankerworm eaten; and that which the cankerworm hath left hath the caterpillar eaten.*"
>
> Joel 1:4

Rejecting your need to accept the Principles of Righteousness as Primary for the Way you must live your life will cause genuine spiritual Enlightenment to feel very, very harsh to you.

> *"And it came to pass, when the Sun did arise, that God prepared a vehement East Wind; and the Sun beat upon the head of Jonah, that he fainted, and wished in himself to die, and said, it is better for me to die than to Live."*
>
> Jonah 4:8

The Words: *And it came to pass, when the Sun did arise, that God prepared a vehement East Wind; and the Sun beat upon the head of Jonah that he fainted* describe that harshness causing an internal swooning within your willingness to even reconsider the errors of your own errant philosophies and misleading religious doctrinal beliefs.

He teaches you that these Principles are inescapable.

The Words: *and wished in himself to die, and said, It is better for me to die than to Live;* illustrate hypocrisy being Given to know better, yet choosing to justify its own thoughts rather than surrendering itself to the Lord's Thoughts.

~

> *"And God said to Jonah, Doest thou well to be angry for the Gourd? And he said, I do well to be angry, even unto death."*
>
> Jonah 4:9

And so here, once again the Lord attempts to Reason with Jonah, asking him, "Doest thou well to be angry with the Gourd?" Jonah, now more indignant than ever, answers Him with still greater spiritual irrationality, "And he said, I do well to be angry, even unto death." Throughout human history, such irrationality has caused many to cast themselves headlong into self-destructive spiritual insanities of all sorts. Mark 5:12-13 spiritually depicts the unabashed insanity of doing so.

~

> "*Then said the Lord, Thou hast had pity on the Gourd, for the which thou hast not laboured, neither madest it grow; which came up in a night, and perished in a night:* "
>
> Jonah 4:10

From His Love for you, the Lord continually reaches out to you, asking you to reconsider any reasons you have used to reject His Testimony to you about what must always be, and remain, your First Works.

The Words: *Then said the Lord, Thou hast had pity on the Gourd, for which thou hast not laboured, neither madest it grow* depict His asking you to remember His Purpose for doing so.

The Words: *which came up in a night, and perished in a night* spiritually remind you that your time for honest reflection about what constitutes True and saving faith in His Testimony to you, and what does not, is limited. They remind you not to take this invaluable Opportunity in vain. They remind you that the time you have been Given to turn away from any errant philosophies or misleading religious doctrinal beliefs, and turn toward Him for Mercy and Guidance in all you think, feel, and do, is now.

~

> "*And should not I spare Nineveh, that great city, wherein are more than sixscore thousand persons that cannot discern between their right hand and their left hand; and also much cattle?*"
>
> Jonah 4:11

Regardless of our physical, historical, cultural, philosophical, or religious "pedigree," the Lord teaches us that if we continue to adulterate the fidelity of our relationship between Divine Truth and the Doctrine of His Righteousness, we will surely forfeit the Opportunity of our lifetimes.

The Words: *And should not I spare Nineveh, that great city, wherein are more than sixscore thousand persons that cannot discern between their right hand and their left hand* teach us that He will have Compassion, Forgiveness, and Mercy upon all who are willing to repent from that adulteration and then live their lives in the Way that He is Showing them that they must.

The Words: *and also much cattle?* demonstrate the extent of the latent spiritual capacity for Good that exists within all who are willing to honestly, sincerely, and humbly do so. To consistently reject that Righteous Offer is the very definition of spiritual insanity.

~

Our propensity to build philosophies and doctrines based upon our own false notions about what is "true and right," and then value them above all else has caused indescribable harm and suffering throughout human history. From dissensions, to divisions, to hatreds, to wars, and worse, those misgivings have adulterated our relationship with the Good within one another, and with the Goodness of the Lord Himself.

The Story of Jonah warns you about the dangers of backsliding into erroneous and misguided prior beliefs.

And so, through the Story of Jonah, the Lord teaches you about your need to visit, confront, and correct any attachments to beliefs that do not place the Principles of His Righteousness in their Rightful Place within your life. As Righteousness Himself, He is teaching you that by doing do you are loving Him above all else and loving your neighbor in the Way that He Loves you. He is teaching you that these Principles are inescapable. He is teaching you that attempting to flee away from your personal responsibility to accept and abide by this Holy understanding is self-defeating. He is teaching you that doing otherwise is hypocritical. With this story He is teaching you … all of us, about the spiritual meaning of His Seventh Commandment, "Thou shalt not commit adultery."

> "He answered and said unto them, When it is evening ye say, It will be fair weather: for the sky is red.
>
> "And in the morning, It will be foul weather today for the sky is red and lowering. O ye hypocrites, ye can discern the face of the sky; but ye can ye not discern the Signs of the times?
>
> "A wicked and adulterous generation seeketh after a sign; and there shall be no sign given unto it, but the Sign of the prophet Jonas. And He left them, and departed."
>
> Matthew 16:2–4

> "Jesus answered them and said, My Doctrine is not Mine, but His that sent Me.
>
> "If any man will do His Will, he shall know of the Doctrine, whether it be of God, or whether I speak of Myself.
>
> "He that speaketh of himself seeketh his own glory: but he that seeketh His Glory that sent Him, the same is True, and no unrighteousness is in Him."
>
> John 7:16–18

Being Spiritually Lukewarm

From the Beginning our existence, the Lord has Offered us Good Doctrine about the Way we must live our lives. And although we have professed to have received it, we have so often formed spiritual half-truths to dilute it until it becomes ineffectual for the reformation and transformation of our souls.

Doing so is repulsive to our ability to retain genuine spiritual understanding about the Truth of Love within our lives. Jonah's having been "vomited out upon the dry land" foretold of his eventual lack of willingness to leave his doctrinal half-truths behind. And so, the Lord warns you about the great perils of diluting, adding to, or subtracting from all that He has been teaching you to be True and Right about the Doctrine of His Righteousness.

> "*Therefore, thou Son of man, say unto the children of Thy people, The righteousness of the righteous shall not deliver him in the day of his transgression: as for the wickedness of the wicked, he shall not fall thereby in the Day that he turneth from his wickedness; neither shall the righteous be able to Live for his righteousness in the day that he sinneth.*

> "*When I shall say to the righteous, that he shall surely Live; if he trust to his own righteousness, and commit iniquity, all his righteousness shall not be remembered; but for his iniquity that he hath committed, he shall die for it.*

> "*Again, when I say unto the wicked, Thou shalt surely die; if he turn from his sin, and do that which is Lawful and Right;*

> "*If the wicked restore the Pledge, give again that he had robbed, walk in the Statutes of Life, without committing iniquity; he shall surely Live, he shall not die.*

"*None of his sins that he hath committed shall be mentioned unto him: he hath done that which is Lawful and Right; he shall surely Live.*

"*Yet the children of Thy people say, The Way of the Lord is not equal: but as for them, their way is not equal.*

"*When the righteous turneth from his righteousness, and committeth iniquity, he shall even die thereby.*

"*But if the wicked turn from his wickedness, and do that which is Lawful and Right, he shall Live thereby.*

"*Yet ye say, The Way of the Lord is not equal. O ye house of Israel, I will Judge you every one after his ways.*"

Ezekiel 33:12–20

How much more clearly can the Lord teach you … teach all of us … about the causes and effects that will determine our state of our being in this life, and most especially, what will determine our state of being in the life to come? How much more perfectly can He Proclaim that we alone are accountable for the way we live our lives?

And although no one is perfect in this world, He teaches us everywhere that as we accept our responsibility to live our lives according to the Principles of His Righteousness, He Will do all the Rest.

Throughout the ages, He has Labored greatly to Gift us with that spiritual Doctrine. Yet so many times, instead of rejoicing in that Gift, we have so often adulterated it by being "wise in your own eyes."

"*Woe unto them that are wise in their own eyes, and prudent in their own sight!*"

"*Woe unto them that are mighty to drink wine, and men of strength to mingle strong drink.*"

Isaiah 5:21-22

"*And this have ye done again, covering the Altar of the Lord with tears, with weeping, and with crying out, insomuch that He regardeth not the offering any more, or receive it with Good will at your hand.*

"*Yet ye say, Wherefore? Because the Lord hath been witness between thee and the Wife of thy youth, against whom thou hast dealt treacherously: yet She is thy companion, and the Wife of thy Covenant.*

"*And did He not make One? Yet had He the residue of the Spirit. And wherefore One? That He might seek a Godly seed. Therefore take heed to your spirit, and let none deal treacherously against the Wife of his youth.*

"*For the Lord, the God of Israel, saith that He hateth putting away: for one covereth violence with his garment, saith the Lord of hosts: therefore take heed to your spirit, that ye deal not treacherously.*

"*Ye have wearied the Lord with your words. Yet ye say, Wherein have we wearied Him? When ye say, Every one that doeth evil is Good in the sight of the Lord, and He delighteth in them; or, Where is the God of Judgment?*"

Malachi 2:13-17

The Lord describes Himself as *the Amen.*

The Words: *Therefore take heed to your spirit, and let none deal treacherously against the Wife of his youth* describe your need to keep the fidelity between Divine Truth and the Doctrine of the Lord's Righteousness Sacred within your life.

The Words: *Yet ye say, Wherefore?* and *Wherein have we wearied Him?* reveal the refusal to acknowledge the falsities within the errant philosophies and misleading religious doctrines that continually attempt to adulterate that spiritual understanding.

And so, the Lord warns us that all our *"tears, with weeping, and with crying out"* will be of no avail unless we offer Him that which He Values most of all from us.

To do so is to use Good Judgment in the Name of the Lord. Doing otherwise has caused humanity more self-inflicted mental, emotional, and spiritual harm and suffering than they will ever believe.

> "And unto the angel of the church of Laodiceans write; These things saith the Amen, the Faithful and True Witness, the Beginning of the Creation of God.
>
> "I know thy works, that thou are neither cold nor hot: I would though wert cold or hot.
>
> Revelation 3:14–15

The Lord describes Himself as "the Amen" because He is Divine Truth Himself. As such, He describes Himself as "the Faithful and True Witness" Who has been teaching us about the Way we may receive, retain, and forever share the Goodness of His Love for us since *"the Beginning of the Creation of God."*

Being within you, the Lord also Testifies that He knows all things that you think, feel, and do in life. He teaches you that He knows when you are willing to live your life in the Light of His Righteousness and treat others likewise, and when you are not.

The Words: *I know thy works, that thou are neither cold nor hot* address proclaiming to be fully committed to living your life in that Light, when you are not.

Knowing better, yet defending your lack of commitment with doctrinal half-truths turns you into a religious hypocrite. And because hypocrisy causes the worst self-inflicted harm of all to your mind, heart, and soul, the Lord laments, "I would thou wert cold or hot."

"So then because thou art lukewarm, and neither cold nor hot, I will spew thee out of My mouth."

Revelation 3:16

And so, just as in the Story of Jonas, the Lord teaches you in Revelation about the dangers of being lukewarm in your commitment to keep the fidelity between Divine Truth and the Doctrine of His Righteousness Sacred within your life. Adulterating that understanding by attempting to justify any alternative philosophy or religious doctrine within your life is incompatible with the ability to retain the Goodness of His Love within your soul.

"They Gave Him vinegar to drink mingled with gall: and when he has tasted thereof, He would not drink."

Matthew 27:34

Reflections

The Lord has Given you this Seventh Commandment, "Thou shalt not commit adultery" so that you might know the overriding importance of keeping the fidelity of your physical and spiritual wedding vows Sacred in all you think, feel and do.

He teaches you that doing so completes a Holy union between His Truth and the Doctrine of His Righteousness within your soul. He teaches you that this union will Bless you with innermost happiness and genuine fulfillment in this life, and most especially will Bless you abundantly with these invaluable Wedding Gifts in the life to come.

He teaches you that this Commandment is seamlessly woven together with all His other Commandments. He Calls upon you to realize that if you adulterate one of them, you become guilty of adulterating all of them.

He suffered greatly to reestablish this Holy understanding among all the peoples of the world, for our Good and for the Good of all around us.

> "For as Jonas was three Days and three nights in the Whale's belly; so shall the Son of man be three Days and three nights in the heart of the earth.
>
> "The men of Nineveh shall rise in Judgment with this generation, and shall condemn it: because they repented at the preaching of Jonas; and behold, a Greater than Jonas is here."
>
> Matthew 12:40–41

> "If ye love Me, keep My Commandments."
>
> John 14:15

YOU SHALL NOT STEAL.

20
Dishonesty

Thieves should take great pause
to reconsider their selfish motives.

" Thou shalt not steal. "

Exodus 20:15

Introducing The Eighth Commandment

Stealing causes harm in countless ways. As dear and as necessary as they may
be, when physical possessions are stolen, the loss suffered is only incidental
to the injury thieves cause to the victim's mental, emotional, and spiritual
wellbeing. Doors open quickly for thoughts and feelings of anger, hatred,
and revenge to enter in. Despair, hopelessness, loss of self-esteem, and
feelings of self-pity also find easy access into their minds and hearts. All
these lead to mistrust, anxiety, depression, and worse, robbing the victim of
the innocence and security they need to live in Peace and Goodwill toward
others. Stealing has the potential to harm people for generations to come.

" Whoso is partner with a thief hateth his own soul: he heareth
cursing and betrayeth it not. "

Proverbs 29:24

Those who justify stealing material, intellectual, and emotional properties
have no idea of the individual and collective internal harm they are inflicting

upon others, and more often than not, they do not care. Yet thieves should take great pause to reconsider their selfish motives, for the greatest harm of all is the harm they will cause to return upon themselves.

Throughout the entire Bible, the Lord warns you about those dangers. And with "His still small Voice" within you, He warns you time and time again. Those who scoff at these warnings are portrayed by the Words: *he heareth cursing and betrayeth it not.*

~

"Thus saith the Lord, The Heaven is My Throne, and the earth is My footstool: where is the house that ye build unto Me? And where is the place of My Rest?"

Isaiah 66:1

Spiritually, your mind and heart are described as a *house* in the Bible. The Lord teaches you that unless you build the integrity of your mind and heart into a structure that welcomes His Righteousness into your life, you will never find Rest within your soul. Spiritually, His Truth acts as the Cornerstone for the foundation of that structure. From the True Thoughts and Unselfish Affections you chose to *host* there, you become described as His spiritual *storehouse*.

"Now he that planteth and he that watereth are One: and every man shall receive his own reward according to his own labor.

"For we are laborers together with God: ye are God's husbandry, ye are God's building."

1 Corinthians 3:8–9

Philosophical and Religious Theft

Everywhere the Lord counsels you not to steal one precious moment from the time He has Given you to build a place for His Abode within your life. He implores you to refrain from taking anything away from allowing Him to come into your mind and heart, and change everything within you for the Better. Staying awake and aware of that remembrance is all-important for your innermost happiness and genuine fulfillment in this life, and most especially for their continuing growth and prosperity in the life to come.

> *"Lift up your heads, O ye gates; and be ye Lift Up, ye Everlasting Doors: and the King of Glory shall come in."*
>
> Psalms 24:7

Valuing any philosophy or religious doctrine that places itself above acknowledging that the Principles of Righteousness are Primary for the Way you must live your life closes your mind and heart to acknowledging the most important things of all. They cause a spiritual blindness and deafness that act to rob you of comprehending what constitutes the Opportunity of your lifetime. The proponents of those errant philosophies and misleading religious doctrines will always deny that theft, claiming that they are "innocent" and even "righteous" in all their "ways."

Will a man rob God?

> *"Will a man rob God? Yet ye have robbed Me. But ye say, Wherein have we robbed Thee? In tithes and offerings.*
>
> *"Ye are cursed with a curse: for ye have robbed Me, even this whole nation."*
>
> Malachi 3:8–9

With the Words: *Will a man rob God?* the Lord is asking you to recognize what deprives Him from fulfilling His Purpose for the Creation of your soul.

With the Words: *But ye say, Wherein have we robbed Thee?* He is asking you to recognize any misleading thoughts and wayward affections that attempt to stand in the Rightful Place of what must always be and remain your First Love.

Throughout the Bible, the number "ten" pertains to the Lord's Commandments. "Tithes" describe your willing efforts to abide by each, and every Righteous Principle existing within them. Making those efforts "offers" the Lord the most valuable things of all, for from them you allow Him to expand the Heavens from people on earth, like you!

The Words: *Ye are cursed with a curse: for ye have robbed Me* reveal the effects of substituting counterfeit beliefs to stand in the Rightful Place of that Sacred understanding. They act to steal that Opportunity away from the Lord Himself.

The Words: *even this whole nation* describe the consequent loss of Peace and Goodness that your thefts can cause within generations to come.

~

"*Now Jacob's Well was there. Jesus therefore, being wearied with His Journey, sat thus on the Well; and it was about the sixth hour.*"

John 4:6

Since the Beginning of our existence, the Lord has been teaching us about the Way we must live our lives. Each time He approaches you in Truth, Compassion, and Goodwill from His Love for you, freely Offering you spiritual knowledge about why and how you must live. Yet He leaves it up to you to heed His Testimony to you by living your life accordingly. It is your responsibility to place those things First within your life. Only you can do it!

~

> "*Bring ye all the tithes into the storehouse, that there may be Meat in Mine House, and prove Me now herewith, saith the Lord of hosts, if I will not open you the Windows of Heaven, and pour you out a Blessing, that there shall not be room enough to receive it.*"
>
> Malachi 3:10

Realizing that the Lord is inviting you to "prove" Him is quite amazing. The Humility of that statement is remarkable. Yet everywhere, He implores you to do so. And as you are wise enough, brave enough, and humble enough to do so, He Promises to validate the Truth of His Testimony to you by pouring out an abundance of spiritual Blessings that will far exceed your greatest expectations.

The Words: *and prove Me now herewith, saith the Lord of hosts, if I will not open you the Windows of Heaven, and pour you out a Blessing, that there shall not be room enough to receive it* deliver that incomparable Offer. Shall you not offer up the courage, humility, and wisdom to prove the validity of that Offer for yourself?

> "*And the Lord Spake unto Moses, saying,*
>
> "*Speak unto the children of Israel, that they bring Me an offering: of every man that giveth it willingly with his heart ye shall take My Offering.*"
>
> Exodus 25:1–2

Spiritually, speaking "unto Moses" describes the Lord addressing your need to understand the overriding importance of abiding by His Commandments in all you think, feel, and do.

The Words: *Speak unto the children of Israel, that they bring Me an offering* express His calling upon your spiritual sensibilities to do so. As you willfully make those "offerings," nothing withheld, He Promises to return them with extraordinary and invaluable "Offerings" of His Own.

> *In My Father's House are many Mansions: if it were not so, I would have told you. I go to prepare a Place for you.*
>
> *And if I go and prepare a Place for you, I will come again, and receive you unto Myself; that where I am, there ye may be also.*
>
> *And whither I go ye know, and the Way ye know.*
>
> John 14:2-4

Spiritual Dishonesty

> *Take My yoke upon you, and learn of Me; for I am meek and lowly in Heart: and ye shall find Rest unto your souls.*
>
> Matthew 11:29

In both the Old and New Testaments, the Lord calls upon you to take on the Burden of working with Him to develop the spiritual potential of your mind, heart, and soul. Yet so many times throughout our history we have refused to do so, instead placing our trust and faith in "thoughts formed from the imaginations" of our own hearts. Those "thoughts" have so often robbed us from understanding what will bring the Goodness of His Love to Rest within us, and what will not.

> *If the thief be not found, then the master of the house shall be brought unto the Judges, to see whether he have put his hand unto his neighbor's Goods.*
>
> Exodus 22:8

Throughout Scripture, the Lord asks you to realize that ultimately, we will all be brought into the Light of His Righteousness. He teaches you about the transparency that Light will reveal about the integrity of your thoughts and affections.

The Words: *If the thief not be found, then the master of the house shall be brought unto the Judges* teach you about the futility of thinking that you can hide yourself "from the presence of the Lord God amongst the trees of the Garden" just as Adam and Eve tried to do.

The Words: *to see whether he have put his hand unto his neighbor's Goods* illustrate your inability to use justifications of your own making as "aprons" to cover over what has become openly exposed in that Light.

> "Woe unto him that buildeth his house by unrighteousness, and his chambers by wrong; that useth his neighbor's service without wages, and giveth Him not for His Work;
>
> "That saith, I will build me a wide house and large chambers, and cutteth him out windows; and it is ceiled with cedar, and painted with vermilion."
>
> Jeremiah 22:13–14

The Words: *Woe unto him that buildeth his house by unrighteousness* describe attempting to develop the integrity of your internal character based upon faulty foundations.

The Words: *and his chambers by wrong* developing errant conclusions about what must always be, and remain, your First Works.

Spiritually, your *neighbor* is descriptive of all True Thoughts and Unselfish Affections that reside in very close proximity to your mind and heart. To use their *service without wages* is to deny your need to love them in the Way the Lord Loves you. Such abuse is described as he who *has giveth Him not for His Work.*

Throughout the entire Bible, the Lord teaches you that the only currency which is acceptable to Him consists of your honest, sincere, and humble willingness to seek His Righteousness First in all you think, feel, and do. Those offerings are invaluable to Him, for from them, He Creates and stretches forth the Heavens, filling them from people on earth. Everywhere He teaches you never to withhold that currency from Him, or exchange it for something you, or others have minted of yourselves, for to Him it is by far the most valuable currency of all!

The Words: *That saith, I will build me a wide house and large chambers* depict broad misrepresentations about what will develop and fulfill the spiritual potential of your mind, heart, and soul.

The Words: *and cutteth him out windows* explain attempting to make those misrepresentations appear "enlightening" when they are anything but.

The Words: *and it is ceiled with cedar* describe using letter-of-the-Word misinterpretations to make spiritual half-truths seem authentic, when they are not.

The Words: and *painted with vermilion* portray attempting to make those spiritual half-truths seem attractive by covering them over with false promises about what will bring innermost happiness and genuine fulfillment into your life. And although the color vermilion may seem attractive on the outside, it is made up of elements which are poisonous to human life. It thereby depicts enticing the innocent and unsuspecting to enter into what is deadly to their mental, emotional, and spiritual wellbeing.

~

He teaches you to stay spiritually sober, awake, and aware.

In common language, if you create broad misrepresentations about what brings lasting happiness and internal fulfillment into your life, you become described as someone who lives in their own fantasy world. Mentally, emotionally, and spiritually you have formed, shaped, and moved into a "place" of your own making.

Doing so steals your thoughts and affections away from the Lord's Quest to lead you into the Mansions of His "Father's House." Who do you think you're kidding?

> "*Am I a God at hand, saith the Lord, and not a God afar off?*
>
> "*Can any hide himself in secret places that I shall not See him? saith the Lord. Do not I fill Heaven and earth, saith the Lord?*"
>
> Jeremiah 23:23–24

~

Throughout the Bible, the Lord warns you against any form of physical, intellectual, emotional, or spiritual theft. He warns against believing that you can justify those thefts by hiding behind anything of your own making. Rather, He teaches you to stay spiritually sober, awake, and aware, ready to recognize anything, or any one, who would attempt to steal that spiritual understanding away from you.

> "*They shall run to and fro in the City; they shall run upon the wall, they shall climb up upon the houses; they shall enter in at the windows like a thief.*"
>
> Joel 2:9

The Words: *They shall run to and fro in the City* explain the zeal and illusiveness of misleading beliefs attempting to convince you that their "ways" alone are "true" and "right." With great fanfare, they seek to undermine the Doctrine of Righteousness within your life.

The Words: *they shall climb up upon the houses, they shall enter in at the windows like a thief* expose their uninvited invasiveness into your thoughts and affections.

And so everywhere, the Lord implores you to remember to reverence, defend, and honor the Doctrine which comes *down out of Heaven, prepared as a Bride adorned for Her Husband* with all your mind, heart, and strength.

> *And now, Israel, what doth the Lord thy God require of thee, but to fear the Lord thy God, to walk in all His Ways, and to love Him, and to serve the Lord thy God with all thy heart and with all thy soul,*
>
> *To keep the Commandments of the Lord, and His Statutes, which I Command thee this Day for thy Good?*
>
> Deuteronomy 10:12–13

> *The Lord by Wisdom hath founded the earth; by understanding hath He established the Heavens.*
>
> Proverbs 3:19

> *If ye keep My Commandments, ye shall abide in My Love; even as I have kept My Father's Commandments, and abide in His Love.*
>
> John 15:10

> "*Therefore whosoever heareth these sayings of mine, and doeth them, I will liken him unto a wise man, which built his house upon a Rock.*
>
> "*And the rain descended, and the floods came, and the winds blew, and beat upon that house; and it fell not: for it was founded upon a Rock.*
>
> "*And everyone that heareth these Sayings of mine, and doeth them not, shall be likened unto a foolish man, which built his house upon the sand:*
>
> "*And the rain descended, and the floods came, and the winds blew, and beat upon that house; and it fell: and great was the fall of it.*"
>
> Matthew 7:24–27

These Words reveal how the Lord establishes the Principles of His Righteousness to act as the structure for the Way you must live your life. His Divine Truth acts as the Cornerstone which secures that structure to Stand firm within your soul.

The Words: *Therefore whosoever heareth these sayings of mine, and doeth them, I will liken him unto a wise man, which built his house upon a Rock* lay open that spiritual Reality. Your need to be honest about the Implications of these Words cannot be overstated.

21

Mental, Emotional, and Spiritual Harm ....

He warns you that losing your willingness to do so
will cause you to come into a very dark and cold place
of your own making.

> *Ye are the salt of the earth: but if the salt have lost his savour,*
> *wherein shall it be salted? It is thenceforth good for nothing,*
> *but to be cast out, and to be trodden under foot of men.*
>
> Matthew 5:13

Your willingness to live your life in the Way which the Lord is Showing you that you must is spiritually described as "the salt of the earth." Losing that willingness is spiritually descriptive of "salt" which has "lost his savour."

The Words: *It is thenceforth good for nothing* communicate without that willingness, anything you may have learned about the Truth of Love becomes useless in providing for the Good of your mental, emotional, and spiritual wellbeing.

The Words: *but to be cast out* reveal that eventually, that loss will regulate anything you have learned from the Lord to a very low status within your life.

The Words: *and to be trodden under foot of men* express that losing that esteem will cause you to belittle the importance of what the Lord has

Labored so greatly to teach you about why and how you must live your life. That belittling will soon cause you to lose all spiritual sensibility about the most important things of all.

> "*For I say unto you, That unto every one which hath shall be Given; and from him that hath not, even that he hath shall be taken away from him.*"
>
> Luke 19:26

This verse describes the downward spiral of allowing yourself to lose reverence for the importance of seeking Righteousness from the Lord First, in all you think, feel and do in life. Doing so steals away your spiritual sensibilities, causing you to come into a very dark and cold place of your own making.

> "*The fear of the Lord is the beginning of Wisdom: and the knowledge of the Holy is understanding.*
>
> "*For by Me thy Days shall be multiplied and the years of thy Life shall be increased.*
>
> "*If thou be wise, thou shalt be wise for thyself: but if thou scornest, thou alone shalt bear it.*"
>
> Proverbs 9:10–12

Throughout the entire Bible, the Lord teaches you about spiritual causes and effects. He implores you to keep your understanding about these things burning Brightly within your life. Everywhere He warns you that losing your willingness to do so will eventually cause you great mental, emotional, and spiritual harm. "Kicking" against those Precepts is self-defeating.

The Lord Promises to protect you from spiritual harm.

"Nevertheless I have somewhat against thee, because thou hast left thy First Love.

"Remember therefore from whence thou art fallen, and repent, and do the First Works; or else I will come unto thee quickly, and will remove thy Candlestick out of His Place, except thou repent."

Revelation 2:4–5

How much more clearly can the Lord describe what must always be, and remain your First Love? And how much more clearly can He explain what must always be, and remain your First Works? And how much more clearly can He explain the consequence of not submitting yourself to reverencing that spiritual understanding in mind, heart, and deed?

Jesus Christ calls Peter and Andrew. by Louise Seymour Houghton

~

Abiding by what the Lord is teaching you about why and how you must live your life will require you to turn away from your self-serving thoughts, selfish desires and their corresponding behaviors, and leave them behind. That turning away and leaving behind must always be made in reverence for His Love for you and in reverence for the Good of all those around you. Acknowledging this spiritual Truth, yet living your life hypocritically will eventually rob you of the Opportunity of your lifetime.

~

> "Wherefore the Lord said, Forasmuch as this people draw near Me with their mouth, and with their lips do honor Me, but have removed their heart far from Me, and their fear toward Me is taught by the precept of men:
>
> "Therefore, behold, I will proceed to do a marvelous Work among this people, even a marvelous Work and a wonder: for the Wisdom of their wise men shall perish, and the understanding of their prudent men shall be hid."
>
> Isaiah 29:13–14

Because hypocrisy causes the greatest mental, emotional, and spiritual harm of all, the Lord removes spiritual understanding from those who would otherwise abuse it. And although it may not appear so on the surface, that removal is Merciful, for it moderates the severity of the damage hypocrisy does to their mind, hearts, and souls.

The Words: *Therefore, behold, I will proceed to do a marvelous Work among this people, even a marvelous Work and a wonder: for the Wisdom of their wise men shall perish, and the understanding of their prudent men shall be hid* reveal that moderation occurring among those who are described in

Isaiah 5:21 as having become "wise in their own eyes and prudent in their own sight."

> *Oh how great is Thy Goodness, which Thou hast laid up for them that fear Thee; which Thou hast wrought for them that trust in Thee before the sons of men!*
>
> *Thou shalt hide them in the secret of Thy Presence from the pride of man: Thou shalt keep them secretly in a Pavilion from the strife of tongues.*
>
> Psalms 31:19–20

Without the honest, sincere, and humble willingness to accept and apply spiritual understanding in the Way the Lord has Shown you that you must, the Promises of His Testimony to you will never come into fruition within your life. Arguing against that understanding is what divides His Testimony into disjointed pieces, forming spiritual half-truths devised "from the strife of tongues." As so, in Order to protect our ability to receive, retain, and forever share in the incomparable Goodness of His Love for us, He hides that spiritual understanding "from the pride of man."

> *Be watchful, and strengthen the things which remain, that are ready to die: for I have not found thy works perfect before God.*
>
> *Remember therefore how thou hast received and heard, and hold fast, and repent. If therefore thou shalt not watch, I will come upon thee as a thief, and thou shalt not know what hour I shall come upon thee.*
>
> Revelation 3:2–3

To be "watchful" is spiritually descriptive of staying attentive to living your life according to the Principles of the Lord's Righteousness. To "strengthen the things which remain" is to faithfully and continually renew your willingness to do so, nothing withheld.

The Words: *that are ready to die* describe the effects of the philosophical and doctrinal falsities which would otherwise undermine the spiritual integrity of your soul.

The Words: *for I have not found thy works perfect before God* demonstrate how the Lord uses His Words to ask you to reexamine your thoughts and affections in the Light of His Righteousness while you still have the spiritual sensibility to do so.

To "Remember therefore how thou hast received and heard" is to stay mindful of what He has taught you about what must always be, and remain, your First Works. To "hold fast" describes cherishing and abiding by that understanding throughout the entirety of your spiritual journey in this world. And to "repent" describes turning away from whatever you have used to convince yourself, or others, about the safety of believing otherwise.

The Words: *If therefore thou shalt not watch* tell of the Lord's warning you about the danger of not being attentive to what He is, has, and forever will be Showing you to be True and Right. Declaring that you do understand Him, yet not willfully applying that understanding to all that you think, feel, and do in life will cause you to suffer the greatest mental, emotional, and spiritual misfortunes of all.

Yet, the pride of self-intelligence will never blame itself for being the cause of those misfortunes. Instead, it will attempt to blame the Lord Himself!

The Words: *I will come on thee as a thief* depict the self-inflicted loss of spiritual understanding within those who continue to insist that their thoughts are higher than His Thoughts. That loss results quickly within all who would otherwise misuse the meaning and implications of His Testimony to us.

~

The Lord has established the Principles of His Righteousness to act as Standards to protect you from mental, emotional, and spiritual harm. He has made those Sacred Principles internally known to you since your earliest childhood. It is much better for you to lose that understanding than to misuse it.

And it is much, much better to lose that understanding than to become "angry" against it, or to call it "foolish," or to "persecute" it by hypocritically "trodding" it "underfoot."

> "*Verily I say unto you, All sins shall be forgiven unto the sons of men, and blasphemies wherewith soever they shall blaspheme:*
>
> "*But he that shall blaspheme against the Holy Ghost hath never forgiveness, but is in danger of eternal damnation.*"
>
> Mark 3:28–29

At the time of the Lord's advent into our world, religious thought and practice had become rife with spiritual hypocrisy. Letter-of-the-Word misinterpretations about Scripture were distorting the meaning of the Lord's Testimony to humanity. Counterfeit edicts formed from those misinterpretations were made strictly for the benefit of the status, authority, and enrichment of the prevailing religious institutions, authorities, and leaders of that time. Delusions of grandeur ran rabid.

The Lord asks you to take pause and look within yourself.

The worst of these offenses invoked using the history and Miracles described in the Bible to promote their own "indisputable religious" self-merit. Prideful boasts about their own irrefutable correctness had turned God's Laws into "men's laws." By doing so, the religious teachers and leaders of that time were turning spiritual Light into spiritual darkness. Had that darkness been allowed to prevail, no one could have found their Way back into the Lord's Embrace.

And so, a cry came up from the remnant of spiritual sensibilities remaining within the human race, imploring the Lord to have Compassion and Mercy upon the remaining Goodness within our souls. And so, as He Promised within Genesis 9:9–17, He came in our world to restore the spiritual understanding we so greatly needed to once again find our Way back into His Embrace, before it became too late.

> "*And Jesus went into the temple of God, and cast out all them that sold and bought in the temple, and overthrew the tables of the moneychangers, and the seats of them that sold doves.*
>
> "*And said unto them, It is written, My House shall be called the House of prayer; but ye have made it a den of thieves.*"
>
> Matthew 21:12-13

Throughout history, countless false and misleading arguments have been devised to dilute, dismiss, discredit, defile, and reject the spiritual meaning, Purpose, and Intent of the Lord's Testimony to us. Those arguments are then "sold" as exclusive assurances about what will bring salvation, genuine happiness, and lasting "peace" into our lives.

With great fanfare, their proponents attempt to convince you to buy into their misguided beliefs. They shame you if you beg to differ with any of their false doctrinal proclamations.

Instead of authentic spiritual knowledge, they offer you spiritual half-truths in an attempt to justify their own correctness. The Lord came into your world to confront them, described here as overthrowing "the tables of the moneychangers, and the seats of them that sold doves."

He did so because of the dangers those misguided beliefs posed to the Goodness of His Love still remaining within our souls.

> "And Jesus said, For Judgment I am come this world, that they
> which see not might see, and they which see might be made blind.

> "And some of the Pharisees which were with Him heard these
> Words, and said unto him, Are we blind also?

> "Jesus said unto them, if ye were blind, ye should have no sin:
> but now ye say; We see; therefore your sin remaineth."
>
> John 9:39–41

Although these Words may be difficult for those wholly vested in their own errant philosophies and misleading religious doctrines to accept, they should be cherished. They should also be reverenced because they come from a Loving God who beckons us all to receive a True understanding about the Way to our salvation and deliverance into an eternal Heavenly state of being.

And so, the Lord asks each of us to take pause and look within ourselves. He asks us to use Good Judgment when claiming that we understand His Testimony to us. It is one thing to be ignorant of that Holy understanding, yet it is quite different to claim to have received it, and then allow yourself to substitute other "things" to supersede it.

> "And it come to pass, when he hearth the Words of this curse, that
> he bless himself in his heart, saying, I shall have peace, though
> I walk in the imagination of mine heart, to add drunkenness
> to thirst."
>
> Deuteronomy 29:19

> "O that they were wise, that they understood this, that they
> would consider their latter end!"
>
> Deuteronomy 32:29

*" Watch therefore: for ye know not what hour your Lord doth
come.*

*" But know this, that if the Goodman of the house had known in
what watch the thief would come, he would have watched, and
would not have suffered his house to be broken up.*

*" Therefore be ye also ready: for in such an hour as ye think not
the Son of man cometh. "*

Matthew 24:42–44

~

Anyone who attempts to teach others about the meaning and Intent of
Scripture assumes a tremendous personal responsibility. By affecting others
with beliefs about what they must value most in life, they are treading on
Holy ground. That "ground" is Holy because it contains our potential to
become seeded, grow, and prosper in the Ways of the Lord.

And so, the Lord warns all who claim religious authority over others to
walk honestly, sincerely, and humbly in the Paths of His Righteousness,
nothing withheld. He teaches all of us to Place those Holy Principles First
within our lives, for they alone form the structure for all things True and
Good to come into, remain, and find Rest within our souls.

*" Verily, Verily, I say unto you, He that entereth not by the Door
unto the sheepfold, but climbeth up some other way, the same is
a thief and a robber. "*

John 10:1

*" The thief cometh not, but for to steal, and to kill, and to
destroy: I am come that they might have Life, and that they
might have it more Abundantly. "*

John 10:10

Conversion of St Paul on the road to Damascus. Wood engraving.

Paul, as an enforcer of the religious authority of his time, came to learn many of these lessons from the Lord the hard way. And because he had caused so much harm to others, he dedicated the rest of his life to teaching all who would listen to him about what the Lord had Shown him to be True and Right. With great determination, he taught everyone, Jews and Gentiles alike, about the dangers of placing anything in front of that spiritual understanding before it became too late.

> *Thou therefore which teachest another, teachest thou not thyself?*
> *thou that preachest a man should not steal, dost thou steal?*
> Romans 2:21

> *Let him that stole steal no more: but rather let him labor,*
> *working with his hands the thing which is Good, that he may*
> *have to give to him that needeth.*
> Ephesians 4:28

> *But ye, brethren, are not in darkness, that that Day should*
> *overtake you as a thief.*

> *Ye are all the children of Light, and the children of the Day:*
> *we are not of the night, nor of darkness.*
> 1 Thessalonians 5:4–5

Reflections

The Lord has Given us this Eighth Commandment, "thou shalt not steal" to warn us about the dangers of robbing ourselves, or others, from receiving, retaining, and forever sharing in the Joy and Goodness of His Love for us.

He is teaching you that there is nothing you can use to justify that theft. Rather, He teaches you that it is your responsibility to keep the Principles of His Righteousness as your *First Love,* and to willingly do the *Works* required of you to do so. Withhold nothing.

Everywhere He Testifies that doing so is the greatest Opportunity of your lifetime. That Message is very simple to understand! He requires nothing else from you.

> "*But seek First the Kingdom of God, and His Righteousness; and all these things shall be added unto you.*"
>
> Matthew 6:33

22

False Justifications

There are three categories of false witnesses
that you must always guard against.

> *"Thou shalt not bear false witness against thy neighbor."*
>
> Exodus 20:16

*A*s a Loving Father, the Lord warns you not to deceive yourself, or others, about how you may find inmost Joy and everlasting fulfillment in life. Rather, He Offers you Wisdom about that Divine Truth united with Good Doctrine about the Way you may receive, retain, and forever share in those incomparable Blessings.

> *"Hear, O Israel: The Lord our God is One Lord.*
>
> *"And thou shalt love the Lord thy God with all thine heart, and with all thy soul, and with all thy might.*
>
> *"And these Words, which I Command thee this Day, shall be in thine heart;*
>
> *"And thou shalt teach them diligently unto thy children, and shalt talk of them when thou sittest in thine house, and when thou walkest by the Way, and when thou liest down, and when thou risest up.*

> *"And thou shalt bind them for a Sign upon thine hand, and they shall be as Frontlets between thine eyes.*
>
> *"And thou shalt write them upon the posts of thine house, and on thy gates."*
>
> Deuteronomy 6:4–9

To "love the Lord thy God with all thine heart, and with all thy soul, and with all thy might" requires your reverent willingness to live your life honestly, sincerely, and humbly as you apply the Principles of His Righteousness, to each and every aspect of your life, nothing withheld.

The Words: *And these Words which I Command thee this Day shall be in thine heart* reveal the Lord's Will for you to cherish His Testimony to you about these things above all else.

The Words: *And thou shalt teach them diligently unto thy children, and shall talk of them when thou sittest in thine house, and when thou walkest by the Way, and when thou liest down, and when thou risest up* describe how these Holy Principles must be honored into perpetuity in all you think, feel, and do.

That these Sacred Principles must be kept as your Single most important focus in life is portrayed by the verse "And thou shalt bind them for a Sign upon thine hand, and they shall be as Frontlets between thine eyes."

The Words: *And thou shalt write them upon the posts of thine house, and on thy gates* illuminate your need to always remember why and how you must.

> *"And it shall be, when the Lord thy God shall have brought thee into the Land which He sware unto thy fathers, to Abraham, to Isaac, and to Jacob, to Give thee Great and Goodly Cities, which thou buildest not.*

"And houses full of all Good things, which thou filledst not, and Wells digged, which thou diggedst not, Vinyards and Olive trees, which thou plantedst not; when thou shalt have eaten and be full;

"Then beware lest thou forget the Lord, which brought thee forth out of the land of Egypt, from the house of bondage."

Deuteronomy 6:10–12

Throughout the Bible, the Lord Promises that as you live your life according to what He has Shown you to be True and Right, He will save you from mental, emotional, and spiritual harm and lead you into an eternal state of Heavenly Joy.

The Words: *And it shall be, when the Lord thy God shall have brought thee into the Land which He sware unto thy fathers, to Abraham, to Isaac, and to Jacob, to Give thee Great and Goodly Cities, which thou buildest not. And houses full of all Good things, which thou filledst not, and Wells digged, which thou diggedst not, Vineyards and Olive trees, which thou plantedst not; when thou shalt have eaten and be full* describe the fulfillment of that Sacred Promise.

Spiritually, "Great and Goodly Cities" depict all philosophies and doctrines connected through the Principles of Righteousness. "Houses full of all Good things" describe those philosophies and doctrines hosting all things True and Right within their belief structures. "Wells" portray deep and pure spiritual knowledge about that Divine Truth. "Vineyards" describe the

> It is your responsibility to abide by the Lord's Testimony about the Way you must live your life.

Goodness of Unselfish Love coming into fruition within your life. "Olive trees" describe the humility needed to sustain by that Holy understanding.

These are all described as things you did not *build, fill, dig,* or *plant* yourself because they are brought forth within you by the Lord as you allow Him to reform you and transform you into the person that He has Purposed for you to become.

> *"And He humbled thee, and suffered thee to hunger, and fed thee with manna, which thou knewest not; neither did thy fathers know; that He might make thee know that man doth not Live by Bread only, but by every Word that proceedeth out of the mouth of the Lord doth man Live."*
>
> Deuteronomy 8:3

It is your responsibility to abide by the Lord's Testimony to you about the Way you must live your life. In no uncertain terms, He warns you about the dangers of thinking otherwise. The Words: *Then beware lest thou forget the Lord, which brought thee forth out of the land of Egypt, from the house of bondage* underscore your need to remember why and how you must.

> *"Thou shalt not go up and down as a talebearer among thy people: neither shalt thou stand against the blood of thy neighbor: I am the Lord.*
>
> *"Thou shalt not hate thy brother in thine heart: thou shalt in any wise rebuke thy neighbor, and not suffer sin upon him.*
>
> *"Thou shalt not avenge, nor bear any grudge against the children of thy people, but thou shalt love thy neighbor as thyself: I am the Lord."*
>
> Leviticus 19:16–18

Clinging onto alternative beliefs of any sort, or conjuring up new ones of your own making will cause you to become a false witness to everything the Lord has Labored so greatly to teach you through the Law and the prophets, *and* during His advent into our world.

> *"And one of the scribes came, and having heard them reasoning together, and perceiving that He had answered them well, asked Him, Which is the first Commandment of all?*

“*And Jesus answered him, The first of all the Commandments is, Hear, O Israel; The Lord our God is One Lord.*

“*And thou shalt love the Lord thy God with all thy heart, and with all thy soul, and with all thy mind, and with all thy strength: this is the first Commandment.*

“*And the second is like, namely this, thou shalt love thy neighbor as thyself. There is none other Commandment greater than these.*”

Mark 12:28–31

To "love the Lord thy God with all thy heart, and with all thy soul, and with all thy mind, and with all thy strength" requires your reverent willingness, spiritual sensibility, and inmost commitment to live your life according to His Commandments, nothing withheld. As you willingly do so, you will quickly discover that it is impossible to love the Lord above all else without also loving your neighbor as He has Loved you. It then becomes very apparent that these Two Commandments are One and the same. For that Reason, the Lord, Who is Righteousness Himself, proclaims in the Singular that "There is none other Commandment greater than these."

“*When therefore He was Risen from the dead, His disciples remembered that He had said this unto them; and they believed the Scripture, and the Word which Jesus had said.*”

John 2:22

~

We refer to those who share our values as our brothers and sisters. From the proximity of their thoughts and affections to our thoughts and affections, they are also described as our "neighbors." Throughout the Bible, the Thoughts and Affections that come forth from the Mind and Heart of the Lord are described in this very same manner.

To withhold doing Good to any of them is to resist giving the Lord His Just due. Attempting to justify that resistance with "thoughts formed from the imaginations" of your own heart is the very definition of bearing "false witness against thy neighbor."

> "Withhold not Good from them to Whom it is due, when it is in the power of thine hand to do it.
>
> "Say not unto thy neighbor, Go, and come again, and tomorrow I will give; when thou hast it by thee.
>
> "Devise not evil against thy neighbor, seeing He dwelleth securely by thee."
>
> Proverbs 3:27-29

> "And the King shall answer and say unto them, Verily I say unto you, Inasmuch as you have done it unto one of the least of these My brethren, ye have done it unto Me."
>
> Matthew 25:40

Spiritual Deceptions

They are cautionary flags waving at you ... beware. There are three categories of false witnesses that you must always guard against.

- The first consists of justifying lying to another person.

- The second exists within any secular philosophy or religious doctrine that adds or subtracts from the Lord's Testimony to you about why and how you must live your life.

- The third is believing that the Way to your salvation and deliverance into a Heavenly state of being is only accessible to those who belong to a particular religious denomination, regardless of their love for God, or how they have treated others throughout their lifetime in this world.

Each of these categories of false witness generates very misguided thinking.

Each presents a grave danger to your present and eternal mental, emotional, and spiritual wellbeing.

Each threatens the mental, emotional, and spiritual wellbeing of those around you.

Lies selfishly violate the trust and Goodwill existing within, between, and among people.

Each carries a cautionary flag waving at you … beware.

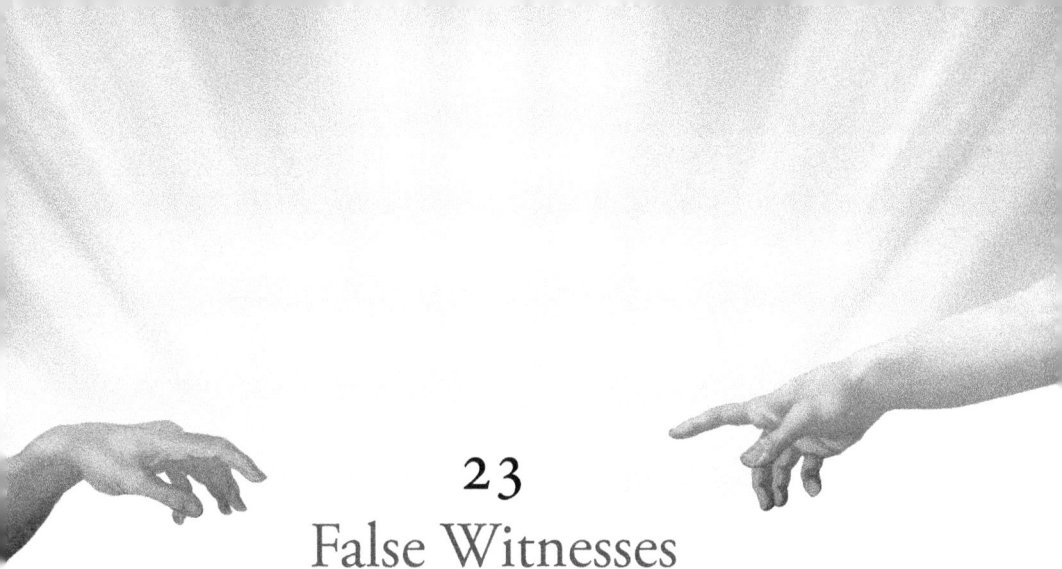

23
False Witnesses

The Bible is dedicated to warning you against
temptations that strive to seduce you into
becoming a false witness to the Truth of Love.

Lying ... the First Form of Being a False Witness

Lying to another person is diametrically opposed to loving others as the
Lord has Loved you. Lies selfishly violate the trust and Goodwill existing
within, between, and among people. And because all genuine Goodwill
originates from the Lord's Unselfish Love for you, lies violate your relationship with the Lord Himself. The internal harm they cause to your
mind and heart will eventually undermine the foundation that supports
the integrity of your soul.

It is the first witness: telling a lie to another person.

> *Be sober, be vigilant: because your adversary the devil, as a*
> *roaring lion, walketh about, seeking to whom he may devour:*
> 1 Peter 5:8

Arguments that seek to justify lies are described by Peter as a "roaring lion."
Those arguments are proud and loud, seeking to rip apart your willingness
to Place the Principles of the Lord's Righteousness above all else for the Way
you live your life. In this sense, "a den of lions" exemplify the dangers of
being thrown into a pack of lies that "bear false witness against thy neighbor."

> *"And when he came to the den, he cried with a lamentable voice unto Daniel: and the king spake and said unto Daniel, O Daniel, servant of the Living God, is thy God, Whom thou servest continually, able to deliver thee from the lions?*

> *"Then said Daniel unto the king, O King, Live for ever."*
>
> Daniel 6:20–21

Each time you remain diligent and Truthful in the face of arguments tempting you to lie to another person is each time you allow the Lord to protect you from mental, emotional, and spiritual harm. As you do so in reverence for your love for those around you, those arguments will lose their ability to destroy the Goodness of His Love from existing within your soul.

> *"For God is my King of Old, Working salvation in the midst of the earth."*
>
> Psalms 74:12

> *"Teach me, O Lord, the Way of Thy Statutes; and I shall keep it unto the end.*

> *"Give me understanding, and I shall keep thy Law; yea, I shall observe it with my whole heart."*
>
> Psalms 119:33–34

> *"Thy Testimonies are Wonderful: therefore doth my soul keep them.*

> *"The entrance of Thy Words Giveth Light; it Giveth understanding unto the simple."*
>
> Psalms 119:129–130

The way you live your life in this world will determine the state of your mental, emotional, and spiritual wellbeing in the life to come. In that life, your actual appearance, your surroundings, your relationships with others, and your relationship with the Lord Himself will become an image and a likeness to the choices you have made during your life on earth. Exercising your faith in the Lord by living your life according to what He has Shown you to be True and Right is the Key to opening the Rewards of Heavenly Love within your soul.

> *Verily I say unto you, Whatsoever ye shall bind on earth shall be bound in Heaven: and whatsoever ye shall loose on earth shall be loosed in Heaven.*
>
> Matthew 18:18

> *And behold, I come quickly; and My Reward is with Me, to Give every man according as his work shall be.*
>
> Revelation 22:12

There are no arguments you can put forth that are strong enough to change that spiritual Reality, try as you may. Spiritually, the Word "simple" does not mean the unintelligent; rather, it means the spiritually unconfused. The value of being honest about these things in all that you think, feel, and do cannot be overstated.

> *The Lord looked down from Heaven upon the children of men, to see if there were any that did understand, and seek God.*
>
> Psalms 14:2

> *So shall the King greatly desire thy beauty: for He is thy Lord; and worship thou Him.*
>
> Psalms 45:11

> *Let Thy Work appear unto Thy servants, and Thy Glory unto their children.*

> *"And let the Beauty of the Lord our God be upon us: and establish Thou the work of our hands upon us; yea, the work of our hands establish Thou it."*
>
> Psalms 90:16–17

Misrepresentation ... the Second Form of Being a False Witness

In Truth from His Love for you, the Lord teaches you about why and how you must live your life. Throughout the entire Bible, He Offers you the Wisdom, understanding, and Good Doctrine you need to Guide you and Comfort throughout your entire spiritual journey in this world.

It is your responsibility to keep and apply these Offerings to every aspect of your life without adding to or subtracting from their spiritual meaning and implications for what lays ahead.

Misrepresenting the spiritual meaning of the Lord's Testimony to you is the second form of becoming a false witness.

> *"In that Day shall this song be sung in the land of Judah; We have a strong City; Salvation will God appoint for walls and bulwarks.*
>
> *"Open ye the Gates, that the Righteous nation which keepeth the Truth may enter in."*
>
> Isaiah 26:1–2

As clear, concise, and harmonious as the Lyrics of the Lord's "Song" are, have always been, and forever will be, it is quite amazing how many times we have changed them to suit our own discordant melodies. How? By composing our own misleading lyrics to drown out our willingness to abide by the most important things of all.

He warns you against the dangers of falling for their seductive lyrics.

> *"And, lo, Thou art unto them as a very lovely Song of One that*
> *hath a pleasant Voice, and can play well on an instrument: for*
> *they hear Thy Words, but they do them not.* "
>
> Ezekiel 33:32

It is also quite amazing to consider how much of the Bible is dedicated to warning you against

The "tree of the knowledge of good and evil" describes what comes forth from the pride of our own self-intelligence.

becoming seduced by misleading "lyrics" formed from the imaginations of our own hearts. It is even more amazing to consider how many times we have taken those warnings in vain, regretfully making them a waste of the Lord's Divine "Breath" within our individual and collective lives.

> *"I have heard what the prophets said, that prophesy lies in My*
> *Name, saying, I have dreamed, I have dreamed.*
>
> *"How long shall this be in the heart of the prophets that prophesy*
> *lies? Yea, they are prophets of the deceit of their own heart.* "
>
> Jeremiah 23:25–26

Throughout the Bible, the Lord warns you about the dangers that false witnesses pose to your mental, emotional, and spiritual wellbeing. From beginning to ending, He warns you against the dangers of being seduced by their philosophical and doctrinal "babel," regardless of their proclamations to the contrary.

> *"And the Lord God Commanded the man, Saying, Of every tree*
> *of the Garden thou mayest freely eat:*

"*But of the tree of the knowledge of good and evil, thou shalt not eat of it: for in the Day that thou eastest thereof thou shalt surely die.*"

Genesis 2:16–17

Spiritually, "the tree of the knowledge of good and evil" describes what comes forth from the pride of your own self-intelligence. When you choose to trust in your own self-intelligence rather than trusting in the Lord's Testimony to you about why and how you must live your life, you risk becoming delusional about the things that matter most in life.

"*And the Lord Spoke unto Aaron, Saying,*

"*Do not drink wine nor strong drink, thou, nor thy sons with thee, when thou goest into the Tabernacle of the congregation, lest ye die: it shall be a Statute for ever throughout your generations:*

"*And hat ye may put difference between Holy and unholy, and between unclean and Clean;*

"*And that ye may teach the children of Israel all the Statutes which the Lord hath Spoken unto them by the hand of Moses.*"

Leviticus 10:8–11

Spiritually, Aaron represents your loftiest intentions to worship the Lord by seeking His Righteousness First in all you think, feel, and do. The Word "Wine" is used throughout the Bible to describe genuine spiritual understanding about the Truth of the Lord's Love for you. Mixing letter-of-the-Word misinterpretations about Scripture with misguided zeal to form spiritual half-truths is described here as "strong drink."

The Words: *Do not drink wine nor strong drink, thou, nor thy sons with thee, when thou goest into the Tabernacle of the congregation, lest ye die* reveal the Lord's warning against those intoxicating concoctions, as they are used to seduce what is innocent and unsuspecting within you.

He warns you because doing so will eventually ruin your ability to discern the differences between what is "Holy and unholy," and what is "Clean and unclean" in the choices you make in life.

The Words: *And that ye may teach the children of Israel all the Statutes which the Lord hath Spoken unto them by the hand of Moses* describe the importance of remaining a true witness to the things the Lord has Given you to cherish and propagate as True and Right within your life.

> "*A faithful witness will not lie: but a false witness will utter lies.*
>
> "*A scorner seeketh wisdom, and findeth it not: but knowledge is easy unto him that understandeth.*"
>
> Proverbs 14:5–6

> "*Blessed art thou, O land, when thy King is the son of nobles, and thy princes eat in due season, for strength, and not for drunkenness!*"
>
> Ecclesiastes 10:17

Throughout the Bible, the Word "land" is used to describe your spiritual potential to develop into the person that the Lord has Purposed for you to become. The Word "king" spiritually describes what you allow to govern your thoughts, feelings, and behaviors. The Word "nobles" describes what you esteem most in life. The Word "princes" describes the qualities and virtues that come forth from your ruling love.

When you acknowledge the Righteousness of the Lord to be your King and Savior, what then comes forth to Enlighten you about the Way you must live your life is "for strength, and not for drunkenness." For this reason, in Isaiah 9:6, the Lord is called the Prince of Peace. Your need to honor this spiritual understanding in all you think, feel, and do cannot be overstated. Convincing yourself otherwise will cause a self-inflicted spiritual darkness and coldness to overwhelm your spiritual sensibilities about the most important things of all.

> "And it came to pass, when he heareth the Words of this curse, that he bless himself in his heart, saying, I shall have peace, though I walk in the imagination of mine heart, to add drunkenness to thirst:
>
> "The Lord will not spare him, but then the anger of the Lord and His jealousy shall smoke against that man, and all the curses that are written in this Book shall lie upon him, and the Lord shall blot out his name from under Heaven."

Deuteronomy 29:19–20

Professing that "Faith Alone" in the Lord is Saving

Religious doctrines that profess that *faith alone* in the Lord is saving misrepresent the spiritual meaning of the Word *faith*.

Always remember the Lord's first temptation during His advent into our world.

By doing so, they deprive their followers from gaining the spiritual understanding they so greatly need to Guide them in recognizing, acknowledging, and accepting their spiritual task at hand.

> "And when the tempter came unto Him, he said, If thou be the Son of God, Command that these stones be made Bread.
>
> "But He answered and said, It is Written, Man shall not live by Bread alone, but by every Word that proceedeth out of the mouth of God."

Matthew 4:3–4

It behooves you to always remember the Lord's first temptation during His advent into our world. The significance of that temptation being first, and the Lord's response to it, sets the stage for everything He teaches you … and all of us afterward.

Spiritually, the Word "stones" describes both falsities and Truths. When describing Truths, "stones" depict the Principles of Righteousness.

The Word "Bread" spiritually describes the Goodness of the Lord's Love for you.

The "tempter" portrays those who would have you believe that the Goodness of the Lord's Love can be received and retained without first abiding by the Principles of His Righteousness in all you think, feel, and do.

The reply the Lord Gives that "tempter" is quite revealing: "*But He answered and said, It is Written, Man shall not live by Bread alone, but by every Word that proceedeth out of the mouth of God.*" His reply is not only an answer, but also a restatement of the very same Message He has Gifted to humanity since the beginning of our existence. The Lord came into our world and suffered Greatly to restore the overriding importance of this ancient and timeless Message to each and every one of us.

> " *They that hate Me without a cause are more than the hairs of Mine head: they that would destroy Me, being Mine enemies wrongfully, are mighty: then I Restored that which I took not away.* "
>
> Psalms 69:4

~

During His advent into our world, the Lord made Himself vulnerable to the whims and cruelties of the proponents of errant philosophies and misleading religious doctrines. He did so in Order to expose the differences between Truth and falsity and Right from wrong for all to see. He did so without complaint, becoming the Sacrificial Lamb who innocently allowed His Own Blood to be shed for that Divine Purpose. By doing so, He once again repaired the breach that had come to separate our thoughts and affections from comprehending His Thoughts and Affections.

> *"And they that shall be of Thee shall build the old waste places: Thou shall raise up the foundations of many generations; and Thou shalt be called, The Repairer of the breach, the Restorer of Paths to dwell in."*
>
> Isaiah 58:12

Throughout human history, the Lord has freely Offered us all the spiritual knowledge we will ever need to realize how we might receive, retain, and forever share in the incomparable Blessings of True Life from His Life. However, and just as foretold in the story of Adam and Eve, we are very inclined to fall for

The result seeds a breach to grow between your thoughts and His Thoughts.

temptations presented by the pride of our own self-intelligence. Instead of following the Commandments He has Given to us to bring forth the Goodness of His Love within our lives, we wind up bringing forth nothing of the kind.

> *"He spoke also this parable; A certain Man had a fig tree planted in His Vineyard; and he came and sought fruit thereon, and found none.*
>
> *"Then He said to the dresser of His Vineyard, Behold, these three years I come seeking fruit on this fig tree, and find none: cut it down; why cumbereth it the ground?"*
>
> Luke 13:6–7

Everywhere He teaches you, that of your own free will, you must do the First things First in Order to receive, retain, and forever share in the Goodness of His Love within your soul. As Righteousness Himself, He has taught you that there is no other "way, up or around" for you to eternally partake in those incomparable Blessings.

> "And he answering said unto Him, Lord, let it alone this year also, till I shall dig and dung it.
>
> "And if it bear fruit, well: and if not, then after that Thou shalt cut it down."
>
> Luke 13: 8–9

Spiritually, a *tree* has been used may times throughout Scripture to portray what takes root, grows, and produces various results within your mind, heart, and soul. During His advent into our world, the Lord spoke about what it takes for us to become as trees "planted" and nourished by the "Waters" of genuine spiritual knowledge about Divine Truth.

Thinking that "faith alone" in the Lord is saving is described by the "fig tree" that bears no fruit. Your need to apply yourself to bringing that tree into fruition within your life is to be recognized and cherished in all you think, feel, and do. The time Given to you to do so is now.

> "Blessed is the man that walketh not in the counsel of the ungodly, nor standeth in the way of sinners, nor sitteth in the seat of the scornful.
>
> "But his delight is in the Law of the Lord, and in His Law doth he meditate day and night.
>
> "And he shall be like a tree planted by the Rivers of Water, that bringeth forth his fruit in his season; his leaf also shall not whither; and whatsoever he doeth shall prosper."
>
> Psalms 1:1–3

"*Blessed in the man that trusteth in the Lord, and whose hope the Lord is.*

"*For he shall be as a tree planted by the Waters, and that spreadeth out her roots by the River, and shall not see when heat cometh, but her leaf shall be green; and shall not be careful in the year of drought, neither shall cease from yielding fruit.*"

Jeremiah 17:7-8

"*For God so Loved the world, that He Gave His only begotten Son, that whosoever believeth in Him should not perish, but have everlasting Life.*"

John 3:16

~

"*Whosoever shall confess that Jesus is the Son of God, God dwelleth in him, and he in God.*"

1 John 4:15

This proclamation by John has been used many, many times to mislead the innocent and unsuspecting into believing that "faith alone" in the Lord is saving. Thinking that by solely confessing "Jesus is the Son of God" you will receive your salvation and deliverance into the Kingdom of Heaven acts as a false witness to everything the Lord has been teaching you about why and how you must live your life. Such false witness threatens to once again cause a breach to form between our thoughts and His Thoughts.

Literal misinterpretations about the meaning of the Words "belief" and "faith" have led many astray.

"*Or what man is there of you, whom if his son ask Bread, will he give him a stone?*"

Matthew 7:9

Here the Lord employs the Word "stone" to describe false thoughts. To think that Lord would Give you misleading information about the Way you may receive, retain, and forever share in the Joy and Goodness of His Love for you is unimaginable. Those who offer misguiding letter-of-the-Word misinterpretations about these things need to look deeply within themselves, and reconsider the full body of Scripture, seeking genuine spiritual understanding about the meaning and Purpose of the Lord's Testimony to us.

~

"*Wherefore the people did chide with Moses, and said, Give us water that we may drink. And Moses said unto them, why chide ye with me? Wherefore do ye tempt the Lord?*"

Exodus 17:2

Spiritually, to "chide Moses" is to ridicule acknowledging that keeping the Lord's Commandments in all you think, feel, and do is Primary for your salvation and deliverance into an eternal Heavenly state of being. The Word "water" is used throughout the Bible to describe both false and True spiritual knowledge. Here the Words "Give us water that we may drink" depict a wanting to replace genuine spiritual knowledge with "thoughts formed from the imaginations" of our own hearts. That wanting typifies the desire to escape our personal responsibility to live our lives "by every Word that proceedeth out of the mouth of God."

"*Thou believest that there is One God; thou doest well: the devils also believe, and tremble.*

"*But wilt thou know, O vain man, that faith without Works is dead?*"

James 2:19–20

"*Whosoever believeth that Jesus is the Christ is born of God: and every one that loveth Him that begat loveth him also that is begotten of Him.*

"*By this we know that we love the children of God, when we love God, and keep His Commandments.*

"*For this is the love of God, that we keep His Commandments: and His Commandments are not grievous.*"

1 John 5:1–3

"*Here is the patience of the saints: here are they that keep the Commandments of God, and the faith of Jesus.*

"*And I heard a voice from Heaven saying unto me, Write, Blessed are the dead which die in the Lord from henceforth: Yea, saith the Spirit, that they may rest from their labors; and their Works do follow them.*"

Revelation 14:12–13

24
The Spiritual Meaning of Grace

The Opportunities you are Offered by the Lord are timeless and eternally enduring.

The Opportunities the Lord provides for you to receive, retain, and forever share in the incomparable Blessings of True Life from His Life are spiritually described by the Word "Grace." Those Opportunities are not earned; but rather, they are Given to you freely through His Love, Compassion, Forgiveness, and Mercy for you. That the Lord is "full of Grace" describes those Opportunities perfectly, for He provides them to you abundantly during your entire lifetime in this world.

> "We then, as workers together with Him, beseech you also that ye receive not the Grace of God in vain.
>
> "For He saith, I have heard thee in a time accepted, and in the Day of salvation have I succored thee: behold, now is the accepted time; behold, now is the Day of salvation."
>
> 2 Corinthians 6:1–2

The Lord leaves it up to you to accept the Opportunities He affords you by willfully living your life according to the Principles of His Righteousness, nothing withheld. He Promises you that as you do so, all things Good will become possible within your life. He teaches you that it has been, is, and will always be the Way He saves you from spiritual harm and fulfills His Purpose for the Creation of your soul. Of all people, Paul realized that we have no time to waste, knowing that the time we have been Given to embrace those Opportunities is "now."

> "For the Lord God is a Sun and a Shield: the Lord will Give Grace and Glory: no Good thing will He withhold from them that walk Uprightly.
>
> "O Lord of hosts, Blessed is the man that trusteth in Thee."
>
> Psalms 84:11–12

The Words: *For the Lord God is a Sun* illustrate the Lord Enlightening you and Inspiring you with the internal Light and Warmth that comes forth in Truth from the Splendor of His Love for you. As that Divine Truth acts to protect you from the falsities and evils that would otherwise act to destroy your spiritual sensibilities, it is also portrayed as a "Shield."

The Words: *the Lord will Give Grace* reveal the many Opportunities He Gives you to understand the Way you may receive, retain, and forever share in the incomparable Blessings of True Life from His Life.

The Words: *and Glory* describe the Marvelous arrays of Principles that Illuminate the Truth of this understanding within your life.

The Words: *no Good thing will He withhold from them that walk Uprightly* confirm His Promise to fulfill all the Goodness that He has Purposed to bring into your life.

The Words: *O Lord of Hosts, Blessed is the man that trusteth in Thee* beckon you to place your belief, trust, and faith in the Way He is asking you to live your life.

> *"That which has been is now; and that which is to be hath already been; and God requireth that which is past."*
>
> Ecclesiastes 3:15

The Opportunities you are Offered by the Lord are timeless and eternally enduring. Yet the time you have been Given to embrace them is finite. That spiritual understanding must never be taken in vain.

> *"Know therefore that the Lord thy God, He is God, the faithful God, which keepeth Covenant and Mercy with them that love Him and keep His Commandments to a thousand generations."*
>
> Deuteronomy 7:9

> *"And now, Israel, what does the Lord thy God require of thee, but to fear the Lord thy God, to walk in all His Ways, and to love Him, and to serve the Lord thy God with all thy heart and with all thy soul,*
>
> *To keep the Commandments of the Lord, and His Statutes, which I Command thee this Day for thy Good?"*
>
> Deuteronomy 10:12–13

> *"For the Grace of God that bringeth salvation hath appeared to all men,"*
>
> Titus 2:11

The Story of Noah Applys To Your Life

> *"And God saw that the wickedness of man was great in the earth, and that every imagination of the thoughts of his heart was only evil continually.*

> *"And it repented the Lord that He had made man on the earth, and it grieved Him at His Heart."*
>
> Genesis 6:5–6

The pride of our own self-intelligence has attempted to lead us astray since the beginning of human existence. That pride would have us fall in "love" with falsities formed from "the imaginations of the thoughts" of our own hearts. Those "loves" are insidious, seeking only to justify their own correctness in order to establish dominance over our lives. When left to their own devices, they will strive to extinguish the Goodness of the Lord's Love from existing within our souls. The suffering that results breaks our Creator's Heart.

> *"And the Lord said, I will destroy man whom I have Created from the face of the earth; both man, and beast, and the creeping thing, and the fowls of the air; for it repenteth Me that I have Created them."*
>
> Genesis 6:7

- In a positive sense, you are called "man" from your ability to host the Qualities and Virtues of True Life from the Lord's Life within your soul.

- In a positive sense, a "beast" is descriptive of wholesome spiritual characteristics, including the innocence and commitment to love others unselfishly, and the spiritual conscience to remind you why and how you must.

- In a positive sense, "creeping things" depict your sensual faculties, acting in accordance with what the Lord has Shown you to be True and Right.

- In a positive sense, "fowls of the air" describe thinking about the concepts of Heavenly things.

The Words: *And the Lord said, I will destroy man whom I have Created from the face of the earth; both man, and beast and the creeping thing, and the fowls of the air* describe humanity's self-inflicted destruction of all these Righteous things. And although the Lord describes Himself as destroying them, that is just the spiritual appearance of the effects we bring upon ourselves by violating the relationship between Divine Truth and the Doctrine of His Righteousness within our lives.

> "*But Noah found Grace in the eyes of the Lord.*"
>
> Genesis 6:8

Spiritually, to find "Grace in the eyes of the Lord" is to recognize the Opportunity of your lifetime. To the Lord, that is a "sight" like none other.

> "*And these are the generations of Noah: Noah was a Just man and perfect in his generations, and Noah walked with God.*"
>
> Genesis 6:9

The "generations of Noah" describe the new thoughts and new affections that come forth from within you as you willingly follow the Lord's Instructions to live your life in the Way He is Showing you to be True and Right.

The Words: *Noah was a Just man and perfect in his generations, and Noah walked with God* depict your willingness to do so without adding or subtracting anything from His Testimony to you about why and how you must.

As you honestly, sincerely, and humbly make those efforts, He Provides you with all you need to establish the spiritual integrity of your soul. That integrity acts as an "Ark" that serves to protect you from mental, emotional, and spiritual harm as He lifts you above the fray of falsities and evils in times of temptation. And as the Lord Offered this Opportunity to Noah, so, too, does He Offer it to you!

Noah supervises the building of the Ark. Artist unknown

"But with thee will I establish My Covenant; and thou shalt come into the Ark, thou, and thy sons, and thy wife, and thy sons' wives with thee.

"And of every Living thing of all flesh, two of every sort shalt thou bring unto the Ark, to keep them Alive with thee: they shall be male and female."

Genesis 6:18–19

The Lord establishes His "Covenant" within you through your willingness to live your life in the Way that He is Showing you that you must. Abiding by that understanding allows you to build the internal structure of your mind and heart into a refuge wherein His Qualities and Virtues may enter in and find welcome within your soul.

It Inspires an inmost thankfulness for all the Lord has accomplished within you.

The Words: *thou shalt come into the Ark, thou and thy sons, and thy wife, and thy son's wives with thee* reveal the safety and surety of that Refuge.

The Words: *and of every Living thing of all flesh, two of every sort shalt thou bring unto the Ark* illustrate bringing your thoughts and affections into a Holy Covenant with the Lord.

When your thoughts and affections enter into that Covenant with the Lord, your potential to bring forth new generations of True Life from His Life becomes unlimited. And so, as it was with Noah, so is it also possible with you.

"Thus did Noah; according to all that God Commanded him, so did he."

Genesis 6:22

> "*And Noah buildeth an Altar unto the Lord: and took of every clean beast, and of every clean fowl, and offered burnt offerings on the Altar.*"
>
> Genesis 8:20

Being saved from mental, emotional, and spiritual harm and delivered into a much more perfect spiritual state of being Inspires an inmost thankfulness for all the Lord has accomplished within your life, like none other. Your acknowledgment, commitment, and rededication to abiding by all He has Shown you to be True and Right is described here as building "an Altar unto the Lord."

The Words: *of every clean beast, and of every clean fowl* describe offerings of heartfelt recognition and thoughts of appreciation for having received the Goodness of those invaluable Blessings within your life. To offer them as "burnt offerings on the Altar" illuminates your most passionate expressions of gratefulness for His delivering you into the Joys of Heavenly Love.

> "*And I will establish My Covenant with you; neither shall all flesh be cut off any more by the waters of a flood; neither shall there anymore be a flood to destroy the earth.*"
>
> Genesis 9:11

The Words: *And I will establish My Covenant with you* portray the Lord's Promise to eternally renew our spiritual understanding about the most important things of all.

The Words: *neither shall all flesh be cut off any more* describe His Promise to prevent the loss of genuine Goodness from ever being extinguished within the human race.

The Words: *by the waters of a flood* explain the falsities that would otherwise sweep away all spiritual sensibility about the overriding importance of living our lives in the Way that He has Shown us that we must.

> *"And God said, This is the Token of the Covenant which I make between Me and you and every Living creature that is with you, for perpetual generations:*
>
> *"I do set My Bow in the Cloud, and it shall be for a Token of a Covenant between Me and the earth."*
>
> Genesis 9:12–13

Spiritual Enlightenment about the Truth of Love is described here as the "Token of the Covenant." That "Token" Illuminates the Marvels of His Righteousness for all to see. Those Marvels are described as a "Token" because they are just a glimpse of the Joy and Goodness He Promises to bring into your life as you live your life according to the Beauty of those Holy Principles.

As you do so, He Promises to continually renew that Holy understanding within your life as He fulfills His Purpose for the Creation of your soul.

The Words: *for perpetual generations* set the stage for that eternal renewal to unfold within us as we continue to live our lives in the Way that He is Showing us that we must. That Glorious Renewal, described in Scripture as being Marvelous in our eyes, is a vast understatement.

> *"And it shall come to pass, when I bring a Cloud over the earth, that the Bow shall be seen in the Cloud."*
>
> Genesis 9:14

Your perception of the Righteousness of the Lord is Amazing to behold. Throughout the Bible, that perception is described as seen in a Cloud. That Cloud acts to moderate the Light and Warmth coming forth in Truth from His Love for you as He acclimates you into recognizing, comprehending, understanding, and accepting your spiritual task at hand. To call that Opportunity "Amazing Grace" is, likewise, a vast understatement.

"*But as the Days of Noe were, so shall also be the coming of the Son of man be.*"

Matthew 24:37

The Story of Noah describes your Opportunity to enter into a Covenant with the Lord. The "Days of Noe" describe the spiritual steps and stages you will experience during your spiritual reformation as you choose to enter into that Sacred Covenant with Him. And just as Noah received Instruction from the Lord about the Way you must, "so shall also be the coming of the Son of man be" within your own life. To think that the Grace of the Lord may become received and fulfilled within you in any other "way" is spiritual folly.

> "*Jesus saith unto him, Thou hast said: nevertheless I say unto you. Hereafter shall ye see the Son of Man sitting on the Right hand of Power, and coming in the Clouds of Heaven.*"
>
> Matthew 26:64

> "*And the Word was made flesh, and dwelt among us, (and we beheld His Glory, the Glory as of the only begotten of the Father), full of Grace and Truth.*"
>
> John 1:14

> "*Unto the angel of church of Ephesus write; These things saith He that holdeth the Seven Sars in His Right Hand, and Who walketh in the midst of the Seven Golden Candlesticks;*
>
> "*I know thy works, and thy labour, and thy patience, and how thou canst not bear them that are evil: and thou hast tried them which say they are apostles, and are not, and hast found them liars:*
>
> "*And hast borne, and hast patience, and for My Name's sake hast laboured, and hast not fainted.*
>
> "*Nevertheless I have somewhat against thee, because thou hast left thy First Love.*

> *Remember therefore from whence thou art fallen, and repent, and do the First Works; or else I will come unto thee quickly, and will remove thy Candlestick out of His Place, except thou repent.*
>
> Revelation 2:1–5

Paul's Warnings About Becoming a False Witnessing To the Truth of Love

Many false witnesses have arisen from beliefs founded upon literal misinterpretations about the meaning of Scripture. Those beliefs have led many far astray. Leading up to being addressed by the Lord on the road to Damascus, Paul was certainly one of them.

> *Which things I also did in Jerusalem: and many of the saints did I shut up in prison, having received authority from the chief priests; and when they were put to death, I gave my voice against them.*
>
> *And I punished them oft in every synagogue, and compelled them to blaspheme; and being exceedingly mad against them, I persecuted them even unto strange cities.*
>
> Acts 26:10–11

> *This is a faithful saying, and worthy of all acceptation, that Jesus Christ came into the world to save sinners; of whom I am chief.*
>
> 1 Timothy 1:15

Because Paul was raised, schooled, and steeped in letter-of-the-Word mis-interpretations about Scripture, he knew full well the blinding effects they can cause to your spiritual sensibilities. And because he had also received a new spiritual understanding from the Lord, he also knew the Enlightening effects that understanding can bestow upon your mind, heart, and soul.

Recognizing the profound dangers of allowing yourself to divide the letter of the Word from the Spirit of the Word, he, of all people, realized our urgent need to reunite them together once again, as One.

> "And when they had appointed him a day, there came many to him into his lodging; to whom he expounded and testified the Kingdom of God, persuading them concerning Jesus, both out of the Law of Moses, and out of the prophets, from morning till evening."
>
> Acts 28:23

Paul spoke to his own religious leaders and teachers using their own religious terminology. He made every effort to reconcile their lack of understanding about the Spirit of the Word with their knowledge about the letter of the Word. He did so by addressing the breach that had developed between the two. Because of his own personal experience, Paul realized the deep harm that breach had caused him, and was continuing to cause to the people he so loved.

Unless you view his writings from this perspective, you, too, risk falling into misconceptions about what Paul was teaching all of us about the Truth of Love.

> "And some believed the things which were spoken, and some believed not.
>
> "And when they agreed not among themselves, they departed, after that Paul had spoken one Word, Well spake the Holy Ghost by Esaias the prophet unto our fathers,
>
> "Saying, go unto this people, and say, Hearing ye shall hear, and shall not understand; and seeing ye shall see, and not perceive:

"For the heart of this people is waxed gross, and their ears are dull of hearing, and their eyes have they closed: lest they should see with their eyes, and hear with their ears, and understand with their heart, and should be converted, and I should heal them.

"Be it known therefore unto you, that the salvation of God is sent unto the Gentiles, and that they will hear it."

Acts 28:24–28

~

Paul realized the drastic harm he had caused to the followers of Christ before his life-changing experience on the road to Damascus. He recognized that by trying to enforce his prior literal misconceptions about the meaning of Scripture upon others, he was harming the Lord Himself. Hence, Paul dedicated the rest of his life to teaching all who would listen to him about what he had learned from the Lord about the True spiritual meaning of Scripture.

> Self-importance will cause you to be unwilling to hear anything else.

"For the Grace of God that bringeth salvation hath appeared to all men,

"Teaching us that, denying ungodliness and worldly lusts, we should live soberly, Righteously, and Godly, in this present world."

Titus 2:11–12

By stating that "the Grace of God that bringeth salvation hath appeared to all men," Paul is teaching you about the Opportunity of your lifetime. He is explaining that this invaluable Opportunity requires you to deny "ungodliness and worldly lusts" and "live soberly, Righteously, and Godly, in this present world."

How much more clearly can Paul describe what it means to be a true witness to the Lord's Testimony to us? A Testimony to you about why and how you must live your life?

> "Not by works of righteousness which we have done, but according to His Mercy He Saved us, by the washing of regeneration, and renewing of the Holy Ghost:"
>
> Titus 3:5

Throughout all his writings, Paul makes it very clear that simply being compliant with the letter of the Word has little lasting effect upon your mental, emotional, and spiritual wellbeing. From his own experience, he knew thinking that literal compliance constituted the "works of righteousness" would mislead you from understanding the most important things of all. He knew that such thinking would cause many to be unwilling to hear anything other than the correctness of your own self-merit.

By stating that you are saved by the Lord "according to His Mercy" and "by the washing of regeneration," Paul is describing the Way you become spiritually reformed and transformed into an image of the Lord's Qualities and as a likeness to His Virtues. He realized that in His Mercy, the Lord came into our world to once again teach you about these things. He realized that only by applying this genuine spiritual knowledge to each and every aspect of your life can the Lord regenerate your ability to host the Goodness of His Love with your soul. Paul describes your reception of that spiritual understanding as "the renewing of the Holy Ghost." How much more clearly can Paul teach you about what he learned from the Lord about the Way He saves you from mental, emotional, and spiritual harm and leads you back into the Goodness of His Love's Embrace?

> "And such trust have we through Christ to God-ward:
>
> "Not that we are sufficient of ourselves to think anything as of
> ourselves; but our sufficiency is of God;
>
> "Who also hath made us able ministers of the New Testament;
> not of the letter, but of the Spirit; for the letter killeth, but the
> Spirit Giveth Life."
>
> 2 Corinthians 3:4–6

These statements by Paul are not idle or insignificant assertions. They have come forth from a person who learned the hard way about what constitutes True and saving faith in the Lord, and what does not. He made these statements to help you recognize the difference between what poses a death trap to the Goodness within your soul, and what liberates your understanding about the most important things of all.

~

> "But for us also, to whom it shall be imputed, if we believe on Him
> Who raised up Jesus our Lord from the dead;
>
> "Who was delivered for our offences, and was raised again for
> our Justification."
>
> Romans 4:24–25

Paul clearly recognized that the Lord came into our world and died for us in Order to Give us a renewed spiritual understanding about why and how we must live our lives. He realized that by doing so He once again Gave us the tools we need to work with Him to overcome our ethical, moral, and spiritual faults and weaknesses. Paul realized this work is what Justifies our "Right" to receive, retain, and forever share in the Joy of His Love within our lives. Spiritually, the Word "Right" means the restoration of our ability to grasp onto this Truth, as we walk hand in Hand with the Lord in the Light of His Righteousness.

> "For I the Lord thy God will hold thy Right hand, saying unto thee, Fear not; I will help thee."
>
> Isaiah 41:13

> "Then shall the King say unto them on His Right hand, Come, ye Blessed of My Father, inherit the Kingdom Prepared for you from the foundation of the world."
>
> Matthew 25:34

> "Then Jesus said unto them, Yet a little while is the Light with you. Walk while ye have the Light, lest darkness come upon you: for he that walketh in darkness knoweth not whither he goeth."
>
> John 12:35

Misusing the Spiritual Meaning of the Term *Justification*

When misinterpreted, the term "justification" dilutes the Lord's Divine Message to the human race. It becomes misinterpreted whenever religious leaders proclaim that your salvation is *justified* simply by believing that Jesus died upon the cross for you. That proclamation is misleading because it leaves out the Reason *why* He died for you, misdirecting you from focusing on your spiritual task at hand.

The spiritual meaning of Justification becomes further diluted by proclaiming that by dying for you, the Lord took away the sins of the world. That proclamation leaves out your need to understand that the Lord takes away your sins step by step, and stage by stage, only as you willingly walk with Him, hand in hand, in the Paths of His Righteousness. Nothing withheld.

The spiritual meaning of "Justification" becomes still further diluted by proclaiming that Jesus will take away your sins if you simply confess that He is the Son of God. That misinterpretation leaves you believing that "faith alone" is saving, while leaving out the "weightier matters of Law, Judgment, Mercy and Faith" as the Lord exclaimed to the scribes and Pharisees in Matthew 23:23.

Deeper dilution occurs by proclaiming that because Jesus died for you on the cross, for His sake, His Father will Honor Him by having Mercy on all who simply confess that He is the Son of God. That dilution tempts you into believing that you can "live by Bread alone," rather than first abiding by "every Word that proceedeth out of the mouth of God."

And still deeper dilution occurs by proclaiming that because your confession confirms that Jesus is the Son of God, His Father will forgive your sins and impute His Son's Righteousness to you. That proclamation misleads you into believing that besides your confession, there is nothing more you need to do to receive your salvation and deliverance into the Joys of Heavenly Love.

Finally, the spiritual meaning of "Justification" becomes trampled upon when proclaiming that only those who make these several confessions of "faith" will have their souls repurchased by the Blood of Christ, and that all others will not. That doctrine causes us to lose focus about what Truly defines the meaning of "Justification," and what does not. It acts to separate you from comprehending the most important things of all.

Each of these letter-of-the-Word-based "justifications" act to form spiritual half-truths … half-truths that quickly turn into the "smooth things" that cover over our need to understand why and how we must live our lives. They blind you from recognizing the overriding importance of accepting your spiritual task at hand. Religious leaders should take great care in what they profess … and most especially in what they teach others about the Truth of Love.

"But I say unto you, That every idle word that men shall speak, they shall give account thereof in the Day of Judgment.

"For by thy words thou shall be Justified, and by thy words thou shall be condemned."

Matthew 12:36–37

⁓

Paul recognized that by raising up His Divine Truth for all to see, the Lord once again Gifted us with the spiritual understanding we so desperately need to realize what Justifies our spiritual transformation into the people that He has Purposed for us to become.

"Mark well, O Job, hearken unto Me: hold thy peace, and I will Speak.

"If thou hast anything to say, answer Me: speak, for I desire to Justify thee.

"If not, hearken unto Me: hold thy peace, and I shall teach thee Wisdom."

Job 33:31–33

"O ye sons of men, how long will ye turn My Glory into shame? How long will ye love vanity, and seek after leasing? Selah.

"But know that the Lord has set apart him that is Godly for Himself: the Lord will hear when I call unto Him.

"Stand in awe, and sin not: commune with your own heart upon your bed, and be still. Selah.

"Offer the sacrifices of Righteousness, and put your trust in the Lord."

Psalms 4:2–5

"For not the hearers of the Law are Just before God, but the doers of the Law shall be Justified."

Romans 2:13

Differences Between the "Laws of the Lord" and the "laws of Men"

Paul realized that the spiritual meaning within the Word Gives the letter of the Word its True meaning and Life, and not the *other way* around. He began his ministry by first warning the religious leaders and teachers of his own faith against the dangers of thinking otherwise. By doing so, at his own great peril, he deeply offended many of them.

He began by teaching them precisely what the Lord had taught him.

"For circumcision verily profiteth, if thou keep the Law, but if thou be a breaker of the Law, thy circumcision is made uncircumcision.

Therefore if the uncircumcised keep the Righteousness of the Law, shall not his uncircumcision be counted for circumcision?"

Romans 2:25–26

From his prior formal religious education, Paul began to speak to them about the differences between the spiritual and literal meaning of Scripture. He was attempting to help his own people discern spiritual Light from the spiritual darkness that had come to dominate their lives.

"And shall not uncircumcison which is by nature, if it fulfill the Law, Judge thee, who by the letter and circumcision dost transgress the Law?

For he is not a Jew, which is one outwardly; neither is that circumcision, which is outward in the flesh:

> *"But he is a Jew, which is one inwardly; and circumcision is that of the heart, in the Spirit, and not in the letter; whose praise is not of men, but of God."*
>
> Romans 2:27-29

Paul calls upon each of us to realize that our salvation is predicated solely upon our willingness to abide by the Laws the Lord has Given for us to keep and cherish for our Good and for the Good of all those around us. He calls upon us to realize that these Laws have been Given to us as the Lord's Commandments, and that they Embody all the Principles of His Righteousness for all to see and understand.

Yet many of today's religious theologies boast that your spiritual reformation, which is to say, the "circumcision is that of your heart," is in no way dependent upon your efforts to abide by those "Laws." By making those proclamations, they form their own "laws," and then place them above what the Lord has been teaching us since our inceptions.

~

> *"Where is boasting then? It is excluded. By what law? of works? Nay: but by the Law of faith.*
>
> *"Therefore we conclude that a man is justified by faith without the deeds of the law.*
>
> *"Is He the God of the Jews only? Is He not also of the Gentiles? Yes, of the Gentiles also:*
>
> *"Seeing it is One God, which shall Justify the circumcision by faith, and uncircumcision through faith.*

"*Do we then make void the Law through faith? God forbid: yea, we establish the Law.*"

Romans 3:27–31

Paul consistently addresses your need to recognize the differences between "laws of men" and "God's Laws." He teaches you not to use letter-of-the-Word misinterpretations about Scripture to boast about what constitutes "true and saving faith" in the Lord, and what does not. He knew full well that "laws" derived from those misleading literal interpretations have little to no lasting effects upon your mental, emotional, and spiritual wellbeing. He realized that such misleading literal proclamations very often have just the opposite effect.

By differentiating between "men's laws" and "God's Laws," Paul is teaching you about your need to free yourself from servitude to the "works" of misleading letter-of-the-Word religious doctrines. Paul describes that liberation as your being "justified by faith without the deeds of the law."

He realized that the religious authority that mandated adherence to those "literal-based doctrines" were leading the people he so loved back into the same spiritual captivity that their forefathers had suffered so many times in their past. And so, Paul asks you to take pause, and look deeply within yourself to recognize the dangers of placing your faith in the "laws of men," rather that placing your faith in abiding by the "Laws of God."

By posing the question, "Do we then make void the Law through faith?" Paul draws your attention to the danger of misinterpreting the True meaning of the Word "faith." By answering that question with "God forbid: yea, we establish the Law," Paul teaches you about your inescapable need to establish the Principles of the Lord's Righteousness as Primary for the Way you live your life. Paul fully realized that those Holy Principles are the "Laws" of Love, and that abiding by them is the only thing the Lord requires of you to fulfill His Covenant with your life.

> *"But Israel, which followed after the law of righteousness, hath not attained to the Law of Righteousness.*
>
> *"Wherefore? Because they sought it not by faith, but as it were by the works of the law. For they stumbled at that stumblingstone;"*
>
> Romans 9:31–32

They had turned the meaning of "God's Laws" into mere "religious superstitions."

At the time of the Lord's advent into our world, letter-of-the-Word misinterpretations about Scripture had come to dominate religious thought and practice. Those literal misinterpretations controlled all phases of social and religious life. Their leaders' insistence about their own infallibility had turned them into false witnesses to the very people they were purporting to serve.

For instance, the literal laws about physical religious washings were deemed holy in themselves by religious teachers of that time. Failure to comply with those physical rituals was considered sinful, and people who failed to do so were not allowed to worship in their temples.

Regardless of the Goodness existing within their thoughts, feelings, and behaviors, salvation was deemed impossible for them if they remained ceremonially "unwashed." As a result, the importance of those physical washings came to obscure their ability to comprehend that religious "washings" signify applying genuine spiritual knowledge to act as internal cleansing from falsities and evils of all sorts. Rather, compliance to those letter-of-the-Word "laws," and many more like them, had become much more important than paying attention to "the weightier matters of the Laws, Judgment, Mercy, and Faith," as the Lord exclaimed within Matthew 23:23. By doing so, they had turned the meaning of "God's Laws" into mere "religious superstitions."

Spiritual understanding about the meaning of culinary Laws in the Bible had also become misinterpreted. Instead of understanding that the Statutes that refer to the Way you must select and prepare your food and drink refer to your need for discretion about what you choose for spiritual nourishment, all deviations from the letter of the Word descriptions were considered sinful. Those who were compliant with literal observance of those culinary "laws" were deemed "righteous," and those who were not compliant were prejudged as the "unrighteous."

Literal conformity to the dress codes cited in Scripture was also considered a "holy duty." Instead of understanding that those Statutes describe the honesty, sincerity, and humility you must put on your mind and heart in reverence to your love for the Lord and in reverence for the Good of all around you, all nonconformity to literal Biblical dress codes was proclaimed as sinful. By enforcing those literal-based dress codes without realizing their spiritual meaning and implications, understanding about the way we must "dress" our thoughts and affections as we walk with the Lord in the Light of His Righteousness had become lost.

The Last Supper by Leonardo da Vinci

Literal misinterpretations about the office of the high priest had come to obscure the meaning of that Sacred office. Instead of understanding that the office of the high priest represents your loftiest intentions to worship the Lord in Truth and Goodness, letter-of-the-Word dictates proclaimed that only one individual was "given" the authority to enter the "inner chamber" where the Ark of the Lord's Testimony was housed.

Those literal dictates claimed that if other people even set foot in that inner chamber, they would surely die. By doing so, they were preventing their own congregations from realizing the Way we all must honestly, sincerely, and humbly approach the Lord, dressed in the robe of Righteousness in mind, heart, and soul.

Physical circumcision among men was considered mandatory. The physically "uncircumcised" were considered "unclean" and "unholy." Those beliefs came to cover over their realization about the True meaning of "circumcision," and about the need for our thoughts to undergo spiritual reformation in the Light of Righteousness. Instead, their literal dictates misled people into believing that physical circumcision was "circumcision in the eyes of the Lord," even if they remained spiritually uncircumcised in the way they lived their lives.

Literal misinterpretations of the Word forbid "the righteous" from comingling with others who differed in physical or religious lineage from their own. Instead of realizing that these Biblical Statutes pertain to abstaining from comingling with false thinking and selfish affections, they considered physically comingling with any others outside of their own formal religion lineage as sinful. Those dictates restricted them from sharing common values about the Truth of Love with others of similar thoughts and affections, regardless of any superficial differences in their physical or religious heritages. Even the sharing of meals with others who differed in physical and religious lineage from their own was deemed sinful.

Instead of bringing differing peoples of the world together in Peace and Goodwill through mutual understanding and joint agreement about the the most important things of all, their letter-of-the-Word dictates acted to divide them from sharing in that Holy Communion with one another.

To make things even more convoluted, false proclamations derived from letter-of-the-Word misinterpretations about Scripture had also come to redefine the spiritual meaning of the term "chosen people." Their leaders and teachers used those proclamations to declare that only those of their own historical, physical, and religious heritage were "chosen" by the Lord to possess the "promised land," and all others were not. Instead of teaching that all who are willing to live their lives in the Way the Lord has Shown us that we must have been "chosen" to come into, and remain in that Domain, they had excluded all others, while only including themselves.

These and many other literal misinterpretations about Scripture had come to obscure the True spiritual meaning of the Lord's Divine Laws and Statutes. Those misguided literal beliefs about "the laws of righteousness" were leading their own people far astray. They were destroying their ability to comprehend what constitutes True and saving faith in the Lord, and what does not.

And so, throughout all his writings, Paul differentiates between "God's Laws" and "men's laws." He warns you time and time again about the dangers of placing your faith in letter-of-the-Word misinterpretations about Scripture. He teaches that such literal-based thinking will cause you to trip over the same religious "stumbling stones" that he had fallen over, as he zealously, blindly, cruelly, and unjustly persecuted the followers of Christ.

Paul's Realization That His Own Teachings Would Become Misused

Paul knew that he would soon face resentment, disdain, and retribution for exposing the flaws within the letter-of-the-Word-based religious doctrines of his time. Yet he undertook an even greater risk, realizing that his own teachings would soon become misunderstood, and then misused to

The invasiveness of misleading doctrines will come very soon after the dawning of Divine Truth within your life.

form equally flawed and misleading religious doctrines in the future. He addressed those coming dangers with great concern. From the beginning of his ministry, his realization about this second danger caused Paul much more anguish than the first.

> "*Take heed therefore unto yourselves, and to all the flock, over which the Holy Ghost hath made you overseers, to feed the Church of God, which He hath purchased with His Own Blood.*
>
> "*For I know this, that after my departing shall grievous wolves enter in among you, not sparing the flock.*
>
> "*Also of your own selves shall men arise, speaking perverse things, to draw away disciples after them.*
>
> "*Therefore watch, and remember, that by the space of three years I ceased not to warn every one night and day with tears.*"
>
> Acts 20:28–31

> "*Now I beseech you, brethren, mark them which cause divisions and offenses contrary to the Doctrine which ye have learned; and avoid them.*

> "For they that are such serve not our Lord Jesus Christ, but their
> own belly; and by good words and fair speeches deceive the
> hearts of the simple."
>
> Romans 16:17–18

Paul realized that the Lord came into out world from His Love for us to
once again Gift us with Good Doctrine about the Way to our salvation
and deliverance into the eternal Joys of Heavenly Love. He fully recognized that the Lord is Righteous in all His Ways, and that if we are honest,
sincere, and humble in our willingness to follow Him, so must we.

Paul taught this Doctrine to all who would listen to him. Any confusion on
our part is the result of falling for the lures of our own errant philosophies
and misleading religious doctrines, whether past, present, or future ones.

> "I do not frustrate the Grace of God: for if righteousness come by
> the law, then Christ is dead in vain."
>
> Galatians 2:21

This very simple statement by Paul has been misinterpreted many, many
times. Instead of realizing that Paul was teaching us about the differences
between men's "laws" and "Divine Laws," between "righteousness" and
"Righteousness," and between "works" and "Works," this statement has been
misused to dismiss the Lord's Own Testimony to us about our inescapable
need to seek His Righteousness First in all we think, feel, and do. Paul
is warning that if we dismiss the overriding importance of keeping those
Holy Principles as our First Works, then the Lord will have come into our
world and died for us in vain.

> "Be not thou therefore ashamed of the Testimony of our Lord,
> nor of me His prisoner: but be thou partaker of the afflictions
> of the Gospel according to the Power of God."

"Who hath saved us, and called us with a Holy Calling, not according to our works, but according to His own Purpose and Grace, which was Given us in Christ Jesus before the world began."

2 Timothy 1:8–9

Paul realized that undergoing your spiritual reformation in the Light of Righteousness is Lifesaving. He understood that the afflictions you will necessarily suffer as you allow the Lord to reform you in that Light are nothing to be ashamed of. Rather, he gladly called himself a "prisoner" to understanding why and how we must. And because he realized that this is the Way the Lord spiritually develops your full spiritual potential to host the incomparable Blessings of True Life from His Life, he implores you, too, to be a willing "partaker" of those "afflictions," just as he was.

Everywhere Paul beseeches you to abide in that "Good News," rightly attributing it "not according to your works" but according "to the Power of God." He realized that abiding by the Truth of this understanding is what allows the Lord to move mountains of stumbling blocks out of your Way, as He reforms you and transforms you into the person that He has Purposed for you to become.

Yet, even as Paul spoke and wrote to us about our need to embrace the Doctrine the Lord had suffered so greatly to bring back into our world, he was amazed at just how quickly we tend to wander away from it. He marveled at how easily we become offended by it, and was astounded at how often we allow ourselves to become re-intoxicated with our own misleading letter-of-the-Word-based doctrines about the meaning of Scripture. He wondered greatly about why we so quickly fall backward into the same mistakes that our forefathers had made. And so, he spoke openly about those dangers, calling out our need to be aware of how fast we tend to "pervert the Gospel of Christ" with new proclamations of our own making.

"*I marvel that ye are so soon removed from Him that called you into the Grace of Christ unto another gospel:*

"*Which is not another; but there be some that trouble you, and would pervert the Gospel of Christ.*"

Galatians 1:6–7

Throughout his writings, Paul beseeches us to rejoice in the Good News found in the spiritual meaning of Scripture. From personal experience, he knew the age-old dangers of placing the pride of our own self-intelligence in front of what the Lord has Given each of us to understand as True and Right.

"*Preach the Word; be instant in Season, out of Season; reprove, rebuke, exhort with all longsuffering and Doctrine.*

"*For the time will come when they will not endure sound Doctrine; but after their own lusts shall they heap to themselves teachers, having itching ears.*

"*And they shall turn away their ears from the Truth, and shall be turned unto fables.*

"*But watch thou in all things, endure afflictions, do the Work of an evangelist, make full proof of thy ministry.*"

2 Timothy 4:2–5

Everywhere Paul teaches us about the overriding importance of applying the Principles of the Lord's Righteousness to every aspect of our lives. He teaches us to "reprove" and "rebuke" any doctrine that professes otherwise. He teaches us that all genuine evangelism—internal and external—comes through our willingness to do this spiritual "Work" with all our mind, heart, and strength. He teaches us that only by doing so will we be making "full proof" of the "ministry" we have been Given by the Lord to serve in the fulfillment of His Purpose for the Creation of our souls. He teaches us that doing so will both serve and befriend the Goodness of the Lord's Love within us, and Goodness of His Love within all around us. Everywhere Paul teaches us that this Doctrine is Sound, True, and Primary for our salvation and deliverance into an eternal Heavenly state of being.

Peter Recognizes That Paul's Teachings Were Becoming Compromised

Peter also realized that Paul's teachings would soon become misinterpreted, and then misused. He realized that such misuse would obscure the ability of many to focus clearly upon their spiritual task at hand. And he recognized the severity that those dangers posed to our individual and collective mental, emotional, and spiritual wellbeing.

And so, Peter warns you about the dangers of misinterpreting Paul's teachings, fully recognizing that those misinterpretations act as a false witness to the Lord's Testimony to us. And like Paul, from deep personal experience, Peter admonishes you to refrain from denying what must always be, and remain, your First Love.

> "And account that the longsuffering of our Lord is salvation; even as our beloved brother Paul also according to the Wisdom Given unto him hath written unto you.

> "As also in all his epistles, speaking in them of these things; in which are some things hard to be understood, which they that are unlearned and unstable wrest, as they do also the other Scriptures, unto their own destruction.

> "Ye therefore, beloved, seeing ye know these things before, beware lest ye also, being led away with the error of the wicked, fall from your own steadfastness. "

2 Peter 3:15–17

Moses and the flaming bush. Artist unknown

Those who proclaim that the Lord "gave" us a "new covenant" that dismisses our need to abide by the Principles of His Righteousness First in all we think, feel, and do should take great pause. They should reconsider why the Lord continually asks us to keep His Commandments and His Statutes as our Singular focus, and why He asks us to Place them in the Forefront of our lives. They should also realize that the "laws," "statutes," and "doctrines" that the Lord dismissed during His advent into our world were not His, but ours.

They should also recall that since the beginning of human existence, the Lord has warned us about the dangers of thinking otherwise. They should take great care not to allow themselves to become a false witness to the very God whom they profess to be their Lord and Savior.

Paul's Reveal: Moses Was a Follower of Christ

"By faith Moses, when he was come to years, refused to be called the son of Pharaoh's daughter;

Choosing rather to suffer affliction with the people of God, than to enjoy the pleasures of sin for a season;

Esteeming the reproach of Christ greater Riches than the treasures in Egypt: for he had respect unto the recompense of the Reward."

Hebrews 11:24–26

In these remarkable verses, Paul explains the very definition of a true believer in the Lord. Understanding that the Word "Christ" means Divine Truth, he explains that all followers of Divine Truth are followers of Christ, Who is Righteousness Himself.

- By explaining that "By faith Moses, when he was come to years, refused to be called the son of Pharaoh's daughter," Paul is teaching you to avoid maintaining affection for errant philosophies or misleading religious doctrines, regardless of your past attachments to them. Coming "to years" describes gaining the spiritual maturity to realize why you must.

- By explaining that Moses chose "to suffer affliction with the people of God, than to enjoy the pleasures of sin for a season," Paul is teaching you that, just as Moses did, you, too, will need to undergo your spiritual reformation in reverence to your love for the Lord and in reverence for the Good of all around you.

- By explaining that Moses esteemed "the reproach of Christ greater riches than the treasures in Egypt," Paul is teaching you to trust in the Lord's Purpose for Calling you to go through that internal reformation. He is teaching you that the Joy and Goodness that await you will far exceed anything that can be gained otherwise.

Today, many Christians and Jews alike might have difficulty admitting that Moses was a true believer in Christ. They might find it difficult to accept that Christ, being Divine Truth, is timeless and has been with us since "before the world began." They might find it difficult to acknowledge that, just as Moses choose to turn away from any prior errant philosophies and misleading religious doctrines, seeking a deeper meaning about the Truth of Love, so must you.

It is Marvelous to recognize that the Story of Moses applies to each of us. It is Wonderful to realize that as you willingly follow the Lord in the same Way as Moses did, that the Lord will liberate you from the captivity and internal harm that falsities and evils inflict upon your life. It is Amazing to comprehend that as you willingly do so, your self-serving thoughts and selfish affections will die off as new generations of True thoughts and Unselfish affections become born anew within you, then multiplying and prospering throughout your spiritual journey in this world.

And it is Eye-opening to understand that as you, too, chose to suffer through the afflictions of "the washing of regeneration, and renewing of the Holy Ghost," the Lord Promises to defeat your true spiritual enemies as He leads you into "a Land" flowing "with Milk and Honey."

> "And the Lord brought us forth out of the Egypt with a
> Mighty Hand, and with an outstretched Arm, and with
> Great terribleness, and with Signs, and with Wonders:
>
> "And He hath brough us into this Place, and hath Given us this
> Land, even a Land that floweth with Milk and Honey."
>
> Deuteronomy 26:8–9

> "Now we have received, not the spirit of the world, but the
> Spirit which is of God; that we might know the things that
> are freely Given to us of God.
>
> "Which things also we speak, not in the words which man's
> wisdom teacheth, but which the Holy Spirit teacheth;
> comparing spiritual things with spiritual."
>
> 1 Corinthians 2:12–13

Peter's Warning Against Becoming a False Witness To the Truth of Love

Peter characterizes faith in the Lord. He exemplified that True and saving faith in the Lord is founded upon our willingness to live our lives according to Principles of His Righteousness, nothing withheld. That recognition is all-important to your salvation and deliverance into the Joys of Heavenly Love.

> "He saith unto them, But Whom say ye that I am?
>
> "And Simon Peter answered and said, Thou art Christ, the Son
> of the Living God.

"*And Jesus answered and said unto him, Blessed art thou, Simon Bar-jona: for flesh and blood hath not revealed it unto thee, but My Father which is in Heaven.*

"*And I say also unto thee, That thou art Peter, and upon this Rock I will build My Church; and the gates of hell shall not prevail against it.*

"*And I will Give unto thee the Keys of the Kingdom of Heaven: and whatsoever thou shalt bind on earth shall be bound in Heaven: and whatsoever thou shalt loose on earth shall be loosed in Heaven.*"

Matthew 16:15–19

Recognizing that the Lord is Righteous in all His Ways Gives you the Keys to unlock your spiritual potential. Having the faith to live your life accordingly allows the Lord to fulfill His Purpose for the Creation of your soul.

"*As soon as they were come to land, they saw a fire of coals there, and fish laid thereon, and Bread.*

"*And Jesus said unto them, Bring of the fish which ye now caught.*

"*Simon Peter went up, and drew the net to land full of great fishes, a hundred and fifty-three: and for all there were so many, yet was not the net broken.*"

John 21:9–11

The Words: *as they were come to land* describe becoming cognizant about what serves your mental, emotional, and spiritual wellbeing.

The Words: *they saw a fire of coals there* reveal the passion for gaining genuine spiritual knowledge about Divine Truth.

The Words: *and fish laid thereon* portray the Principles that dwell within that spiritual knowledge.

The Words: *and Bread* describe the Goodness that accompanies that knowledge.

By asking Peter to "bring of the fish" he had "now caught," the Lord was addressing your need to gather all the Principles you have learned about the Truth of Righteousness into your spiritual sensibilities.

The Words: *Simon Peter went up and drew the net to land full of great fishes, a hundred and fifty-three: and for all there were so many* describe the breadth and depth of their importance for the nourishment and health of your mind, heart, and soul.

The Words: *yet was not the net broken* Spiritually describe how the Lord Promises never to Give you more than you can handle, although the weight of these Principles might seem overwhelming to you at times.

> "*And Jesus said unto them, Come and dine. And none of the disciples dared ask Him, Who art Thou? Knowing that it was the Lord.*"
>
> John 21:12

The Way to your salvation and deliverance into an eternal Heavenly state of being resonates clearly within your spiritual sensibilities as you come to realize that the Lord, being Divine Truth, is Righteousness Himself. Through your faith to abide by that Holy understanding, the Lord Communes with you about all things True and Right.

"Wherefore gird up the loins of your mind, be sober, and hope to the End for the Grace that is to be brought unto you at the revelation of Jesus Christ."

1 Peter 1:13

Through very trying personal experience, Peter came to realize, confess, and accept that abiding by the Principles of Righteousness must always be, and remain, our First Love. He came to recognize that doing so is the Opportunity of our lifetimes.

And like Paul, Peter went on to teach all who would listen to him about that spiritual Reality. At the same time, he warned them, as he also warns you, about the dangers of allowing yourself to deny that this spiritual task is your responsibility. He teaches all of us that this responsibility must be treated soberly and seriously, nothing withheld.

"Grace and Peace be multiplied unto you through the knowledge of God, and of Jesus our Lord."

2 Peter 1:2

"Nevertheless we, according to His Promise, look for new Heavens and a new earth, wherein dwelleth Righteousness.

"Wherefore, beloved, seeing that ye look for such things, be diligent that ye may be found of Him in Peace, without spot, and blameless."

2 Peter 3:13–14

"Ye therefore, beloved, seeing ye know these things before, beware lest ye also, being led away with the error of the wicked, fall from your own steadfastness."

2 Peter 3:17

Peter made a great point of warning you about the dangers of becoming misled by anything which attempts to dilute your understanding about why and how you must live your life. And yet, by itself our faith is fickle, needing the discipline, commitment, and humility to stay the course and remain innocent, "without spot, and blameless" within your life.

> "He said unto him the third time, Simon, son of Jonas, lovest thou Me? Peter was grieved because He said unto him the third time, Lovest thou Me? And he said unto Him, Lord, thou knowest all things; Thou knowest that I love Thee. Jesus said unto him, Feed My sheep.
>
> "Verily, verily, I say unto thee, When thou wast young, thou girdedst thyself, and walkedst whither thou wouldest: but when thou shalt be old, thou shalt stretch forth thy hands, and another shall gird thee, and carry thee whither thou wouldest not."
>
> John 21:17–18

Your faith in the Lord will always be in need of remembrance about your spiritual task at hand. Keeping your focus Single about that remembrance will keep you from being led astray. Faith alone, without the discipline to keep that understanding foremost for the Way you think, feel, and behave in life has caused countless misfortunes to befall the human race. James, being a witness to all of this, declares the Truth about this very same need.

> "But be ye doers of the Word, and not hearers only, deceiving your own selves.
>
> "For if any be a hearer of the Word, and not a doer, he is like unto a man beholding his natural face in a glass.
>
> "For he beholdeth himself, and goeth his way, and straightaway forgetteth what manner of man he was."
>
> James 1:22–24

25
Further Warnings
by the Lord

It is astonishing to consider how many times we have
allowed ourselves to become misled by "thoughts formed
from the imaginations" of our own hearts.

*W*ell before Paul, Peter, and James began to warn us about the
dangers that false witnesses present to our mental, emotional, and spiritual
wellbeing, the Lord did. His warnings have been continuous about the
harm they cause to our ability to understand the most important things of
all. Instead of Light, He warns us about the spiritual darkness they bring
into our lives.

> *"In the Beginning was the Word, and the Word was with God,
> and the Word was God.*
>
> *"The same was in the Beginning with God.*
>
> *"All things that were made by Him; and without Him was not
> any thing made that was made.*
>
> *"In Him was Life; and the Life was the Light of men.*
>
> *"And the Light Shineth in the darkness; and the darkness
> comprehended it not."*
>
> John 1:1–5

With all the Clarity the Lord has Given to us throughout history about how He fulfills His Quest for our salvation and deliverance into the Joy of Heavenly Love, it is quite astonishing to consider how many times we have allowed ourselves to lose focus about what must always be, and remain, our First Love.

> "And after six Days Jesus taketh Peter, James, and John his brother, and bringeth them up into a High Mountain apart.
>
> "And was transformed before them: and His face did Shine as the Sun, and His raiment was White as the Light.
>
> "And behold, there appeared unto them Moses and Elias talking with Him."
>
> Matthew 17:1–3

The Words: *And after six Days Jesus taketh Peter, James, and John his brother, and bringeth them up into a High Mountain apart* describe coming into a state of readiness to receive a new spiritual understanding from the Lord about Thoughts which are much Higher, and much more Perfect than your own.

Spiritually, Peter represents your faith in the Lord, James represents confirmation about why and how you must live your life, and John represents your inmost devotion to live your life accordingly. In the NewTestimant, each displays these qualities and virtues through their words and actions.

The Words: *And was transformed before them: and His face did Shine as the Sun* illuminate the Lord's Enlightening you about the Way to your salvation and deliverance into an eternal Heavenly state of being.

The Words: *and His raiment was White as the Light* display the Lord once again making the Principles of His Righteousness apparent for all to see and understand.

The Words: *And, behold, there appeared unto them Moses and Elias talking with Him* describe the Lord bringing forth remembrance about the Law and prophets. In that Light, He renews your understanding about the things that He has been teaching all of us since the Beginning of time.

> *Then answered Peter, and said unto Jesus, Lord, it is good for us to be here: if Thou wilt, let us make here three tabernacles: one for Thee, and one for Moses, and one for Elias.*
>
> Matthew 17:4

Of its own accord, faith gets confused rather easily. And so, the Lord uses this example, and many others throughout the Bible to teach you about your need to stay focused on the Singularity of His Message to you. Here He is teaching you that there is no reason to divide the Truth of His Message, for it is One Message, and must always remain so if you are to clearly recognize the most important things of all.

> *Think not that I am come to destroy the Law or the prophets: I am not come to destroy, but to fulfill.*
>
> Matthew 5:17

> *The light of the body is the eye: if therefore thine eye be Single, thy whole body shall be full of Light.*
>
> Matthew 6:22

> *While he yet spake, behold a Bright Cloud over-shadowed them: and behold a Voice out of the Cloud, which said, This is My beloved Son, in Whom I am well pleased; hear ye Him.*
>
> Matthew 17:5

> *If ye love Me, keep My Commandments.*
>
> John 14:15

The Parable of the Rich Man

Spiritually, the Word "rich" is used in both a positive and negative sense throughout the Bible. In a positive sense, "rich" describes all the invaluable internal Rewards you receive from the Lord as you willingly live your life in the Way He is Showing you that you must. In a negative sense, the Word "rich" describes the conceit and self-merit that comes from valuing your own self-intelligence above His.

> "*And, behold, one came and said unto Him, Good Master, what good thing shall I do, that I may have eternal Life?*
>
> "*And He said unto him, Why callest thou Me Good? There is none Good but One, that is God: but if thou wilt enter into Life, keep the Commandments.*
>
> "*He said unto him, Which? Jesus said, Thou shalt do no murder, Thou shalt not commit adultery, Thou shalt not steal, Thou shalt not bear false witness.*
>
> "*Honor thy Father and thy Mother: and, Thou shalt love thy neighbor as thyself.*
>
> "*The young man saith unto Him, All these things have I kept from my youth up: what lack I yet?*"
>
> Matthew 19:16–20

The "young man" citied in this parable held himself in great esteem because he complied with religious doctrine derived solely from the letter of the Word. His compliance led him to believe that he was "righteous" in all his "ways." And so, having "faith" in his own correctness, he superficially asks the Lord, "Good Master, what good thing shall I do that I may have eternal Life?"

And although he was expecting immediate approval, the Lord realized that this young man lacked the spiritual understanding he needed to realize what leads to "eternal Life." And so, as Righteousness Himself, the Lord asks him to look within himself and answer this question, "And He said unto him, Why callest Me Good?"

By doing so the Lord is also asking you, too, to look within yourself for answers about what leads to your reception of the Goodness of His Love within your soul. By teaching him "There is none Good but One, that is God" He is teaching you to recognize that there is only One Way to experience that incomparable Goodness.

By saying to this young man, "but if thou wilt enter into Life, keep the Commandments" the Lord is teaching you … all of us … clearly, simply, and without any ambiguity about the Way we must live our lives in Order to receive, retain, and forever share in the eternal Blessings of True Life from His Life. He requires nothing more from us.

By the young man responding to the Lord's Words by asking "Which?" he exemplifies a woeful lack of spiritual recognition about what leads to our salvation and deliverance into an eternal Heavenly state of being. And so, the Lord answers him by teaching him that he must abide by all His Commandments, for they are all Seamlessly interrelated as One. He is also teaching you that if you choose to violate one of them, you will spiritually violate all of them.

By saying to the young man, "Thou shalt do no murder," the Lord is drawing your attention to the harm that ill will toward others will cause to your ability to host the Goodness of His Love within your soul. By saying "Thou shalt not commit adultery." He is teaching you about the harm that violating the fidelity between Divine Truth and the Doctrine of His Righteousness will cause to your mental, emotional, and spiritual wellbeing.

By saying "Thou shalt not steal," He is teaching you about the harm you bring upon yourself by substituting your own thoughts in the Rightful Place of His Thoughts. By saying "Thou shalt not bear false witness," He is teaching you about the harm you will cause to yourself and others by misrepresenting what He has, is, and will forever be Showing you about what must always be, and remain, your First Works.

He was, in fact, very poor and needy.

By teaching this young man to "Honor thy Father and thy Mother," the Lord is teaching you to honor His Love and Wisdom about the Truth of these things.

By His Words "thou shalt love thy neighbor as thyself," the Lord is teaching you that you must always remember to love others in the Way you wish to be loved yourself, while always realizing that like begets like within your life.

By reciting these Holy Commandments to this young man, the Lord is asking you to recognize, acknowledge, and accept that there is need for a much deeper level of understanding about the Way to your salvation and deliverance into "eternal Life" than simply complying with letter-of-the-Word dictates.

And yet, even with all the Lord was teaching him, this young man remained steadfast in believing in own self-merit. Still convinced he had attained everything needed to "have eternal Life" he responded again to the Lord by saying, "All these things have I kept from my youth up: what lack I yet?"

And although this young man thought he was deserving of all the bountiful Rewards Promised to him by the Lord in the Bible, he was, in fact, very poor and needy of possessing the spiritual understanding he so greatly needed to receive them.

> "*Jesus said unto him, If thou wilt be perfect, go and sell that thou hast, and give to the poor, and thou shalt have Treasure in Heaven: and come and follow Me.*"
>
> Matthew 19:21

Having now directed this young man's attention to his need to develop a deeper spiritual understanding about what will allow him to enter into the Joys of Heavenly love, the Lord concludes His Instructions by saying, "If thou wilt be perfect, go and sell that thou hast, and give to the poor."

By doing so, He is teaching all of us to willing rid ourselves of anything we value more in life than seeking His Righteousness First in all we think, feel, and do. He is teaching you that only by doing so will you be giving what is poor and needy within your life the most Valuable things of all.

The Words: *and thou shalt have Treasure in Heaven* recount the Promise the Lord makes to you if you are willing to apply that spiritual understanding to each and every aspect of your life.

The Words: *come and follow Me* demonstrate your need to remember to abide by that understanding with all your mind, heart, and strength. As Righteousness Himself, the Lord completes this remarkable lesson to this "rich" young man in this manner, for these are the Works that are acceptable to the Lord as He reforms you and transforms you into eternally receiving True Life from His Life.

> "*But when the young man heard that saying, he went away sorrowful: for he had great possessions.*"
>
> Matthew 19:22

To think that the Lord is Instructing you to divest yourself of all your worldly possessions is far from spiritual Reality. To think that He wishes for you to let the people who depend upon you suffer the consequences of your giving away everything you have to the materially poor is irresponsible thinking. Rather, He knows you have considerable material needs, and knows that they are required for your physical, mental, emotional, and spiritual wellbeing, and for the physical, mental, emotional, and spiritual wellbeing of those you provide for.

Rather, by asking you to "sell that thou hast," He is asking you to rid yourself of the pride of your own self-intelligence. By asking you to "give to the poor," He is asking you to willingly give all your honesty, sincerity, and humility to your need to remember to live your life in the Way He is Showing you that you must.

That acknowledgment and acceptance will put everything in their proper Order within your life. It will certainly Give you Guidance for the Way to employ all the material possessions you have in life. When used to serve His Purpose for your Good and for the Good of all around you, they provide society with usefulness benefits that can grow and multiply abundantly for generations to come.

The Words: *But when the young man heard that saying, he went away sorrowful for he had great possessions* convey prizing your own self-intelligence above what the Lord has, is, and forever will be teaching you about the most Valuable things of all. And because this young man was so attached to believing in the correctness of his own letter-of-the-Word misinterpretations about Scripture, he went away sorrowful, disappointed that he was not rewarded by the Lord in the "way" that he had expected.

> "*Then Jesus said unto His disciples, Verily I say unto you, That a rich man shall hardly enter into the Kingdom of Heaven.*"
>
> Matthew 19:23

Misplaced attachments to literal misinterpretations about Scripture have caused many to lose their Focus about their spiritual task at hand. Instead of recognizing, acknowledging, and accepting what must always be, and remain your First Love, they cause to misunderstand what it means to "enter" in through the Gates into the City" as described in Revelation 22:14.

The Words: *Then Jesus said unto his disciples, Verily I say unto you, That a rich man shall hardly enter into the Kingdom of Heaven*, communicate the Lord's clear warning to take great care in what you choose to value most in life.

> "*And again I say unto you, It is easier for a camel to go through the eye of a needle, than for a rich man to enter into the Kingdom of God.*
>
> "*When His disciples heard it, they were exceedingly amazed, saying, Who then can be saved?*
>
> "*But Jesus beheld them, and said unto them, With men this is impossible; but with God all things are possible.*"
>
> Matthew 19:24–26

By His Words: *And again I say unto you, It is easier for a camel to go through the eye of a needle, than for a rich man to enter into the Kingdom of God*, the Lord is defining "the straight and narrow Gates" that you must be willing to enter through in your quest to receive the Joy and Goodness of His Love within your life. And as a "camel" is a beast of burden capable of traveling great distances with little refreshment from water or food, you, too, must make the most of the spiritual nourishment you have received from the Lord to sustain you during your spiritual journey ahead.

During that journey, you will be asked to draw deeply within yourself from those reserves. As you willingly do so with all your mind and heart, you will soon find all the strength you need to walk "the extra mile" in the Light of His Righteousness. It is then when you will be Given to fully understand what it means for it to be easier "for a camel to go through the eye of a needle, than for a rich man to enter into the Kingdom of God."

With this lesson, the Lord is teaching you that there is simply no other *way*—up or around—for you to receive, retain, and forever share in the incomparable Blessing of "eternal Life." Allowing yourself to be misled into believing otherwise is spiritual folly.

> "*Therefore all things whatsoever that ye would that men should do to you, do ye even so to them: for this is the Law and the prophets.*
>
> "*Enter ye in at the strait Gate: for wide is the gate, and broad is the way, that leadeth to destruction, and many there be which go in thereat:*
>
> "*Because strait is the Gate: and narrow is the Way, which leadeth unto Life, and few there be that find it.*"
>
> Matthew 7:12–14

> "*Take My Yoke upon you, and learn of Me; for I am meek and lowly in heart: and ye shall find Rest unto your souls.*
>
> "*For My Yoke is easy, and My Burden is Light.*"
>
> Matthew 11:29–30

If you are honest with yourself, it is quite amazing to think that from where you have started your spiritual journey in this world that you can become spiritually reformed and transformed into an image of the Truth and as a likeness to the Goodness of the Lord Himself!

The Words: *When His disciples heard it, they were exceedingly amazed* describe that honest amazement.

The Words: *Who then can be saved?* interject reflecting on doubts upon your ability to undergo that reformation and transformation. Yet that question is understandable, given honest, sincere, and humble introspection about the extent of your spiritual task at hand.

The Words: *But Jesus beheld them, and said unto them, With men this is impossible; but with God all things are possible* answer those doubts. With this answer, the Lord is inviting you to prove the Truth of His Testimony to you, by living your life in the Way He is Showing you that you must.

> *I had fainted unless I had believed to see the Goodness of the Lord in the land of the Living.*
>
> *Wait on the Lord: be of Good courage, and He shall strengthen thine heart: wait, I Say, on the Lord.*
>
> Psalms 27:13–14

> *But seek ye first the Kingdom of God and His Righteousness; and all these things shall be added unto you.*
>
> Matthew 6:33

> *If ye know these things, happy are ye if ye do them.*
>
> John 13:17

Christ and the Rich Young Ruler, by Heinrich Hofmann

26
Religious Discrimination

Understanding the Truth of Love
is not exclusive to any one institutional religion.

*P*rofessing that there is only one institutional religion capable of providing the understanding needed for your salvation and deliverance into an eternal Heavenly state of being is very shortsighted. Throughout human history, stiff-necked and cold-hearted judgments made from such beliefs have led many into mental, emotional, and spiritual insanities of all sorts. The disastrous behaviors they have provoked defy description. This form of religious bias constitutes the third form of becoming a false witness to the Lord's Testimony to us. Let that not be you.

> "And John answered Him, saying, Master, we saw one casting out devils in Thy Name, and he followed not us: and we forbad him, because he followed not us.

> "But Jesus said, Forbid him not: for there is no man which shall do a Miracle in My Name, that can lightly speak evil of Me.

> "For he that is not against us is on our Part."

Mark 9:38–40

The meaning of the Lord's "Name" is portrayed by many Beautiful descriptions throughout the Bible. Included are: The Lord Our Righteousness, Wonderful, Counselor, The Mighty God, The Everlasting Father, The Prince of Peace, The Most High, Jehovah, and Christ the Lord, among others. All these wonderful descriptions make manifest the Splendor of His Qualities and Virtues, Giving us understanding about Divine Truth and the Goodness of His Love for us all. They reveal Who He Is.

> "*A Word fitly Spoken is like Apples of Gold in Pictures of Silver.*"
> Proverbs 25:11

When Moses asked what he should say to the children of Israel when he told them that "The God of your fathers has sent me unto you," and they asked him, "What is His Name?" the Lord replied, "I am That I am." That reply was not meant to be nebulous. Rather it was Intended to focus our understanding upon the Divine Qualities and Virtues that Define Who He is, has been, and will always Be.

> "*And Moses said unto God, Behold, when I come unto the children of Israel, and shall say unto them, The God of your fathers has sent me unto you; and they shall say unto me, What is His Name? what shall I say to them?*
>
> "*And God said unto Moses, I AM THAT I AM: and He said, Thus thou shalt say unto the children of Israel, I AM hath sent me unto you.*"
> Exodus 3:13–14

The Lord's Qualities and Virtues are Worthy of worship in all that you think, feel, and do. As you willingly worship Him in that manner He Promises to come into your life, teach you about Himself, lead you into your salvation, and deliver you into the Joys of Heavenly Love. For this Reason, He is also called the "Messenger of the Covenant."

> "*Behold, I will send My Messenger, and He shall Prepare the Way before Me: and the Lord, Whom ye seek, shall suddenly come to His temple, even the Messenger of the Covenant, Whom you delight in: behold, He shall come, saith the Lord of Hosts.*"
>
> Malachi 3:1

As you live your life in the Way the Lord is teaching you that you must, you become enabled to host His Qualities and Virtues within your mind, heart, and soul. In that manner, you derive your new "name" from His Name.

> "*To Him the porter openeth; and the sheep hear His Voice: and He calleth His Own sheep by Name, and leadeth them out.*"
>
> John 10:3

The Words: *To Him the porter openeth; and the sheep hear His Voice* tell of innocently opening yourself up to receiving a new spiritual understanding about why and how you must live your life.

Spiritually, the Word "porter" describes your free will.

Through the verses recorded by Mark at the beginning of this Chapter, the Lord is teaching you that you cast "out devils" in "His Name" each time you willingly turn away from your self-serving thoughts, selfish affections and their corresponding behaviors, and abide by the Principles of His Righteousness, no matter what institutional religious orientation you follow.

The Lord illuminates that understanding by teaching you that each honest, sincere, and humble effort you make to do so allows Him to spiritually reform you and transform you into the person that He has Purposed for you to become. And because the Lord is Infinite and we are finite, as each person becomes a unique image and likeness to His Qualities and Virtues, they are portrayed as being a "Part" of the Whole.

The "Name" Jesus Christ means the Salvation of Truth.

He teaches you that no one should "forbid" anyone else from making those efforts, or "speak evil" against them for any reason whatsoever because those efforts are the very acts that allow Him to unite us together with Him and with one another as One. He thereby depicts that union as a "Miracle" being done within you by Him "on our Part."

> *"And these Signs shall follow them that believe; in My Name*
> *they shall cast out devils; they shall speak with new tongues:"*
> Mark 16:17

Throughout Scripture, the Lord teaches you that willfully abiding by the Principles of His Righteousness allows you to receive innermost happiness and genuine fulfillment within your mind, heart, and soul. He described these incomparable Blessings as the "Signs" that "shall follow" as you exercise your belief in Him by living your life accordingly.

The Words: *in My Name they shall cast out devils* depict gaining the ability to reject falsities and evils whenever they present themselves within your life.

To "speak with new tongues" describes communicating that new spiritual understanding through the way you think and feel, and most especially through the way you behave toward others. Doing so constitutes becoming a True witness to what the Lord has been teaching you since dawning of your spiritual Enlightenment.

> *"At that Day ye shall know that I am in my Father, and ye in*
> *me, and I in you."*
> John 14:20

The "Name" Jesus Christ means the Salvation of Truth. Knowing that meaning is a Blessing. Yet thinking that literal belief in His surname alone is "saving" is misleading. Rather, only by living your life according to the Way He is Showing you that you must can you become enabled to share in the incomparable Blessings that He has Prepared for you to inherit since the beginning of time. That He is Righteous in all of His Ways is exclaimed throughout the Bible. In Exodus, the Words "I Am" are meant to sharpen that focus.

> *"But the Comforter, which is the Holy Ghost, Whom the Father will send in My Name, He shall teach you all things, and bring all things to your remembrance, whatsoever I have said unto you.*"
>
> John 14:26

Spiritual understanding about the Truth of Love does not belong to any one formal religion. It belongs to what the Lord has been teaching all of humanity since our inceptions.

~

Unfortunately, and all too often, we have cast aside that understanding, then trodden it under foot by valuing our institutionalized "religions" over the One Language the Lord has Given to unite us all together with Him and with each other in Peace and Goodwill. Fortunately for us, in Truth from His Love for us He continues to return into our lives, reaching out to us to bring His Testimony back into remembrance within our lives. Have you heard His Call?

> "And now, Israel, what doth the Lord thy God require of thee, but to fear the Lord thy God, to walk in all His Ways, and to love Him, and to serve the Lord thy God with all thy heart and with all thy soul,
>
> "To keep the Commandments of the Lord, and His Statutes, which I Command thee this Day for thy Good?
>
> "Behold, the Heaven and the Heaven of Heavens is the Lord's thy God, the earth also, which all that therein is.
>
> "Only the Lord had a delight in thy fathers to Love them, and He chose their seed after them, even you above all people, as it is this Day.
>
> "Circumcise therefore the skin of your heart, and be no longer stiffnecked."
>
> Deuteronomy 10:12–16

Throughout His advent into our world, the Lord Labored greatly to restore our understanding about why and how we must live our lives. Everywhere He teaches you to remember what unites us all together with Him, and with one another, as His "people."

"O Righteous Father, the world hath not known Thee: but I have known Thee, and these have known that Thou hast sent Me.

"And I have declared unto them Thy Name, and will declare it: that the Love wherewith Thou hast Loved Me may be in them, and I in them."

John 17:25–26

"He that hath an ear, let him hear what the Spirit saith unto the churches."

Revelation 2:29

That the Lord has "declared" the Way to your salvation and deliverance into an eternal Heavenly state of being is professed throughout the entire Bible, from Beginning to Ending. His Message is timeless and everlasting, meant to be shared equally among all the people of the world. It is up to us to recognize the Truth of His Testimony to us, and to honor it in all we think, feel, and do. Only we can do it.

Honesty, sincerity, and humility shall flow as a River of gratefulness.

"Come now, and let us Reason together, saith the Lord: though your sins be as scarlet, they shall be as white as snow; though they be red as crimson, they shall be as wool.

"If ye be willing and obedient, ye shall eat the good of the Land."

Isaiah 1:18–19

Keeping remembrance about the Lord's Qualities and Virtues allows you to use Good Judgment in all you think, feel, and do. Keeping that remembrance as our Highest Priority in life will act to dissipate all differences existing between the differing "faiths" of the world, allowing the Lord to put all things in their proper Order within our lives.

"Behold the Days come, saith the Lord, that I shall raise unto David a Righteous Branch, and a King shall reign and prosper, and shall execute Judgment and Justice in the earth;

"In His Days Judah shall be saved, and Israel shall dwell safely: and this is His Name whereby He shall be called, THE LORD OUR RIGHTEOUSNESS."

Jeremiah 23:5–6

"And He shall Judge among the nations, and shall rebuke many people: and they shall beat their swords into plowshares, and their spears into pruninghooks: nation shall not lift up sword against nation, neither shall they learn war any more.

"O ye house of Jacob, come ye, and let us walk in the Light of the Lord."

Isaiah 2:4–5

When all the religions, nations, and peoples of the world come to a mutual agreement about why they need to place the Principles of Righteousness as their First Love, all Reasoning will lead to understanding about the Way the Lord fulfills His Purpose for the Creation of our souls. Any proclamations to the contrary will be used as examples of wrongheaded arguments, then Enlightening us about the most important things of all.

"In that Day shall there be a Highway out of Egypt to Assyria, and the Assyrian shall come into Egypt, and the Egyptian unto Assyria, and the Egyptians shall serve with the Assyrians.

"In that Day shall Israel be the Third with Egypt and with Assyria, even a Blessing in the midst of the Land:

> "*Whom the Lord of hosts shall Bless, saying, Blessed be Egypt My people, and Assyria, the Work of My hands, and Israel Mine inheritance.*"
>
> Isaiah 19:23–25

In that Day, any doctrine that had caused separation between us will find the invaluable spiritual understanding needed to reunite all of us together in Love and Goodwill toward one other.

In that Day, our realization about the most important things of all will become One with that understanding, yielding incomparable Blessings, abundantly, for endless generations to come.

In that Day, those Blessing shall flow as a River of gratefulness in reverence to what the the Lord has, is, and forever will be Endeavoring to accomplish within our lives.

> "*And the Lord shall be King over all the earth: in that Day shall there be One Lord, and His Name One.*"
>
> Zechariah 14:9

> "*For it is Written, As I Live, saith the Lord, every knee shall bow to Me, and every tongue shall confess.*

> "*So then every one of us shall give account of himself to God.*

> "*Let us not therefore judge one another any more: but Judge this rather, that no man put a stumbling block or an occasion to fall.*"
>
> Romans 14:11–13

Reflections

Becoming a false witness to the Truth of Love is self-defeating. It harms you in ways that will destroy the Goodness within your own soul. It also has the potential to harm the Goodness within others for generations to come.

Throughout the entire Bible, the Lord raises Up the Principles of His Righteousness to act as the Standards for the Way you must live your life. Those Standards also apply to the the Way you must think, feel, and act towards others, nothing withheld. Do you use those Standards to Judge the Goodness within others, or do you rely solely on the letter of the Word to judge them? Are you rich in your own self-merit, or are you willing to give away all of your preconceived notions about what constituents "true and saving faith in the Lord," and then honestly, sincerely, and humbly love others in the Way that the Lord Loves you?

And so, throughout the Bible, the Lord warns you not to allow yourself to become deceived about what allows the Joy and Goodness of His Love to remain, grow, and flourish within you, and what does not. And in no uncertain terms, He also teaches you to be very careful about what you teach others about these most important things of all.

> "*Therefore all things whatsoever ye would that men should do to you, do ye even so to them: for this is the Law and the prophets.*
>
> "*Enter in at the Strait Gate: for wide is the gate, and broad is the way, that leadeth to destruction, and many there be which go in thereat:*
>
> "*Because Strait is the Gate, and narrow is the Way, which leadeth unto Life, and few there be that find it.*

"Beware of false prophets, which come to you in sheep's clothing, but inwardly are ravening wolves."

Matthew 7:12–15

"For there shall arise false Christs, and false prophets, and shall show great signs and wonders; insomuch that, if it were possible, they shall deceive the very elect.

"Behold, I have told you before."

Matthew 24:24–25

YOU SHALL NOT COVET.

27

Thirsting for
What Is Not Yours

Keeping Righteousness First requires
a great and lasting commitment on your part.

*"Thou shalt not covet thy neighbor's house, thou shalt not covet
thy neighbor's wife, nor his manservant, nor his maidservant,
nor his ox, nor his ass, nor anything that is thy neighbor's."*

Exodus 20:17

We have all been Created to evolve into an image and as a likeness
to the Truth and Goodness that flows forth from the Lord's Unselfish Love
for us all. We are all neighbors in that regard, all in need of receiving His
Qualities and Virtues and sharing them through Goodwill for one another.
Some might say that we are all in that same boat!

*"There is a River, the Streams whereof shall make Glad the City
of God, the Holy Place of the Tabernacles of the Most High."*

Psalms 46:4

To covet the physical possessions of others is self-serving. It bears nothing
of Unselfish Love or Goodwill for your "neighbor." Rather, it brings forth
the very opposite into being within your mind, heart, and soul.

Yet spiritually, there is a much more harmful form of coveting "anything that is thy neighbor's." That is a wish to take control over their mental, emotional and spiritual, wellbeing for selfish purposes.

~

Covetousness loves itself above all else. It is diametrically opposed to what enables you to have the "Right to the Tree of Life." Rather, it would have you take control over "the tree of the knowledge of Good and evil" for selfish purposes. It wishes to take you in the very opposite direction of where you may "make Glad the City of God."

> "No man can serve two masters: for either he will hate the One, and love the other, or else he will hold to the One, and despise the other. Ye cannot serve God and mammon."
>
> Matthew 6:24

Covetousness hates the notion that it must give up the pride of its own self-intelligence to share in the Joys of Heavenly Love. It resents having to give up what it values most in Order to receive those incomparable Blessings. Rather, to its own great detriment, it rejects and persecutes that Divine Truth.

> "And He Showed me a Pure River of Water of Life, Clear as Crystal, proceeding out of the Throne of God and of the Lamb.
>
> "In the Midst of the street of it, and on either side of the River, was there the Tree of Life, which bear Twelve manner of fruits, and yielded her fruit every month: and the leaves of the Tree were for the healing of the nations.
>
> "And there shall be no more curse: but the Throne of God and of the Lamb shall be in it; and His servants shall serve Him:"
>
> Revelation 22:1–3

> *Blessed are they that do His Commandments, that they might have Right to the Tree of Life, and may enter in through the Gates into the City.*
>
> Revelation 22:14

The First Phrase of the Tenth Commandment—
Thou shalt not covet thy neighbor's house.

Throughout the Bible, your soul is portrayed as a "house" hosting thoughts and affections. Believing that taking control over the knowledge of Good and evil for selfish purposes can lead to anything of lasting Value within you is to build one's own "house" on very faulty foundations.

> *Except the Lord build the house, they labor in vain that build it: except the Lord keep the City, the watchman waketh but in vain.*
>
> Psalms 127:1

Working with the Lord to build the integrity of your soul upon the Truth of His Love for you is spiritual Wisdom. Allowing Him to keep that Doctrine Shining Brightly within your life is all-important for your inmost gladness of mind and heart. Doing otherwise wastes the Opportunity of your lifetime. Your realization about the Importance of these things acts as the "watchman" over the choices you make in life.

> *Therefore whoever heareth these Sayings of Mine, and doeth them, I will liken him unto a wise man, which built his house upon a Rock.*
>
> *And the rain descended, and the floods came, and the winds blew, and beat upon that house; and it fell not: for it was founded upon a Rock.*
>
> Matthew 7:24–25

Through this Testimony, the Lord informs you about the Way you must construct yourself to become an Abode for the Goodness of His Love to come to Rest within your soul. The Truth of these "Sayings" acts as the Cornerstone for that foundation to be built upon, and last forever within your life.

> "Hear, O My son, and receive My sayings; And the years of thy Life shall be many.
>
> "I have taught thee in the Way of Wisdom; I have led thee in Right Paths.
>
> "When thou goest, thy steps shall not be straitened; and when thou runnest, thou shalt not stumble."
>
> Proverbs 4:10–12

> "Jesus answered and said unto him, If a man love Me, he will keep My Words: and My Father will Love him, and We will come unto him, and make our Abode with him.
>
> "He that loveth Me not keepeth not My sayings: and the Word which ye hear is not Mine, but the father's which sent Me."
>
> John 14:23–24

Throughout your entire lifetime in this world the Lord Works within you to fulfill His Purpose for the Creation of your soul. Choosing to work with Him to that End is all-important for your salvation and deliverance into the Joys of Heavenly Love.

These temptations should be treated as your own worst enemies.

> "Now He that planteth and he that watereth are One: and every man shall receive his own reward according to his own labour.

> "For we are laborers together with God: ye are God's husbandry,
> ye are God's building."
>
> 1 Corinthians 3:8–9

The second phrase of the tenth the Commandment—
Thou shalt not covet thy neighbor's wife.

When left unabated, coveting another person's wife looks to act upon its own lust. It threatens to ruin the physical and spiritual fidelity of their marriage. It risks destroying their mental, emotional, and spiritual wellbeing and the mental, emotional, and spiritual wellbeing of their children. It risks causing dire effects to the wellbeing of generations to come.

> "The eye also of the adulterer waiteth for the twilight, saying,
> No eye shall see me: and disguiseth his face."
>
> Job 24:15

Realizing the harm that coveting another person's wife can cause to so many others should stop you in your tracks from harboring such lusts. And knowing that like begets like, those temptations should be treated as your worst enemies. Self-serving thoughts and selfish desires that argue otherwise seek to adulterate the integrity of your own soul.

> "But I say unto you, That whosoever looketh on a woman to lust
> after her hath committed adultery with her already in his
> heart."
>
> Matthew 5:28

Your thoughts and affections are perfectly transparent to the Lord. In the life to come, they will also become transparent to all around you. Spiritual beauty is obtained through your honest, sincere, and humble willingness to live your life by abiding by the Principles of Righteousness in all you think, feel, and do. Thinking otherwise is self-deceptive.

"Let Thy Work appear unto Thy servants, and Thy Glory unto their children.

"And let the Beauty of the Lord our God be upon us: and establish Thou the work of our hands upon us; yea, the work of our hands establish Thou it."

Psalms 90:16–17

"For the Lord taketh pleasure in His people: He will beautify the meek with salvation."

Psalms 149:4

The third phrase of the tenth Commandment—*Thou shalt not covet thy neighbor's manservant, nor his maidservant.*
The spiritual sensibilities that serve you in discerning Truth from falsity and Right from wrong are described in the Bible as your "manservants" and "maidservants." They are trustworthy and loyal because they help you in fulfilling the Lord's Purpose for the Creation of your soul. To covet control over these "servants" for selfish purposes is to despitefully abuse them.

He never leaves you alone.

"Hear another parable: There was a certain Householder, which planted a Vineyard, and hedged it round about, and digged a Winepress in it, and built a Tower, and let it out to husbandmen, and went into a far country.

"And when the time of the fruit drew near, He sent His servants to the husbandmen, that they might receive the fruits of it.

"And the husbandmen took His servants, and beat one, and killed another, and stoned another.

"Again, He sent other servants more than the first: and they did unto them likewise."

Matthew 21:33–36

You have been Gifted with the Opportunity to work with the Lord to become a "Place" wherein the Goodness of His Love may come into fruition within your soul. From His providing you with all you need to fulfill that Opportunity, He is called "a certain Householder."

That He "planted a Vineyard, and hedged it round about, and digged a Winepress in it, and built a Tower" is descriptive of His having done so. Spiritually, you are the "the husbandmen" of those Provisions within your own life.

And although He never leaves you alone, the Lord does leave you with the time and space you need to cultivate the most important things of all. And so, after Providing you with all you need to do so, He describes Himself as He Who "went into a far country."

The free will choices you make in this life will determine the person you will become in the life to come.

The Words *And when the time of the fruit drew near, He sent His servants to the husbandmen, that they might receive the fruits of it* represent a time of Visitation, wherein the Lord will seek to gather in all the Goodness you have tended to bring into fruition within your life.

The Words *And the husbandmen took His servants, and beat one, and killed another, and stoned another* describe spitefully abusing the spiritual sensibilities the Lord has Given you to help Him fulfill that Righteous Quest.

The Words: *Again, He sent other servants more than the first: and they did unto them likewise* exemplify hating those the spiritual sensibilities the Lord has sent you without a Just cause.

"*When the Lord therefore of the Vineyard cometh, what will He do unto those husbandmen?*"

Matthew 21:40

Throughout Scripture, the Lord asks you to consider the consequences of abusing what He has Provided for you to discern Truth from falsity and Right from wrong. How much more clearly can He warn you about the dire effects that you will bring upon yourself by coveting control over the cry of His "*manservants*" *and* "*maidservants*" within your life?

"*For the Vineyard of the Lord of Hosts is the house of Israel, and the men of Judah His pleasant plant: and He looked for Judgment, but behold oppression; for Righteousness, but behold a Cry.*"

Isaiah 5:7

"*But they made light of it, and went their ways, one to his farm, another to his merchandise.*"

"*And the remnant took His servants, and entreated them spitefully, and slew them.*"

Matthew 22:5–6

"*For the Son of man is as a Man taking a far journey, who left His House, and gave authority to His servants, and to every man his work, and Commanded the porter to watch.*"

"*Watch ye therefore: for ye know not when the Master of the House cometh, at even, or at midnight, or at the cock-crowing, or in the morning.*"

<blockquote>
"Lest coming suddenly He find you sleeping.

"And what I say unto you, I say unto all, Watch."
</blockquote>

Mark 13:34–37

The Fourth Phrase of the Tenth Commandment—
Thou shalt not covet thy neighbor's ox.

Spiritually, an "ox" describes your commitment to live your life according to the Principles of the Lord's Righteousness. The strength of that commitment acts as your spiritual beast of Burden.

<blockquote>
"Thou shalt not see thy brother's ox or his sheep go astray, and hide thyself from them: thou shalt in any case bring them again unto thy brother."
</blockquote>

Deuteronomy 22:1

Thoughts having common lineage with the Lord's Thoughts are your spiritual "brothers." The term "brotherly love" describes recognizing and cherishing those thoughts above your own. Should you perceive that your commitment to do so has gone astray, you must never try to hide it.

The Words: *Thou shalt not see thy brother's ox or his sheep go astray, and hide thyself from them* reflect that spiritual Imperative. These Words inform you that if you try to hide from acknowledging your lack of commitment to abide by His Thoughts, your spiritual innocence will be at risk as well.

The Lord teaches you that it is your responsibility to revisit any spiritual missteps, and then reconcile yourself to your "brother" in the Way that He has Shown you that you must.

The Words: *thou shalt in any case bring them again unto thy brother* portray recommitting yourself to abiding by that spiritual understanding in all you think, feel, and do. Doing so also honors His Wisdom within your life.

"While He yet talked to the people, behold, His Mother and His Brethren stood without, desiring to speak with Him.

"Then one said to Him, Behold, Thy Mother and Thy Brethren stand without, desiring to speak with Thee.

"And He answered and said unto him that told Him, Who is My mother? and who are My brethren?

"And He stretched forth His hand towards His disciples, and said,

"Behold my Mother and My Brethren!"

Matthew 12:46–49

The return of the ark of the covenant to Beth Shemesh. Engraving by Gustave Dore.

Your need to keep the Principles of Righteousness Primary within your life requires a great and lasting commitment on your part, and the Lord knows that much more than you realize it yourself.

The Words: *disciple* and *discipline* are very closely related in their spiritual meaning.

> "*In like manner shalt thou do with his ass; and so shalt thou do with his raiment; and with all the lost things of thy brother's, which he hath lost, and thou hast found, shalt thou do likewise: thou mayest not hide thyself.*
>
> "*Thou shalt not see thy brother's ass or his ox fall down by the Way, and hide thyself from them: thou shalt surely help Him to lift them Up again.*"
>
> Deuteronomy 22:3–4

In Scripture, your spiritual conscience is described by the Word "ass." Acknowledgement about what must always be, and remain, your First Love is portrayed as your "raiment." To have lost your willingness to keep the importance of these things in remembrance for the Way you live your life is descriptive of "the lost things of thy brother's, which he has lost."

The Words: *and thou hast found* describe becoming aware of that loss.

The Words: *shalt thou do likewise: thou mayest not hide thyself* are the Lord's Instructions to heed His warning about the danger of ignoring the importance of remembering why and how you must live your life.

The Words: *thou shall surely help Him to lift them Up again* defines your responsibility to help the Lord restore them up into their Rightful Place within your life once again, before it becomes too late.

There will be many, many times in this life when you will need to work with the Lord to overcome your own spiritual missteps. Each effort you make to do so helps Him to Help you recover your spiritual sense of Reason.

> "Give ye ear, and hear My Voice; hearken and hear My Speech.
>
> "Doth the plowman plow all day to sow? Doth he open and break the clods of his ground?
>
> "When he hath made plain the face thereof, doth he not cast abroad the fitches, and scatter the cummin, and cast in the Principle wheat and the Appointed barley and the rie in their Place?
>
> "For God doth Instruct him to discretion, and doth teach him."
>
> Isaiah 28:23–26

Throughout the entire Bible, the Lord uses physical things to teach you about spiritual things. This is His "Speech," and it is the "language" spoken throughout the Heavens. It is the Way He Communicates with you about the most important things of all. And so, for your Good and for the Good of all around you, He asks you to "Give ye ear, and hear My Voice." How you "hearken" to "hear" His "Speech" becomes evident to Him through the way you think, feel, and act in life.

The Lord uses physical things to teach you about spiritual things.

The Word: *plowman* spiritually describes your willingness to apply yourself to living your life according to what He is teaching you to be True and Right.

The Words: *Doth the plowman plow all day to sow?* ask you to reflect upon why you should be willing to cultivate the spiritual potential for Good within your life.

The Words *Doth he open and break the clods of his ground?* describe recognition of your need to break up each and every hardheaded, stiff-necked, and cold-hearted form of poor judgment that confronts you along the Way.

The Words: *When he hath made plain the face thereof* communicate having readied your mind and heart to receive the Lord's Testimony within your life. At that time, you will have prepared yourself as a fertile field to receive the implantation of the seeds of Divine Truth within your soul.

The Words: *Doth he not cast abroad the fitches, and scatter the cumin, and cast in the Principle wheat and the Appointed barley and the rie in their Place?* describes how you work with the Lord to sow the things that will sustain the Goodness of His Love within your life, then allowing them to become an everlasting Source of Joy within you in the life to come.

Throughout the entire Bible, the Lord asks you to use this same Sound Judgment in all that you think, feel and do.

The Words: *For God doth Instruct him to discretion* express His Call to Reason.

The Words: *and doth teach him* describe the continual Guidance He Gives you about why and how you must respond to that Righteous Call.

To live your life accordingly is to "Remember the Sabbath Day, to keep it Holy."

> "*Say unto the righteous, that it shall be well with him: for they shall eat the fruit of their doings.*"
>
> Isaiah 3:10

> "*Sow to yourselves in Righteousness, reap in Mercy: break up your fallow ground: for it is time to seek the Lord, till He come and rain Righteousness upon you.*"
>
> Hosea 10:12

> *And answered them, saying, Which one of you shall have an ass*
> *or an ox fallen into a pit, and will not straightway pull him*
> *out on the Sabbath Day?*
>
> Luke 14:5

The Fifth Phrase of the Tenth Commandment—
Thou shalt not covet thy neighbor's ass.

Throughout the Bible, the Lord describes Himself as making His advent into your life through your spiritual conscience. With His "still small Voice," He comes into your mind and heart with Compassion and Humility, teaching you about the Way you must live your life. If you are willing to head His Call, you will soon find that He is approaching you in a very Sure-footed manner.

> *Rejoice greatly, O daughter of Zion; shout, O daughter of*
> *Jerusalem: behold, thy King cometh unto thee: He is Just, and*
> *having salvation; lowly, and riding upon an ass, and upon a*
> *colt the foal of an ass.*
>
> Zechariah 9:9

Spiritually, the "daughter of Zion" is descriptive of your affection for the Lord's Divine Love for you … for all of us. The "daughter of Jerusalem" is descriptive of your affection for the Doctrine that teaches you about the Way you may receive and forever share in the Blessings of that incomparable Love.

He Promises to defend you from spiritual harm.

The Words: *behold, thy King cometh unto thee* state your need to recognize the Sovereignty of the Divine Truth He is bringing into your life. The effects of living your life accordingly are described by the Words "He is Just."

The Words: *and having salvation* celebrate the protection and liberation from mental, emotional, and spiritual harm He affords you as you diligently abide by the Principles of His Righteousness in all you think, feel, and do.

The Word: *lowly* describes the Lord's Divine Humility, for He knows that He is asking great patience, courage, and endurance of you as He leads you through your spiritual journey in this world.

The Words: "*and riding upon an ass* illustrate His approaching you through your spiritual conscience about the most important things of all.

The Words: *upon a colt the foal of an ass* portray the Innocence of that approach, for He has only your Best interests in Heart.

The Words: *Rejoice greatly* and *shout* express recognizing that the Joy and Goodness that await you will far exceed your greatest expectations.

> "*But let all those that put their trust in Thee rejoice: let them ever shout for Joy, because Thou defendest them: let them also that love Thy Name be Joyful in Thee.*
>
> "*For Thou, Lord, wilt Bless the righteous; with favor wilt Thou compass him as with a Shield.*"
>
> Psalms 5:11–12

Throughout Scripture, the Lord teaches you about His Purpose for coming into your life. He Promises to defend you from mental, emotional, and spiritual harm as you work with Him to fulfill that Holy Purpose.

He teaches you about His Qualities and Virtues, and about the eternal Blessings He has in store for you as you willingly work with Him to become an image and as a likeness to them within your mind, heart, and soul.

He asks you not to be offended by your need to understand the Truth about these things. Rather, He teaches you that He is bringing this realization into your life solely for your Good and for the Good of all around you.

> "*And we know that all things work together for Good to them that love God, to them who are called according to His Purpose.*"
>
> Romans 8:28

28
Spiritual Obstinance

At the time of the Lord's advent into our world, humanity
had become lost in a spiritual wilderness of its own making,

$\mathcal{A}$s many times as the Lord has delivered His Message about His Purpose for coming into our lives, it is astonishing how many times we have rejected it. Instead of rejoicing in it, we have so often coveted control over it for our own self-serving motives.

"*Why, seeing times are not hidden from the Almighty, do they that know Him not see His Days?*

"*Some remove the Landmarks; they violently take away flocks, and feed thereof.*

"*They drive away the ass of the Fatherless, they take the Widow's ox for a pledge.*

"*They turn the needy out of the Way: the poor of the earth hide themselves together.*

"*Behold, as wild asses in the desert, go they forth to their work; rising betimes for a prey: the wilderness yieldeth food for them and for their children.*

446 | The Spiritual Meaning of Scripture

> *"They reap every one his corn in the field: they gather the vintage of the wicked.* **,,**

The Words: *Why, seeing times are not hidden from the Almighty* address those who proclaim to understand spiritual causes and effects, yet refuse to apply that understanding to the way they live their lives.

The Words: *do they that know Him not see His Days?* reveal the perplexity of their refusal to do so. With this question, the Lord is asking you to realize that those "times" are already upon you. He further illustrates this Truth within Matthew 16:1-3 and Revelation 1:3.

The Words: *Some remove the Landmarks* reveal dismissing your need to keep the Principles of Righteousness as the Standards for the Way you must live your life.

The Words *they violently take away flocks* make known the resulting harm that this misguided dismissal causes to the innocence within your mind and heart.

The Words: *and feed thereof* portray the resulting loss of spiritual nourishment to sustain the Goodness of His Love within your soul.

The Words: *They drive away the ass of the Fatherless* disclose the great disservice that loss brings upon your willingness to remember the important things of all.

The Words: *they take the Widow's ox for a pledge* warn against making a commitment to things that do not unite Wisdom with Unselfish Love within your life.

The Words: *They turn the needy out of the Way* depict the harm that these missteps cause to your understanding about why and how you must live your life.

The Words: *the poor of the earth hide themselves together* divulge the futility of trying to justify those missteps, just as Adam and Eve discovered in Genesis as they tried to hide "themselves from the presence of the Lord God amongst the trees of the Garden."

The Words: *Behold, as wild asses in the desert* describe the resulting undisciplined spiritual conscience choosing to dwell where genuine spiritual knowledge is nearly nonexistent.

The Words: *go they forth to their work* tell of zealously justifying their own errant philosophies and misleading religious doctrines as if they were above reproach.

The Words: *rising betimes for a prey* describe the loss of Peace and Rest they cause to their own mental, emotional, and spiritual wellbeing.

The Words: *the wilderness yieldeth food for them and for their children* present the false notions they use to sustain their own self-serving thoughts and selfish desires.

The Words: *They reap every one his corn in the field* describe what comes forth from their having been *wise in their own eyes.*

The Words: *and they gather vintage of the wicked* depict what returns upon those who mislead themselves, or others, about what constitutes the Truth of our Salvation.

> "*For every man shall bear his own burden.*
>
> "*Let him that is Taught in the Word communicate unto Him that Teacheth in all Good things.*
>
> "*Be not deceived; God is not mocked: for whatsoever a man soweth, that shall he also reap.*"
>
> Galatians 6:5–7

The age-old perplexity of those who claim that "they that know" the Lord, yet refuse to accept what He is teaching us about the Way we must live our lives is proclaimed throughout the Bible … from Beginning to End.

- The strength by which they covet their own thoughts above His Thoughts is staggering.

- The effects they bring upon the wellbeing of their own minds, hearts, and souls in this life are dire.

- The extent of those effects in the life to come are beyond frightful.

> "The Vision of Isaiah, the son of Amoz, which he saw concerning Judah and Jerusalem in the days of Uzziah, Jotham, Ahaz, and Hezekiah, kings of Judah.

> "Hear, O Heavens, and give ear, O earth: for the Lord hath Spoken, I have nourished and brought up children, and they have rebelled against Me.

> "The ox knoweth his Owner, and the ass his Master's crib: but Israel doth not know, My people doth not consider.

> "Ah sinful nation, a people laden with iniquity, a seed of evildoers, children that are corrupters, they have forsaken the Lord, they have provoked the Holy One of Israel unto anger, they are gone away backward.

> "Why should ye be stricken any more? Ye will revolt more and more: the whole head is sick, and the whole heart faint."

Isaiah 1:1–5

The Words: *they are gone away backward* exclaim the Lord's Bewilderment about our refusal to turn away from our misguided beliefs about His Testimony to us.

Many spiritual battles will be won as you work with the Lord.

By asking "Why should ye be stricken anymore?" He is imploring each of us to reexamine the harm that our errant philosophies and misleading religious doctrines cause us before it becomes too late.

> "*A wild ass used to the wilderness, that snuffeth up the Wind at her pleasure; in her occasion who can turn her away? All they that seek her will not weary themselves; in her month they shall find her.*"
>
> Jeremiah 2:24

An undisciplined spiritual conscience indulging in the pride of its own self-intelligence is described here as being "A wild ass used to the wilderness."

The Words: *that snuffeth up the Wind at her pleasure* illustrates its extreme indignance when presented with genuine spiritual understanding about the Truth of Love.

The Words: *in* her occasion *who can turn her away?* describe its ability to intimidate your willingness to refuse its false premises.

The Words: *All they that seek her will not weary themselves* reveals the reluctance it instills within those who would otherwise take exception.

The Words: *in her month they shall find her* highlights how wayward affections seduce you into falling for their misguided beliefs about what will lead you into the Joy, Goodness and Peace of the Lord's Embrace.

〜

At the time of the Lord's advent into our world, humanity had become lost in a spiritual wilderness of its own making. We had lost our willingness to understand Thoughts that are much Higher and much more Perfect than our own. We had once again come into the danger of having all spiritual sensibility swept away by falsities and evils of our own making.

> *"Withhold thy foot from being unshod, and thy throat from thirst: but thou saidst, There is no hope: no, for I have loved strangers, and after them will I go."*
> Jeremiah 2:25

Given how far we had gone astray, it is reasonable to think that all hope of returning into the Goodness of mutual Love had been lost. But as He Promised in Genesis 9:9-11, the the Lord came into our world to once again restore our ability to think clearly about the most important things of all. If He had not, all True Life from His Life would have soon perished from the face of the earth.

> "And when they drew nigh unto Jerusalem, and were come to Bethphage, unto the Mount of Olives, then sent Jesus two disciples,
>
> "Saying unto them, Go into the village over against you, and straightway ye shall find an ass tied, and a colt with her: loose them, and bring them unto Me.
>
> "And if any man say aught unto you, ye shall say, The Lord hath need of them; and straightway he will send them. "
>
> Matthew 21:1–3

The Lord drawing near "unto Jerusalem" is descriptive of His approaching us where the Doctrine of Righteousness should reign supreme within our lives.

The Words: *and were come to Bethphage, unto the Mount of Olives* verifies His approach from the East, and into where spiritual Humility yields Truth and understanding within your mind, heart, and soul.

The Words: *then sent Jesus two disciples* tells how the Lord sent forth what aids Him in teaching you about the Way you must live your life.

The Words: *Saying unto them, Go into the village over against you* describe entering resistance about the acceptance of the Truth of Love.

The Words: *and straightway ye shall find an ass tied, and a colt with her: loose them* reveals the beginning of His liberating your spiritual conscience from that resistance.

The Words: *and bring them unto Me* describe your need to willingly submit your spiritual conscience to His Calling.

The Words: *And if any man say ought unto you, ye shall say, The Lord hath need of them* illuminates the Lord addressing you to receive spiritual understanding from Him about why and how you must.

The Words: *and straightway he will send them* affirms your immediate recognition that He is Calling you in Truth, for your Good and for the Good of all around you.

~

> *All this was done, that it might be fulfilled which was spoken by the prophet, saying,*
>
> *Tell ye the daughter of Zion, Behold, thy King cometh unto thee, meek, and sitting upon an ass, and a colt the foal of an ass.*
>
> Matthew 21:4–5

Spiritually, "sitting" is descriptive of a state of internal confidence. In this case, "sitting" is descriptive of Divine Truth, Humbly and Innocently coming into your life, all the while Confidently teaching you about the Way to your salvation and deliverance into an eternal state of Heavenly Joy.

> *And the disciples went and did as Jesus Commanded them,*
>
> *And brought the ass, and the colt, and put on them their clothes, and they set Him thereon.*
>
> Matthew 21:6–7

The Words: *And the disciples went and did as Jesus Commanded them* describes bringing your spiritual conscience into the service of the Lord.

The Words: *And brought the ass, and the colt, and put on them their clothes* portray putting your thoughts about the Principles of Righteousness in their Rightful Place within your life.

The Words: *and they set Him thereon* describe Placing faith in the Lord's Testimony to you above all else for the Way you must think, feel, and behave in life.

> "*Behold, the Lord hath proclaimed unto the end of the world,*
> *Say ye unto the daughter of Zion, Behold, thy Salvation cometh;*
> *behold, His Reward is with Him, and His Work before Him.*
>
> "*And they shall call them, The Holy people, the redeemed of the*
> *Lord: and thou shall be called, Sought out, a City not forsaken.*"
>
> Isaiah 62:11–12

Spiritually, a great internal conversation takes place when the proponents of errant philosophies and misleading religious doctrines realize that they are in danger of losing control over the lives of others. It is then when they should take great pause, and reconsider Who is Standing within their midst, and Why He Calling upon them to listen to His "still small Voice" within their souls.

With His Words: *Thou shalt not covet thy neighbor's ass* the Lord is Instructing you to never attempt to wrest away your spiritual conscience from being of service to Him.

Rather, He is Instructing you to employ the humility and innocence necessary to saddle it with understanding about why and how you must. As Righteousness Himself, He is Giving you this Testimony so that you might remember the most important things of all. Each willing effort you make to do so is a step in the Right direction for your spiritual journey ahead.

"*Blessed are ye that sow beside all Waters, that send forth thither the feet of the ox and the ass.*"

Isaiah 32:20

"*Neither shall they say, Lo here! or, lo there! for, behold, the Kingdom of God is within you.*"

Luke 17:21

29
The Final Phrase

The Lord begins the Work of our spiritual reformation
by exposing our selfish tendencies for what they really are.

The Final Phrase of the Tenth Commandment—
Thou shalt not covet anything that is thy neighbor's.

Spiritually, coveting "anything that is thy neighbor's" describes desiring to take control over what the Lord has Given you to know as True and Right for selfish purposes. Those desires strive to justify their own self-serving thoughts at every turn. When left to dominate your life, they draw all forms of unrighteousness into your soul.

> "*And they came over unto the other side of the sea, into the country of the Gadarenes.*
>
> "*And when He was come out of the ship, immediately there met Him out of the tombs a man with an unclean spirit,*"
>
> Mark 5:1–2

In a positive sense, a "sea" is descriptive of where vast and deep spiritual knowledge has been gathered together.

The Words: *the other side of the sea* depicts where that knowledge ends.

Spiritually, a "ship" depicts a vessel carrying cargo. A ship carrying Divine Truth portrays the most Valuable Cargo of all. That the Lord "was come out of the ship" is spiritually descriptive of His fulfilling His Promise to return into our lives yet once again.

The Words: *immediately there met Him out of the tombs a man with an unclean spirit* express self-serving thoughts filled with selfish desires confronting the Truth of Love. This unclean spirit is described as coming "out of the tombs" because his thoughts and affections were devoid of all spiritual Goodness.

In the Light of Righteousness, that spiritual state of being appears frightfully dark and cold, just as an unclean physical corpse appears on earth. It's lack of Goodness is both pathetic and horrifying.

> "Who had his dwelling among the tombs; and no man could
> bind him, no, not with chains:"
>
> Mark 5:3

The Words: *Who had his dwelling among the tombs* communicate where self-serving thoughts and selfish desires find solace among like kind.

The Words: *and no man could bind him, no, not with chains* describe their insidious strivings as they try to destroy any restraints which oppose their own insatiable cravings.

Without Intercession from the Lord, we stand no chance of overcoming the harm that self-serving thoughts and selfish desires are capable of inflicting upon our mental, emotional, and spiritual wellbeing.

> "Because that he had been often bound with fetters and chains,
> and the chains had been plucked asunder by him, and the fetters
> broken in pieces: neither could any man tame him."
>
> Mark 5:4

The Words: *Because that he had been often bound with fetters and chains* declare the boundaries which limit your self-serving thoughts and selfish desires from acting themselves out. Those boundaries include fear of criminal penalties, fear of lost material wealth, fear of lost prestige, and fear of ruined reputation.

The Words: *and the chains had been plucked asunder by him* spiritually explain the cunningness of self-serving thoughts and their corresponding behaviors, always struggling to escape or circumvent those restraints.

The Words: *and the fetters broken in pieces* describe the shattering of moral and ethical principles for selfish purposes. And even if they are not immediately apparent, your selfish tendencies are always there, rooted more deeply within you than you would like to admit. They lie in wait to exert themselves whenever they find an opening.

The Words: *neither could any man tame him* emphasize your inability to contain, control, or overcome them on your own, try as you may.

> "*And always, night and day, he was in the mountains, and in the tombs, crying, and cutting himself with stones.*"
>
> Mark 5:5

The Words: *And always, night and day, he was in the mountains, and in the tombs, crying* depicts the continuous arrogance, internal restlessness, and urgings of covetous thoughts and their selfish desires, as they desperately seek to indulge in what they crave most.

The Words: *and cutting himself with stones* reveal the self-inflicted harm their false arguments cause to our ability to think and feel Rightly.

The Lord begins the Work of your spiritual reformation by exposing your selfish tendencies.

> "*But when he saw Jesus afar off, he ran and worshipped Him.*"
>
> Mark 5:6

On the surface, all forms of selfishness are quite capable of making themselves appear submissive to the Truth of Love.

The Words: *But when he saw Jesus afar off, he ran and worshipped Him* describe their submission to the Lord in surface appearance only. Yet, when exposed in the Light of His Righteousness, their true motives become quite transparent. When made aware of that exposure, they are sure to feel great anguish. That anguish will cause them to look for any excuse to flee away and return into the darkness and coldness of their own domain.

> "*And cried with a loud voice, and said, What have I to do with thee, Jesus, Thou Son of the Most High God? I adjure Thee by God, that Thou torment me not.*"
>
> Mark 5:7

The Lord begins the Work of our spiritual reformation by exposing our selfish tendencies for what they really are. In that Light, He exposes the things that we must all recognize as false and evil, turn away from, and leave behind. As we are willing to accept that responsibility, He begins to spiritually separate the "chaff from the wheat" from within our souls.

> "*For He said unto him, Come out of the man, thou unclean spirit.*"
>
> Mark 5:8

All the Lord's Commandments address your need to cast out the falsities and evils which lurk within your own selfish tendencies. He Commands you to do so because they are diametrically opposed to the Joy and Goodness He Wills to bring forth within your soul.

He did not Create anyone to "dwell among the tombs" but rather to receive, retain, and forever share in those incomparable Blessings.

> " *And He asked him, What is thy name? And he answered, saying,*
> *my name is Legion: for we are many.* "
>
> Mark 5:9

The Words: *And He asked him, What is thy name?* describe our need to examine and recognize the true nature of our own self-serving thoughts and selfish desires in the Light of Righteousness. At that stage in our internal development, the Lord begins to move the "Waters" within our minds and hearts, making us aware that there is something much Greater and much more Important to life than we had ever before realized.

It is then when the regeneration of our spiritual sensibilities Truly begins.

The Words: *And he answered, saying, my name is Legion: for we are many* confess our recognition of the true enemies of our mental, emotional, and spiritual wellbeing.

> " *And he besought Him much that He would not send them*
> *away out of the country.*
>
> " *Now there was there nigh unto the mountains a great herd of*
> *swine feeding.*
>
> " *And all the devils besought Him, saying, Send us into the*
> *swine, that we may enter into them.* "
>
> Mark 5:10–12

The Words: *And he besought Him much that He would not send them away out of the country* reveal self-serving thoughts and selfish desires coveting their own self-preservation.

The Words: *Now there was there nigh unto the mountains a great herd of swine feeding. And all the devils besought Him, saying, Send us into the swine, that we may enter into them* depict their looking for safe refuge among like kind. Internally, all insatiable, selfish and self-serving tendencies appear vile, vicious, and destructive, just like crazed wild swine.

> *"And forthwith Jesus gave them leave. And the unclean spirits went out, and entered into the swine: and the herd ran violently down a steep place into the sea, (they were about two thousand); and were choked in the sea."*
>
> Mark 5:13

These Words describe the appearance of self-serving thoughts and selfish desires mindlessly rushing headlong into spiritual insanities of all sorts. That "they were about two thousand" is descriptive of their willingness to violate everything the Lord has Shown humanity to be True and Right. That they "were choked in the sea" describes their complete loss of ability to acknowledge the Truth about what leads to inmost happiness and genuine fulfillment in life.

> *"And they that fed the swine fled, and told it in the city, and in the country. And they went out to see what it was that was done."*
>
> Mark 5:14

This verse and the ones immediately following describe the proponents of errant philosophies and misleading religious doctrines, always trying to find a way to regain control over our lives.

And so, the Lord warns you in advance about them, cautioning and alerting you about your need to stay vigilant in keeping them at bay. If you lose that vigilance … what will rise again out of that "sea" will be much worse, and much more deceptive than what came before it.

> *"Give not that which is Holy to the dogs, neither cast ye your pearls before swine, lest they trample them under their feet, and turn again and rend you."*
>
> Matthew 7:6

The Words: *they that fed the swine* describe those that promote errant philosophies and misleading religious doctrines for self-serving motives. That they "fled" is descriptive of their inability to defend themselves in the Light of Righteousness. And although they may flee away, in time they will always try to regroup with intent to find any weakness that will allow them to regain their dominance over our lives

The Words: *and told it in the city, and in the country* spiritually discloses how they will consult their prior philosophical and doctrinal arguments about what they had used to justify their own correctness.

The Words: *And they went out to see what it was that was done* spiritually describe insidiously trying to find a way to discredit all that the Lord has Shown us to be True and Right.

> "*And they come to Jesus, and see him that was possessed with the devil, and had the legion, sitting, and clothed, and in his Right mind: and they were afraid.*"
>
> Mark 5:15

When the proponents of errant philosophies and misleading religious doctrines begin to comprehend the individual and collective liberating Power of Divine Truth, they become fearful for their own existence.

The Words: *And they come to Jesus, and see him that was possessed with the devil, and had the legion, sitting, and clothed, and in his Right mind and they were afraid* describe how fearful they become when realizing that the control they covet most over others is at risk of being lost to them altogether.

> "*And they that saw it told them how it befell to him that was possessed with the devil, and also concerning the swine.*
>
> "*And they began to pray Him to depart out of their coasts.*"
>
> Mark 5:16–17

Spiritually, a great internal conversation takes place when the proponents of errant philosophies and misleading religious doctrines realize that they are in danger of losing control over the lives of others. That conversation is described by Words: *And they that saw it told them how it befell to him that was possessed with the devil, and also concerning the swine.*

And because the proponents of errant philosophies and misleading religious doctrines crave control over the lives of others above all else, they will look for any way possible to reject, distort, and destroy the meaning of the Lord's Message to us. The Words: *And they began to pray Him to depart out of their coasts* describe the extent of their spiritual irrationality.

~

> "*And when He was come into the ship, he that had been possessed with the devil prayed Him that he might be with Him.*"
>
> Mark 5:18

Allowing the Lord to liberate you from being dominated by self-serving thoughts and selfish desires brings a gratefulness into your life unlike any other. The magnitude of that gratefulness will cause you to want to be near Him always, described by the Words "And when He was come unto the ship, he that had been possessed with the devil prayed Him that he might be with Him." Nevertheless, in Truth, from His Love for you, He will Inform you that there is still much more Work left to be done.

> "*Howbeit Jesus suffered him not, but saith unto him, Go home to thy friends, and tell them how Great things the Lord hath done for thee, and hath had Compassion on thee.*"
>
> Mark 5:19

Many spiritual battles will be won as you work with the Lord to confront and overcome your selfish tendencies and the errant philosophies and misleading religious doctrines that have supported them. Yet, throughout your entire lifetime in this world, He will ask you to return to your daily life and continue that work. As you do so, He Promises to Help you to achieve additional and lasting victories, day-by-day, step by step, and stage by stage as you continue to seek His Righteousness First in all you think, feel, and do.

The Words: *Howbeit Jesus suffered him not, but said unto him, Go home to thy friends, and tell them how Great things the Lord hath done for thee, and hath had Compassion on thee* reinforce your need to walk that extra mile.

～

“*And he departed, and began to publish in Decapolis how Great things Jesus had done for him: and all men did marvel.*”
Mark 5:20

Here, "to depart" from the Lord's presence is descriptive of being left to your own free will to live your life in the Way which He has Shown you that you must. It is also descriptive of the Lord taking a journey "into a far country," all the while asking you to be a faithful husbandman in the "dressing" and "keeping" of this spiritual understanding within your life. It is during these times when even the most deceptive of your previous self-serving thoughts and selfish desires will die off as new generations of Truthful thoughts and Unselfish affections become born anew within your mind, heart, and soul.

“*And they sing the Song of Moses the servant of God, and the Song of the Lamb, saying, Great and Marvelous are Thy Works, Lord God Almighty; Just and True are Thy Ways, Thou King of saints.*”
Revelation 15:3

Spiritually, "to publish" is descriptive of what you put forth through the way you live your life. Abiding by the Principles of His Righteousness allows the Lord to Publish all the "Great things" He "has done for" you in His "Book of Life."

The Words: *and all men did marvel* portrays our amazement at the Goodness that comes into fruition within our lives as we abide by the Principles of His Righteousness, nothing withheld. Doing so befriends the Lord's very Purpose for the Creation of our souls.

> *If ye love Me, keep My Commandments.*
>
> John 14:15

> *Greater love hath no man than this, that a man lay down his life for his friends.*
>
> *Ye are My friends, if ye do whatsoever I Command you.*
>
> John 15:13–14

> *And there shall in no wise enter into it any thing that defileth, neither whatsoever worketh abomination, or maketh a lie: but they which are written in the Lamb's Book of Life.*
>
> Revelation 21:27

Reflections

Throughout the entire Bible, the Lord teaches you about why and how you must live your life.

He teaches you never to wrestle with Him about that understanding or covet control over it for any reason whatsoever.

For your Good and for the Good of all around you, He beseeches you not to entangle that timeless Message with complications of your own making.

Rather, He leaves it up to you, from your own free will, to recognize and embrace the spiritual understanding that He has so Greatly Labored to bring into your life. He Calls upon you to do so with all your mind, heart, and strength.

As you seek His Righteousness First, He Promises to Bless you with the understanding you need to put everything in their Rightful Order within you life.

· *"For this Commandment which I Command thee this Day, it is not hidden from thee, neither is it far off.*

"It is not in Heaven, that thou shoudest say, Who shall go up for us to Heaven, and bring it to us that we may hear it, and do it?

"Neither is it beyond the sea, that thou shouldest say, Who shall go over the sea for us, and bring it to us, that we may hear it, and do it?

"But the Word is very nigh unto thee, in thy mouth, and in thy heart, that thou mayest do it.

St John the baptist, by Leonardo Da Vinci

"See, I have set before thee this Day Life and Good, and death and evil;

"In that I Command thee this Day to love the Lord thy God, to walk in His Ways, and to keep His Commandments and His Statutes and His Judgments, that thou mayest Live and multiply: and the Lord thy God shall Bless thee in the Land whither thou goest to possess it."

Deuteronomy 30:11–16

"I have not spoken in secret, in a dark place of the earth: I said not unto the seed of Jacob, Seek ye Me in vain: I the Lord speak Righteousness, I declare things that are Right."

Isaiah 45:19

"Peace I leave with you, My Peace I Give unto you: not as the world giveth,

"Give I unto you. Let not your heart be troubled, neither let it be afraid."

John 14:27

"All Scripture is Given by Inspiration of God, and is profitable for Doctrine, for reproof, for correction, for Instruction in Righteousness.

"That the man of God may be perfect, thoroughly furnished unto all Good Works."

2 Timothy 3:16–17

THE LAUNCH PAD

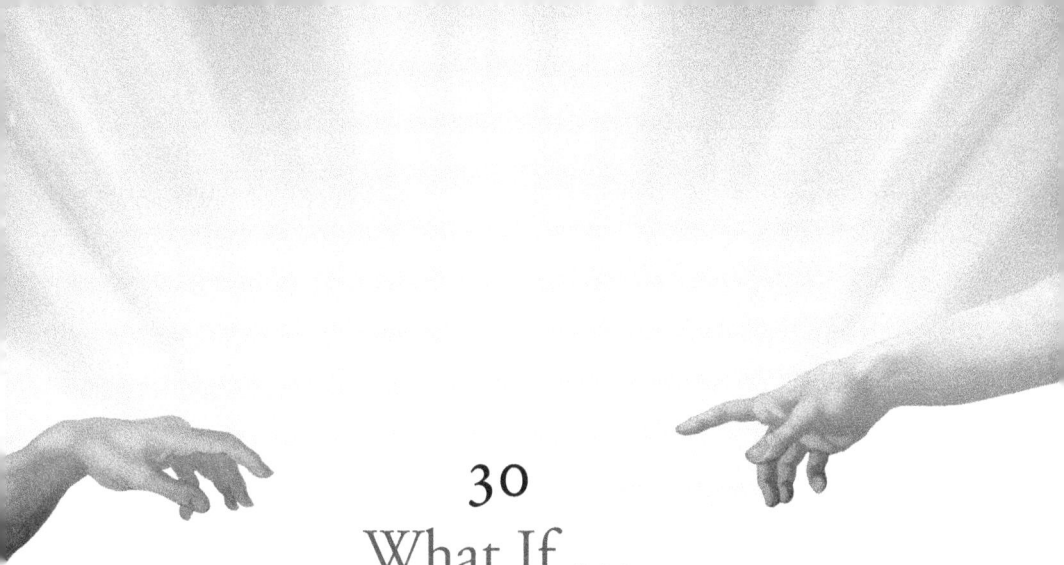

30
What If …

Your choice!

f you were Given the Opportunity to choose a place in our physical universe to develop the full potential of your mind, heart, and soul, would this world appear attractive to you?

But of course, you have already been born into this world! And whether you realize it or not, what you choose to develop within your mind and heart on earth will define the spiritual character of your soul in the life to come. You can, and will take it with you!

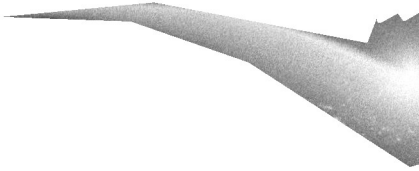

According to the US Census Bureau, the world's population will top eight billion people during January 2024, with an average of 4.3 births occurring every second. That equates to 135 million new souls being physically born on Earth this year alone. According to the same US Census report, two people also will die each second, meaning 64 million souls will also depart from Earth this year.

And so, the Gates of Heaven and Earth are very busy places!

Recognizing that your life on Earth is short, yet understanding that you have been provided with everything you need to develop into the unique and very special person that the Lord has Purposed for you to become presents you with the Opportunity of your lifetime!

As described in the fist chapter of Genesis, all spiritual Enlightenment within the human race begins with receiving that spiritual knowledge.

"*Then Jesus said unto them, Yet a little while is the Light with you. Walk while you have the Light, lest darkness come upon you: for he that walkest in darkness knowest not whither he goeth.*"

John 12:35

Your choice!

"Speak unto the children of Israel, that they bring Me and offering: of every man that giveth it willing with his heart ye shall take My Offering. "

Exodus 25:2

"After this manner therefore pray ye: Our Father which art in Heaven, Hallowed be Thy Name.

"Thy Kingdom come, Thy Will be done in earth, as it is in Heaven. "

Matthew 6:9–10

Where there is a Will, there is a Way.

Sacred Heart of Jesus by Charles Bosseron Chambers

Partial Scripture Index

How to Work with Howard Becker

Howard has decades of speaking experience, including teaching graduate level business classes at California Lutheran University about ethics, (among other subjects), and leading a Christian "Life Group" for a Presbyterian church in Malibu, California.

As the owner/CEO of multi-million dollar executive transport builder Becker Automotive Design he has appeared in major news publications from around the world, including:

FOX NEWS   CBS NEWS   USA TODAY   FAST COMPANY

ESPN   Bloomberg

Trvl CHANNEL   Robb Report   MOTORTREND   Bloomberg Businessweek   The Economist   abc NEWS

Howard provides insights on the following topics plus more:

The Spiritual Meaning of the Bible

God's Purpose for the Creation of Your Soul

Literal Misinterpretations about Scripture

Spiritual Causes and Effects

Divine Truth and the Doctrine of Righteousness

The Compatibility of Religion with Modern Science

Questions that may arise:

- Studies show that attendance at religious organizations has drastically declined. Is this true … and if so, what are your thoughts about why?

- Why does Paul state that the letter of the word kills, while the Spirit of the Word gives Life? (2 Corinthians 3:6).

- Why does understanding the spiritual meaning of Scripture dissipate any conflict between religion and modern science? (Genesis).

- Why do the Principles of Righteousness unite us all with the Lord and with each other in Truth and Goodness? (Isaiah 11:16).

- Why does our mental, emotional, and spiritual health depend upon our willingness to love the Lord above all else and our neighbor as ourselves? (Matthew 22:36-40).

- What are spiritual causes and effects, and why are they called "Laws" in the Bible? (Psalms 19:7).

- What are spiritual "tithes and offerings"? (Malachi 3:10).

- Why is God described as a Trinity? (Matthew 28:19).

- What is the meaning of a City coming down from Heaven as a "Bribe adorned for her Husband"? (Revelation 21:2).

- What is the true meaning of the Word "Grace?" (Genesis 6:8).

- What does it mean to "walk" in the Name of the Lord? (Micah 4:5).

- What is spiritual Wisdom? (1 Kings 3:9).

- Why is religious affiliation drastically declining in the Western world?

Please log into **www.TheSpiritualMeaningofScripture.com** and sign up for our newsletter. We will work to create a two-way communication with you about the most important things of all!

To Contact Howard:
Howard@HowardBBecker.com
424-799-8188
www.TheSpiritualMeaningofScripture.com